MORE PRAISE FOR CONTEMPLATIVE PRACTICES IN HIGHER EDUCATION

"This book is a ... giving them a whole other dimension of experience from which to ... the beauty of their ... ty for themselves. Contemplative practices, integrated ... curriculum of higher education in the ways the authors describe and advocate so skillfully and compellingly, have the capacity to transform our relationship to learning itself, in all its mystery, intimacy, difficulty, and wonder."—Jon Kabat Zinn, author, *Full Catastrophe Living and Mindfulness for Beginners*

"*Contemplative Practices in Higher Education* is truly a breakthrough book, showing how profound attentiveness, intellectual rigor, and self-knowledge can be seamlessly woven together. It offers us a transformed view of a student, a teacher, the academy, and the world."—Sharon Salzberg, author, *Lovingkindness* and *Real Happiness*

"Visionary, yet immensely practical and thorough! Can enhance the skill, understanding, and well-being of students and provide the missing half of education."—Jack Kornfield, author, *A Path with Heart*

"At long last we have a comprehensive overview of the burgeoning field of Contemplative Pedagogy written by two of its leaders and pioneers. This is a must-read for anyone interested in the theory and practice of Contemplative Education."—Harold D. Roth, professor of religious studies and founder and director, Brown University Contemplative Studies Initiative

"Barbezat and Bush set forth a blueprint for a quiet revolution in education—placing student experience at the center of our learning objectives, supporting students in reconnecting with themselves while enabling them to feel their connections with an ever more diverse world. As our problems grow in complexity, the urgent need for such a revolution becomes clear. These pages hold the most practical a ... g what happens in our classrooms, a ... nt at a time."
—Rhonda Magee, p ... eaching Excellence, Univers ...

"This book tells the wonderful and creative way of expanding and increasing the possibilities of higher education through contemplative practices. The authors clearly reveal and express the important and meaningful ties between teaching and learning and the power of contemplative practices, better connecting education to life. The best educators often seek ways to expand and broaden their reach and knowledge—this book will help them achieve that goal."—Bradford C. Grant, director, School of Architecture and Design, and associate dean, College of Engineering, Architecture, and Computer Sciences, Howard University

"A great guide to developing contemplative courses. 'Poetry and Meditation,' the experimental course I taught in Spring 2000 at West Point as a Contemplative Practices Fellow, changed much of what I thought I knew about teaching and learning, and by doing that, changed my life."—Marilyn Nelson, chancellor, Academy of American Poets

"The work represented in this book has been influential and inspirational in opening the doors to a new dimension of learning. The Institute for Jewish Spirituality has brought these contemplative practices—text study, reflection and yoga—into courses in a leading rabbinical school in New York, and thus magnified the impact of its program of spiritual formation of future rabbis and cantors enormously, as well as bringing faculty members together in generative cross-departmental study."—Rabbi Rachel Cowan, Institute for Jewish Spirituality

Contemplative Practices in Higher Education

POWERFUL METHODS TO TRANSFORM TEACHING AND LEARNING

Daniel P. Barbezat
Mirabai Bush

Foreword by Parker J. Palmer
Afterword by Arthur Zajonc

JB JOSSEY-BASS™
A Wiley Brand

Published by Jossey-Bass
A Wiley Brand
One Montgomery Street, Suite 1200, San Francisco, CA 94104-4594—www.josseybass.com

Jossey-Bass books and products are available through most bookstores. To contact Jossey-Bass directly
call our Customer Care Department within the U.S. at 800-956-7739, outside the U.S. at 317-572-3986, or
fax 317-572-4002.

Wiley publishes in a variety of print and electronic formats and by print-on-demand. Some material included
with standard print versions of this book may not be included in e-books or in print-on-demand. If this
book refers to media such as a CD or DVD that is not included in the version you purchased, you may
download this material at http://booksupport.wiley.com. For more information about Wiley products, visit
www.wiley.com.

**Library of Congress Cataloging-in-Publication Data has been applied for and is on file with the Library
of Congress.**

ISBN 978-1-118-43527-4 (paper); ISBN 978-1-118-64688-5 (ebk); ISBN 978-1-118-64692-2 (ebk)

Printed in the United States of America
FIRST EDITION

PB Printing   V10001682_061118

CONTENTS

The Jossey-Bass Higher and Adult Education Series

FOREWORD

Parker J. Palmer

When I think about the reforms needed if higher education is to serve our students and our world faithfully and well, I think there should be a litmus test for every project that claims to strengthen the mission of our colleges and universities. Does this proposal deepen our capacity to educate students in a way that supports the inseparable causes of truth, love, and justice? If the answer is no, we should take a pass and redouble our efforts to find a proposal that does.

Of course, many college graduates go on to do socially constructive, occasionally noble, and sometimes heroic things with their lives. But when I look at the malfeasance of well-educated leaders in business and finance, in health care and education, in politics and religion, I see too many people whose expert knowledge—and the power that comes with it—has not been joined to a professional ethic, a sense of communal responsibility, or even simple compassion.

The reasons for this are many and complex. But one culprit is easily named: the objectivist model of knowing, teaching, and learning that has dominated, and deformed, higher education. Objectivism begins as an epistemology rooted in a false conception of science that insists on a wall of separation between the knower and the known. This, in turn, leads to a pedagogy that keeps students at arm's length from the subjects they learn about. And that, in turn, creates an ethical gap between the educated person and a world that is inevitably impacted by his or her actions, a failure to embrace the fact that one is a moral actor with communal responsibilities. When this trickle-down effect is at its worst, it contributes to the process by which "scholars, artists, lawyers, theologians and aristocrats" end up not just doing wrong but actively collaborating in evil.

These chilling words from Konnilyn G. Feig (1979) are never far from my mind:

> We have identified certain "civilizing" aspects of the modern world—music, art, a sense of family, love, appreciation of beauty, intellect, education . . . [But] after Auschwitz we must realize that being a killer, a family man, and a lover of Beethoven are not contradictions. The killers did not belong to a gutter society of misfits, nor could they be dismissed as just a collection of rabble. They were scholars, artists, lawyers, theologians and aristocrats. (p. 57)

This book is important because it offers a powerful corrective to the chain of philosophical errors that has loosed too many amoral and even immoral educated people on the world. That corrective involves "contemplative practice," a phrase some faculty may find odd or even off-putting in the context of academic culture. Contemplation may sound like something that belongs in the mystical world of religion and spirituality, not in the empirical, rational world of the academy.

But as Daniel Barbezat and Mirabai Bush explain with care—and with the credibility that comes from years of scholarly research and classroom application—the contemplative practices described in this book will deepen, not damage, academic culture. The pedagogical elements found here help students focus more intently on subjects ranging from physics to literature, connect as whole persons with what they are learning, and feel more keenly their responsibilities as educated persons in the larger ecology of human and nonhuman life. These are outcomes that all good teachers strive for and that this book can help teachers in every field achieve.

The contemporary movement to bring contemplative practice back to higher education is now some twenty-five years old. I say "bring contemplative practice back" because contemplation is nothing new in the academy. It was once part and parcel of the intellectual life, a legacy of the monastic schools of the early Middle Ages that are among the ancestors of modern higher education.

At the heart of contemplation is the same quality that is at the heart of all great scholarship: profound attentiveness to the phenomena that one is trying to understand. This is the kind of attentiveness practiced, for example, by Nobel Prize–winning geneticist Barbara McClintock. As Sue V. Rosser (1992) has said, McClintock, who studied maize en route to her breakthrough discoveries related to genetic transposition, "gained valuable knowledge by empathizing with her corn plants, submerging herself in their world and dissolving the boundary between object and observer" (p. 46). Rosser might as well have said that McClintock was a contemplative scientist par excellence, which is exactly what she was.

The philosophers of ancient Greece are also among higher education's ancestry, not least Socrates with his famous dictum, "The unexamined life is not worth living." Here, too, is a lost element of higher education's legacy that can be recovered through contemplative practice, and recover it we must: people who choose to live an unexamined life almost inevitably live in ways that do damage to themselves and to others.

In the Socratic formulation, the focus of contemplation is not McClintock's maize or another subject of study. It is the self of the scholar or the student, the inner dynamics of those who teach and learn—and then, for better or worse, deploy their knowledge as power in the world. Students whose minds and hearts have been formed by contemplation of self as well as world are much more likely to become the kinds of ethical actors we need at a time when basic human values—values the academy arose, in part, to protect—are so widely threatened.

If you are a long-time advocate of contemplative practice in higher education, you will soon find that this is a breakthrough book in the field. If you are an academic who wonders if "contemplation" and "higher education" belong in the same sentence, you may find that this is a breakthrough book for you professionally.

Wherever you find yourself along that continuum, please read on. This is a book that can help thoughtful teachers transform their pedagogies and the lives of their students in ways that will contribute to the transformation of the academy and the making of a better world.

Parker J. Palmer, founder and senior partner of the Center for Courage & Renewal, is a well-known writer, speaker, and activist. He has published nine books, including the best-selling *Let Your Life Speak, The Courage to Teach, A Hidden Wholeness,* and *Healing the Heart of Democracy.* He holds a PhD in sociology from the

University of California at Berkeley, along with ten honorary doctorates, two Distinguished Achievement Awards from the National Educational Press Association, and an Award of Excellence from the Associated Church Press. In 2010, Palmer was given the William Rainey Harper Award, whose previous recipients include Margaret Mead, Elie Wiesel, and Paolo Freire. In 2011, he was named an Utne Reader Visionary, one of "25 people who are changing your world."

PREFACE

Contemplative practices, a vital part of all major religious and spiritual traditions, have long had a place in intellectual inquiry. The predecessors of our colleges and universities in the West, of course, were established as alternatives to monastic schools, where contemplative practices had been central to learning. But even within these new institutions, committed to the pursuit of rational knowledge and later to the scientific method, educators have long been exploring the use of contemplative practices in learning. As we apply these practices to higher education, clearly we must keep them separate from ideology or creed; the invitation must be to explore students' own beliefs and views so that the first-person, critical inquiry becomes an investigation rather than an imposition of particular views. This book is about contemporary contemplative contributions to modern pedagogy.

CONTEMPLATIVE PRACTICE AND THE ACADEMY

Our own journey began in 1995 when a group of leaders in philanthropy, education, health care, and psychology came together to discuss how contemplative practices, which were being used successfully in health and healing programs, could have a beneficial impact on higher education. We formed the Center for Contemplative Mind in Society with coauthor Mirabai Bush as director and, following board chair Charlie Halpern's leadership, decided to offer fellowships for contemplative curriculum development. These fellowships would seek to restore and renew the critical contribution that contemplative practices can make to the life of teaching, learning, and scholarship. At the heart of the program was the belief that bringing contemplative practice into the academy would have pedagogical and intellectual benefits and that contemplative awareness can help to create a more just, compassionate, and reflective society.

Contemplative practices were found only on the fringe of the educational world at that time, but a fellowship program was a conventional way to introduce new ideas, and, to our amazement, the American Council of Learned Societies agreed to administer them. The fellows would receive grants, develop courses that integrated contemplative practices into the curriculum, teach the courses, and write reports about their experience. When we thought about who might apply, we realized that none of us knew even one academic who would want to do this, but we put the announcement out into the world through the *Chronicle of Higher Education* and waited. An astonishing 125 scholars submitted rigorous proposals for innovative courses, from the disciplines of English, philosophy, psychology, architecture, American studies, and law. In 1997, we awarded 16 fellowships. And every year from then until 2009, we received at least 100 applications and awarded at least 10 more fellowships. There are now 152 fellows in more than one hundred colleges and universities.

After a few years, we recognized that we needed a full program, which would include serving those we could not fund through fellowships. Arthur Zajonc, the first academic director, posed this central question: "The university is well-practiced at educating the mind for critical reasoning, critical writing and critical speaking as well as for scientific and quantitative analysis. But is this sufficient? In a world beset with conflicts, internal as well as external, isn't it of equal if not greater importance to balance the sharpening of our intellects with the systematic cultivation of our hearts?"

The program developed this vision for the future:

1. A national community of scholars interested in contemplative practice will exist in diverse fields, linked to and supportive of each other.

2. Contemplative practice will be familiar and acceptable on campuses as a lifestyle and recognized and valued as a way of learning and teaching.

3. A growing body of scholarship will be developed on contemplative practice as a pedagogy and on the history of contemplative practice.

4. A space for silence and contemplative practice will exist on many campuses.

We offered an annual week-long summer session on curriculum development at Smith College and then an annual conference at Amherst College at which professors could present their work to colleagues in this growing field. We formed a membership organization, the Association for Contemplative Mind in Higher Education.

The question of contemplative epistemology is only beginning to be explored (most significantly by Arthur Zajonc, who has called it the "epistemology of love"), but we do know that the contemplative approach is one of inquiry into the nature of things, a scientific suspension of disbelief (and belief) in an attempt to "know" reality through direct observation by being fully present in the moment. Chogyam Trungpa, founder of the first US contemplative center for higher education, Naropa University, said contemplative wisdom is "immediate and nonconceptual insight which provides the basic inspiration for intellectual study." Having seen clearly one's own mind, one has a natural desire to see how others experience reality.

This book is the next ripple outward in providing support for the introduction of contemplative practices into teaching, learning, and research. We have written a brief account of the historical, intellectual, and spiritual/religious context of contemplative practice and pedagogy and provided examples not to imitate but to be inspired by. To do this, we have drawn on the experiences of the fellows and many other teachers who have developed contemplative courses.

ONE ACADEMIC'S PATH TO CONTEMPLATIVE PEDAGOGY

In 2008, coauthor Daniel Barbezat joined the center, first as a contemplative practice fellow and later as executive director. His story of why and how he brought contemplative practice into his teaching illustrates the potential these practices offer for academic renewal.

It is hard to say exactly how it happened, but over the years, I lost my way teaching economics. I knew the material and knew I could do the job of writing down and getting through a syllabus, but I could not say what I was really doing. Was I simply providing signals for the job market? Those students who did well in my class, who could follow instructions and think for themselves—was I training them to be fine hires? Or was I teaching a structured set of information, like those how-to programs available on late-night TV, bundled in a set of five DVDs? Was I guiding the students to think and write creatively, while the material was really immaterial? I could no longer tell. At one point, I realized that I was simply going through the motions and that if I couldn't find myself in my work, I should find other work.

Although I had the realization that I needed a change, I was stuck. I couldn't seem to figure out what I should do. So I called together my close friends to sit and be with me as I stated the issue and tried to work through it. I later realized that this is similar to the seventeenth-century Quaker "clearness committee" process. What I discovered during the weekend was that I was not inquiring about what was most meaningful to me and moving toward that in my work; rather, I was watching my actions and trying to discover what I was doing and getting nowhere.

I resolved to inquire about what mattered most to me and to try and integrate that into my teaching. I realized that contributing to well-being was critically important to me, but I didn't know what that had to do with economics. Well, on close examination, I became clear that it is the core of economics. After all, economics is the study of the allocation of scarce resources to ensure well-being. It is the study of demand (namely, wanting and desire) and supply (what is or is produced). Suddenly my courses opened up to me. I thought of teaching economics in a new way and was looking for new approaches. At the same time, a colleague of mine, Paola Zamperini, told me that there was a strange-sounding center in nearby Northampton, Massachusetts, that was offering fellowships to professors interested in integrating contemplative practices into their classes. I was fortunate to receive a fellowship to create one of my favorite classes to teach, Consumption and the Pursuit of Happiness. In that class and others, I came to realize that I could support environments that allowed students to embark on an inquiry similar to my own. Through the use of the practices, they could come to understand the material in both an abstract, analytical manner and from their own experience. They would find themselves in their own studies and relate what they are learning to what they hold most dear.

Without this grounding, education can be a rather empty process. We should not be shocked by the sort of wanton cheating and indifference that we see on campuses today, including the recent charge of over half of the 250 students in a Harvard course who have been accused of cheating: horrible in one way but a wonderful wake-up call for those willing to hear it. We all miss an important opportunity for self-reflection if we only shake our heads at what has happened to students over the years. These students are the product of our industrial model of education. If courses are merely commodities, then why should students hold them as special? Somehow we have lost our way in higher education and abandoned our mission to create lives of purpose and strong ethical and creative minds. Look at any university or college's mission statement, and you'll see they are filled with that sort of rhetoric. However, in the actual education, where does it happen? It mostly does not. We are cheating our students out of the opportunity to inquire deeply into their own meaning and find themselves in the center of their learning, thus providing them with a clear sense of the meaning of their studies. I hope that the practices in this book can help restore our purpose and make our courses as meaningful and exciting as I know they can be.

HOW TO USE THIS BOOK

In this book, we introduce the use of contemplative and introspective methods that promote the exploration of meaning, purpose, and values and seek to serve our common human future. Personal introspection and contemplation reveal our inextricable connection to each other, opening the heart and mind to true community, deeper insight, sustainable living, and a more just society. As never before, we are faced with challenges that require both an understanding of technical and analytical reasoning and the ability to sustain inquiries into our connections to ourselves and others. Without a context to develop the awareness of the implications of our actions and a clear idea of what is most deeply meaningful to us, we will continue to act in ways that force us into short-term, myopic responses to a world increasingly out of control.

The book is divided into two parts. In part 1, we provide the theoretical and practical background of these practices, and in part 2, we describe and illustrate some of the many kinds of practices.

We begin in part 1 with background material, defining these practices and illustrating the quantitative and qualitative evidence of their benefits. In the past decade, an amazing surge of activity has coursed through neuroscience, cognitive and consciousness studies, health, social work, and education, providing a rich source of methods to assess the efficacy of contemplative practices. Next, we move to an extended, detailed example of these practices in an economics and a social work course. We hope that these examples illustrate how the practices can be tailored to work within the material and intentions of a specific course. Part 1 finishes with a set of cautions and concerns. As with any other practice, a number of problems can arise. Rather than attempt to catalogue all possible problems, chapter 4 addresses some of the main pitfalls.

Part 2 provides guidelines for establishing a contemplative practice of one's own and illustrates many of the practices used in the classroom. It does not attempt to describe every possible practice. Rather, it provides an overview of some of the major contemplative practices and gives some specific examples.

All the quotations from professors, unless otherwise indicated, are from reports and presentations prepared by them for the center.

We hope this book will serve as an introduction to those new to these practices and as a focusing resource for those more familiar with them. May it serve to transform education and foster the flourishing of the human spirit.

ACKNOWLEDGMENTS

Writing a book describing the work of so many people across all of higher education is a daunting and wonderful task. The incredible community that has developed around contemplative pedagogy includes so many inspiring people that the danger of thanking some is to leave out many. To everyone in this growing community, please accept our deepest respect and thanks. Thanks especially to the Center for Contemplative Mind in Society Contemplative Practice Fellows for your work in developing programs, courses, and exercises that have challenged and inspired your students and colleagues. We recognize that we have not described the entire scope of your work here, but we hope this book will foster and deepen the contemplative approaches that you have been engaged in over the years.

Financial support for this book has been generously provided by the Hemera Regnant Foundation. The research and writing of the book was fostered by grants from Hemera, and we appreciate the connection with Ru-Jün Zhou and Caroline Pfohl over the grant period. We are deeply grateful for their guidance and support in the fostering of contemplative practice and perspective in higher education. Their appreciation of the value of practice in cultivating insight, compassion, and wisdom is aligned with our own and has enabled us to promote contemplative pedagogy through this book and associated programs.

David Brightman provided wise, caring, and intelligent editorial advice, which gave us a feeling of great support.

We also are grateful to the Fetzer Institute and the Nathan Cummings Foundation, which funded the Contemplative Practice Fellowships administered by the Center with the American Council of Learned Societies. Much of the work reported in this book was accomplished by these fellows. Fetzer Institute also funded an early draft of this book.

To everyone who has worked with the Center—present and past board members, staff, fellows, and members of the Association for Contemplative Mind in Higher Education—we thank you and have been greatly inspired by your work. Very special thanks go to the visionary work of Charlie Halpern and Rob Lehman who, along with Mirabai Bush, founded the Center and helped stimulate the work that has grown over the past eighteen years.

Of course, the book would not have happened without the pioneering work of Arthur Zajonc. Arthur's work, including his inquiry into the nature of contemplative epistemology, has been the foundation for much of the contemplative work in the academy. We feel blessed to have worked with Arthur as director of the Center's academic program and are honored to consider him a dear friend. We are excited to continue our collaboration with him as president of the Mind and Life Institute. Thank you, Arthur.

Deep gratitude goes to Sunanda Markus for the dedicated work of her research for the book and coordination of the fellows over ten years. She inspired a multidisciplinary collection of diverse scholars to become a contemplative community. Carrie Bergman nourished that community by creating a supportive and beautiful website. Beth Wadham, Lila Mereschuk, Jen Akey, Rose Sackey-Milligan, and Kim Foster also contributed, doing the work of a staff twice our size, and we were constantly impressed and inspired to be working with all of you. Thank you so much. Thanks also to Barbara A. Craig, who wrote an evaluation of the contemplative practice fellows program, providing invaluable information for the book.

Friends of the Center Jon Kabat Zinn, Dan Goleman, Robert Thurman, and Joseph Goldstein gave talks on contemplative education for the Center when the program was just beginning, helping to frame what we were doing before we could name it. Steven Rockefeller wrote a paper for the Center on the potential of meditation in the university that we quoted endlessly.

Daniel Barbezat: I bow to Ellen Kaz, Sam Barbezat, Lia Kaz, and Dante the wonder dog. Thank you for your honesty, integrity, challenge, and support; you have each profoundly affected my work and life. May you all ways (and as you say, Ellen, "all ways and always") feel my great appreciation for you. To Dix McComas, Joe Howe, Gerome Miklau, Johanna Callard, Bill Rohan, Roger King, and Elizabeth Lund, I thank you greatly for your friendship and support in practice and in life. You have made this a far more interesting ride.

I am also deeply grateful to Mirabai for her generosity and graceful mentorship. It has been much fun and rewarding learning and working with you. Thank you, dear Mirabai.

Mirabai Bush: Thanks to Dan for his brilliance, his humor, and his teaching that desire is at the heart of all economic decisions. And much love and appreciation to Charlie Halpern and Rob Lehman for the partnership that grew into the Center and all its good work.

No thanks are enough for my many teachers of contemplative practices and contemplative learning, teaching, and knowing, including Neemkaroli Baba Maharaj, Ram Dass, Chogyam Trungpa Rinpoche, Kalu Rinpoche, David McClelland, Tsoknyi Rinpoche, and Kanai Sensei.

I have special appreciation for Ram Dass, not only for being a dearest friend and wise teacher, but for leaving Harvard, traveling to India, and becoming one of the first in the West to understand and share how contemplative practices deepen and enrich how we learn, teach, awaken, and live our lives. When he helped Chogyam Trungpa start Naropa Institute, the first contemplative university in the United States, one thousand students enrolled in his course to learn a contemplative way of being.

I also bow to my contemplative peers, coteachers, and friends, including Norman Fischer, Joseph Goldstein, Steve Smith, Sharon Salzberg, Jack Kornfield, Rachel Cowan, Surya Das, Sylvia Boorstein, Hal Roth, Jeremy Hunter, Zuleikha, Sun Hee Gertz, Linda Susan Beard, Bokara Legendre, and Chade Meng Tan. Brant Passalacqua and Anna Neiman-Passalacqua inspired me to be on the yoga mat regularly to keep my energy strong yet flexible as I worked on the book.

Joan Konner, Betty Sue Flowers, Deborah Klimburg-Salter, Rhonda Magee, and Carolyn Jacobs helped me remember just how magnificent women in the academy can be. My years of dedication to this work would not have been possible without the seamless support of my loving partner, E. J. Lynch. My commitment to a more meaningful education for future generations has been deepened by my unconditional love and respect for my granddaughter, Dahlia Bush, and her father, Owen.

THE AUTHORS

Daniel P. Barbezat is professor of economics at Amherst College. He has been a visiting professor at Northwestern University and Yale University and has taught in the summer program at Harvard University. In 2004, he won the J. T. Hughes Prize for Excellence in Teaching Economic History from the Economic History Association.

Over the past decade, he has become interested in how self-awareness and introspection can be used in higher education, economic decision making, and creating and sustaining well-being. With the support of a contemplative practice fellowship from the Center for Contemplative Mind in Society in 2008, he has developed courses that integrate contemplative exercises designed to enable students to gain deeper understanding and insight. His approach to these economic classes has been featured in the *Boston Globe, U.S. News & World Report*, as well as on the NPR program *Here and Now*.

Since 2009, he has worked with the Center for Contemplative Mind in Society as a board member, treasurer, and associate director of the academic program. In 2012, he became the executive director of the center. He is working to expand and deepen programs, making the center's work more inclusive and transformative for all in higher education.

Along with his experimental research on choice and awareness, he is editing a group of papers on contemplative pedagogy with Arthur Zajonc and writing (and thinking, thinking, thinking about . . .) a book entitled *Wanting*.

His practice is supported by retreats at Insight Meditation Center and the Forest Refuge in Barre, Massachusetts.

Mirabai Bush is senior fellow and founding director of the Center for Contemplative Mind in Society, a nonprofit organization whose mission is to encourage contemplative awareness in American life in order to create a more just, compassionate, and reflective society. She has designed and led contemplative trainings for corporations from Monsanto to Google, led a national survey of contemplative practice, and directed the contemplative practice fellowship awards program with the American Council of Learned Societies to explore such practices in academic courses. She has directed a study for the US Army on promoting resilience and performance among army medical and chaplain caregivers through meditation training. The center also sponsored a program to bring contemplative practices into social justice organizations and into the profession of law, engaging law students, law faculty, and attorneys in an exploration of the role of contemplative practice in legal education and the practice of law.

She formerly taught writing and English literature at SUNY Buffalo, under the mentorship of Robert Creeley, John Barth, and Lesley Fiedler. She directed an innovative program there for diversifying the university and preparing students of color for academic challenges. She now teaches in the contemplative clinical practice program at the Smith College School for Social Work.

She directed the Seva Foundation Guatemala Project, which supports sustainable agriculture and integrated community development. She codeveloped Sustaining Compassion, Sustaining the Earth, a series of retreats and events for grassroots environmental activists on the interconnection of spirit and action. She is coauthor, with Ram Dass, of *Compassion in Action: Setting Out on the Path of Service*, and editor of *Contemplation Nation: How Ancient Practices Are Changing the Way We Live*. She cofounded and directed Illuminations, Inc., in Cambridge, Massachusetts. Her innovative business practices are available on Working with Mindfulness (CD and download) from morethansound.net.

She is or has been a board member of Shambhala Sun, Omega Institute, Seva Foundation, Military Fitness Institute, Sacred Slam, the Dalai Lama Fellows, and Love Serve Remember.

Her spiritual studies include meditation at the Burmese Vihara in Bodh Gaya, India, with Shri S. N. Goenka and Anagarika Munindra; bhakti yoga with Hindu teacher Neemkaroli Baba; and studies with Tibetan lamas Kalu Rinpoche, Chogyam Trungpa Rinpoche, Kyabje Gehlek Rinpoche, Tsoknyi Rinpoche, and others. She was a student of aikido master Kanai Sensei for five years. She has cotaught with many prominent spiritual teachers including Ram Dass, Surya Das, Sharon Salzberg, Krishna Das, Daido Loori, Bernie Glassman, Norman Fischer, Arthur Zajonc, Clarissa Pinkola Estes, Joan Halifax, Margo Adler, and Terry Tempest Williams.

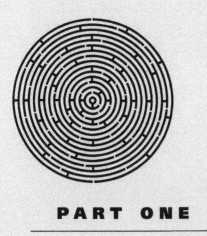

Theoretical and Practical Background

Transformation and Renewal in Higher Education

As teachers, we guide and support our students to become independent thinkers. We endeavor to teach the whole person, with an intention to go beyond the mere transfer of facts and theories. The advent of online learning and the availability of information on the Internet have made our focus on deeper and richer experiences of teaching and learning ever more important. While concentrating on these holistic goals, we also want to challenge and develop students' analytical problem-solving skills as well as provide careful explanations of complicated material. We want to create the opportunity for our students to engage with material so that they recognize and apply its relevance to their own lives, to feel deeply and experience themselves within their education. In other words, while fostering their knowledge base and analytical abilities, we want to present material in a way that supports students in having their own agency so that the material is not simply a set of intellectual hoops for them to jump through but an active opportunity for them to find meaning and develop intellectually.

This is no easy task. Focusing on our students' agency does not mean that our courses should or even could be equal collaborations. Negotiating this divide carefully—on the one hand, wanting to engage with students rather than talk at them, while on the other, knowing that we remain their teachers (however we conceive of that)—is a difficult but worthwhile process. In traversing these two poles, we often err on the side of rigid structure, and we stress the abstract and conceptual.

But concentration on outcomes, abstraction, and narrow information handling has its costs. In her book *Mindfulness*, Ellen Langer writes that perhaps one of the reasons that we become "mindless" is the form of our early education. "From kindergarten on," she writes, "the focus of schooling is usually on goals rather than the process by which they are achieved. This single-minded pursuit of one outcome or another, from tying shoelaces to getting into college, makes it difficult to have a mindful attitude toward life. Questions of 'Can I?' or 'What if I can't do it?' are likely to predominate, creating an anxious preoccupation with success or failure rather than drawing on the child's natural, exuberant desire to explore" (Langer, 1989, pp. 33–34). Indeed, the history of educational reform is full of examples of the responses to the heavy costs of this sort of concentration. It is this sense of deep exploration and inquiry that has led us to develop a pedagogy that uses contemplative methods.

We have often stressed the highly instrumental form of learning to the exclusion of personal reflection and integration. It is understandable how this happens; developing careful discursive, analytical thought is one of the hallmarks of a good education. However, creative, synthetic thinking requires more than this; it requires a holistic engagement and attention that is especially fostered by the student finding himself or herself in the material. No matter how radically we conceive of our role in teaching, the one aspect of students' learning for which they are unambiguously sovereign is the awareness of their experience and their own thoughts, beliefs, and reactions to the material covered in the course. In addition, students need support in discerning what is most meaningful to them— both their direction overall and their moral compass. Without opportunities to inquire deeply, all they can do is proceed along paths already laid down for them.

Researchers and educators have pursued the objective of creating learning environments that are deeply focused on the relationship of students to what they are learning as well as to the rest of the world. We have found that contemplative practices respond powerfully to these challenges and can provide an environment that supports the increasing diversity of our students. While contemplative practices vary greatly, they all have the potential to integrate students' own rich experience into their learning. When students engage in these introspective exercises, they discover their internal relationship to the material in their courses.

To be sure, others have thought about expansive and reflective approaches to teaching. For example, the famous work of John Dewey and Jean Piaget and the radical reframing of education by Paolo Freire all have experiential components at the heart of their systems (Dewey, 1986; Piaget, 1973; Freire, 1970). Dewey, in particular, has keen insights on the relationship between experience and reflection. (See, for example, Rodgers, 2002.) In fact, entire educational systems have been built around experience. For example, the experiential learning theory system of Daniel Kolb posits two sets of related inquiries: concrete experience and abstract conceptualization on the one hand and reflective observation and active experimentation on the other. Indeed, the advocates of the integrative education movement, influenced by the systems of thinkers like Ken Wilbur and Sri Aurobindo, call for the active attention on combining domains of experience and knowing into learning (see, for example, Awbrey, 2006). Thus, our focus on contemplative and introspective practices is not unknown in academia; what distinguishes the experience and integration discussed in this book is that the experience is focused on students' introspection and their cultivation of awareness of themselves and their relationship to others. The exercises are relatively simple and mainly conducted in their own minds and bodies, relating directly to their personal experience discovered through attention and awareness, yet these private investigations yield increased empathy for others and a deeper sense of connection with the world (Birnie, Speca, & Carlson, 2010).

CONTEMPLATION, INTROSPECTION, AND REFLECTION

In this book, we will be talking about contemplative practices and pedagogy, sometimes using *introspection, reflection*, or other terms interchangeably. Although the range of these practices is very broad, all of them have an introspective, internal focus. Whether they are analytical exercises asking students to examine a concept deeply or opportunities to simply attend to what is arising, the practices all have an inward or first-person focus that creates opportunities for greater connection and insight. Although students might be silent or speaking, still or in motion, the practices all focus on the present experience, either physical or mental. The practices certainly include meditation, but not all are meditative in the traditional sense. They range from carefully beholding chemical mappings and making observations, to sitting in stillness, to imagining the impacts of distributing different proportions of goods to loved ones and to strangers. They include both simple and complex concentration practices that sometimes require periods of calm and quiet and sometimes sustained analytical thinking. The critical aspect is that students discover their own internal reactions without having to adopt any ideology or specific belief. They all place the student in the center of his or her learning so that the student can connect his or her inner world to the outer world. Through this connection, teaching and learning is transformed into something personally meaningful yet connected to the world.

We recognize that the idea of a first-person focus has complex ontological and epistemological implications. In essays like Hans-Georg Gadamer's "On the Problem of Self-Understanding" (1976) and Evan Thompson's "Empathy and Consciousness" (2001) the metacognition necessary for evaluative self-awareness is examined and evaluated. While these inquiries are fascinating and important in considering the nature of awareness, self-conception, and knowing, we will not consider them here. Here we are stimulating the inquiry.

RESPONDING TO THE CALL

By legitimizing students' experience, we change their relationship to the material being covered. In much of formal education, students are actively dissuaded from finding themselves in what they are studying; all too often, students nervously ask whether they may use "I" in their papers. A direct inquiry brought about through contemplative introspection validates and deepens their understanding of both themselves and the material covered. In this way, they not only understand the material more richly but also retain their knowledge better once they have a personal context in which to frame it. Questions about how the material fits "into the real world" or is in some way relevant to their lives don't arise. The presentation of the material is approached in a manner in which students themselves directly discover its impact on their lives. Since they are conducting the inquiry with their classmates, they also realize their connection with each other, without any forced discussion of relatedness. This process builds capacity, deepens understanding, generates compassion, and initiates an inquiry into their human nature.

Remarkably these exercises can be used effectively throughout the curriculum: in sciences like physics, chemistry, and neuroscience; in social sciences, like sociology, economics, history, and psychology; in humanities such as art history, English, and philosophy; and in professional schools, including nursing, social work, architecture, business, law, and medicine. Their exact use changes from discipline to discipline, but as we shall see, the diverse practices are deeply connected.

The form and function of education are greatly influenced by the policy goals that underlie its purpose. Most higher education institutions are nonprofit enterprises and are highly subsidized, including financial aid to students. Even students who pay the full tuition and fees are being subsidized since fees are well below per-student average costs. In fact, one of the ways of thinking about alumni gifts to the institution is a repayment of the subsidies they received as students (Winston, 1999). Since these institutions are not focused on profit, they must be able to justify the subsidies and the appeals for charitable contributions in other ways. Some schools have religious orientations, which provide their vision and purpose, but the visions and aspirations of secular schools come from a sense of the common good that they are supporting. As teachers in these institutions, we consider our intentions for each course we teach, but we rarely step back and inquire about our overall vision of the education we are providing. With the pressure of ever increasing costs, the viability of higher education depends on our ability to articulate these aspirations. Contemplative exercises provide a means to engage in this inquiry.

In recent years, a steady stream of books has been published about the crisis in higher education and how colleges and universities are failing to educate students. It is argued again and again that we have failed to provide needed skills and have lost sight of our true calling. In *Academically Adrift: Limited Learning on College Campuses* (2010), Richard Arum and Josipa Roksa claim that nearly half of college students demonstrated no significant improvement in a range of skills—critical thinking, complex reasoning, writing, and so on—after the first two years of college. While colleges and universities have been attacked on the provision of skills, they have been criticized even more harshly for not providing students with a vision of how their studies might affect society at large. In *Crisis on Campus: A Bold Plan for Reforming Our Colleges and Universities* (2010), Mark Taylor argues that "the curriculum [has] become increasingly fragmented, and the educational process loses its coherence as well as relevance for the broader society" (p. 4). In an especially damning critique, Harry Lewis, former dean of Harvard College, writes, "Universities have forgotten their larger educational role for college students. They succeed, better than ever, as creators and repositories of knowledge. But they have forgotten that the fundamental job of undergraduate education is to . . . help [students] grow up, to learn who they are, to search for a larger purpose for their lives, and to leave college better human beings" (2006, p. xii).

We believe that it is not too late to address these problems. In fact, contemplative modes of instruction provide the opportunity for students to develop insight and creativity, hone their concentration skills, and deeply inquire about what means the most to them. These practices naturally deepen understanding while increasing connection and community within higher education. We believe that at its core, the academy must provide students with the opportunity to initiate and pursue an inquiry into their role in society, an inquiry that makes learning personal, meaningful, and relevant. Like John Dewey, social reformers and education theorists began thinking of education as the means to promote personal agency and economic opportunity. Dewey began to see that schools functioned powerfully in "prevailing structures of power." Contemplative practices place the students at the center of their own learning, shifting the balance of power in the classroom in a meaningful and engaged manner.

These practices also directly address essential learning protocols. In *How Learning Works: Seven Research-Based Principles for Smart Teaching*, Susan A. Ambrose, Michael Bridges, Michele DiPietro, Marsha Lovett, and Marie Norman (2010) evaluate the latest research on effective teaching. Many of the key findings relate directly to contemplative practices. Among their many strategies to improve teaching and learning, they advocate the importance of holistic student development and emotional regulation, the advantages of self-awareness and self-monitoring, and the central role of metacognition (personal reflective activity). Not only is emotional and social learning fundamental to student productivity, this type of learning during the college years is actually considerably greater than intellectual gains. As we shall see in the next chapter, contemplative practices support and sustain emotional regulation by allowing students to recognize triggers and be less reactive. This increases learning outcomes in the short run and produces better-balanced citizens in the long run. Contemplative practices are self-reflective practices; they support and sustain the types of self-monitoring activities that research has found crucial for student development and learning. Studies have shown that students who monitor their progress and explain to themselves what they are learning have greater learning gains and were better problem solvers than those who do not (Ambrose et al., 2010). In addition, without practice, we have a tendency to overestimate our abilities, making it less likely that students needing remedial attention will seek it. Finally, both learning and teaching requires sitting back and surveying the big picture, making sure that our strategies are achieving course-level goals and providing students broad gains for their development within and beyond the course (Ambrose et al., 2010).

Beyond these gains, contemplative practices can be designed to focus on various types of learning. For example, the practices can be visual, auditory, cognitive, or physical. While it is true that students might favor one mode over another (say, visual explanations rather than verbal ones), the evidence seems mixed about how much benefit is attained from presentations solely geared to styles associated with certain students. Researchers led by Rita Dunn and Kenneth Dunn at St. Joseph's University reported significant gains from tailoring teaching to learning style preferences. This certainly has captured the imagination of teachers and schools of education and does make intuitive sense. However, Kenneth A. Kavale, Steven R. Forness, and others have shown that the results do not seem statistically robust and that whatever gains exist result simply from the extra attention placed on personal instruction—efforts that when placed elsewhere might have similar effects (Kavale & Forness, 1987).

While the overall benefits from learning style–based teaching are somewhat controversial, there is a broader consensus on adjusting presentation to the content. Certain topics lend themselves rather naturally to types of presentation: for example, visual information like form and color is probably best conveyed with visual examples, while if you were teaching about how honeybees communicate the location of nectar-filled flowers, you might incorporate movement to help students understand the "honey bee dance language" and how it differs from explanations based on odor.

INTROSPECTIVE AND CONTEMPLATIVE PRACTICES

Contemplative pedagogy uses forms of introspection and reflection that allow students to focus internally and find more of themselves in their courses. The types of contemplation are varied, from guided introspective exercises to open-ended, multistaged contemplative reading (i.e., *lectio divina*) to simple moments of quiet, as are the ways in which the practices are integrated into classrooms. What unites them is a focus on personal awareness, leading to insight.

As an introduction, the tree of contemplative practices (figure 1.1) created by the Center for Contemplative Mind in Society illustrates the diversity of practices. This is not an exhaustive summary but does give an excellent overview of the basic categories and the practices within each.

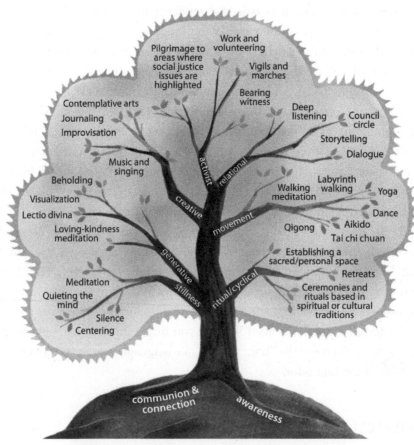

Figure 1.1 Tree of Contemplative Practices

Source: Center for Contemplative Mind in Society. Reprinted with permission.

Practices from different categories can also be combined; for example, meditation can be combined with freewriting or journaling, or a movement exercise can be combined with activist activities. The exact form of the practices depends on the context, the intent, and the skills of the facilitator.

These practices, which can take many forms, are highly adaptable to different contexts throughout the curriculum. In March 2011, Amherst College and the Center for Contemplative Mind in Society hosted a conference in which practitioners from physics, chemistry, religious studies, English, music, economics, psychology, environmental science, and law presented papers on how they had integrated contemplative practices into their teaching. These presentations (in preparation for a forthcoming collected volume to be published under the title *Cultivating Attention, Understanding, Connection and Insight: Contemplative Practices Across the Disciplines in Higher Education*) demonstrated how practices have been woven into the fabric of courses throughout the curriculum, in every kind of educational institution, and in just about every facet of higher education. From law schools to community colleges, liberal arts colleges, and large research universities, contemplative practices are being used in the classroom as well as in student and health services, counseling centers, teaching and learning centers, athletics, and administration. We hope this book will help guide you to your own effective use of these practices.

STRUCTURE AND OBJECTIVES

Broadly speaking, classroom introspective and contemplative exercises have a variety of objectives, including these:

1. Focus and attention building, mainly through focusing meditation and exercises that support mental stability

2. Contemplation and introspection into the content of the course, in which students discover the material in themselves and thus deepen their understanding of the material

3. Compassion, connection to others, and a deepening sense of the moral and spiritual aspect of education

4. Inquiry into the nature of their minds, personal meaning, creativity, and insight

Some of the practices are focused rather narrowly on only one of these objectives, and others are combinations of several. Most often they focus on one, and then naturally open into the others on reflection. A simple meditation, focusing on the breath, can lead to an inquiry into the source of intervening thoughts, an inquiry into the nature of our self-determination. It can indeed be a profound moment for students to realize they are fully in control of neither their thoughts nor their overall experience.

Attention and Analytical Problem Solving

One of the claims of higher education, and particularly of liberal arts colleges, is that we teach students how to think. What does this actually mean? Surely our students can think, so in what sense do they need to be taught to think? Maybe it means that we aid them in developing their analytical problem-solving skills and their ability to integrate different aspects of situations creatively. Certainly one of the goals of contemplative exercises is to develop these skills.

A key element in solving any problem is attention. Anyone who has attempted to solve complex problems knows the intense concentration and attention required. Contemplative exercises hone this skill. Many of them are directly aimed at cultivating concentrated attention. Of course, concentration develops by concerted effort. Musicians, dancers, and athletes, for example, all acquire high levels of concentration. However, problem solving also often requires thinking about a problem from various angles, so while attention is important, so is the ability to let go of what is not working while focusing on (but not clinging to) another. Thus, clear and flexible attention is required to solve more open-ended insight problems—those that require an "aha" moment. These problems require thinking in different ways. For example, suppose you were asked to describe how to throw a ball so that it would travel a short distance, come to a complete stop, and then reverse itself. You are not allowed to bounce it off any surface or tie anything to it. As long as you think of the ball moving horizontally, you will not be able to describe the motion. Being keenly aware of the directions, however, you note that nothing in the problem states in which direction the ball should go. Once you realize this, you can think outside the constraint of throwing a ball as you normally do. If you think about how objects suspend for a moment when thrown up, you realize that throwing the ball up in the air would cause it to rise, stop, and then reverse. Psychologists M. Aisling Murray and Ruth Byrne (2005) argue that in order to solve these sorts of problems, people must have the capacity to hold alternative possibilities along with the ability to switch their attention between them. These abilities are especially refined and honed by contemplative practices.

Logical analytical modes of thinking are just one aspect of our broad abilities, however. For many years, it was taken for granted that each person had a given level of intelligence that determined cognitive ability, often referred to as the index "*g*." Teachers could support students in living up to the potential of their given level of intelligence, but essentially it was immutable. This view has come under serious criticism for a variety of reasons. First, the notion that a single metric could capture a meaningful notion of intelligence does not seem possible. As Howard Gardner, Robert Sternberg, David Perkins, and others have argued, humans have different kinds of intelligence, most prominently captured by Gardner's idea of multiple intelligences (Gardner, 2004). Second, whatever the intelligence might be, the notion that it is fixed within very tight bounds for all time has also shown to be incorrect. Stephen Jay Gould argues convincingly in *The Mismeasurement of Man* (1996) that such a static metric does not capture how our abilities change over time. Indeed, in their rather conservative review of this issue, even the task force designated by the American Psychological Association concluded that "a given person's intellectual performance will vary on different occasions, in different domains" (Neisser et al., 1996, p. 77).

Robert Sternberg's *Beyond IQ: A Triarchic Theory of Human Intelligence* (1985) divides intelligence into three areas: analytical, creative, and practical. Contemplative exercises support analytical intelligence through stabilization of the mind and increased ability to focus. Logical problem solving involves clear, focused linear thinking, requiring the ability to concentrate and not be distracted. Yet it also requires being open to inspiration and intuition. Creative aspects of problem solving are more synthetic, requiring an awareness of many possible solutions. Complex problems demand being able to see outside the constraints of strong initial attempts or useful heuristics that do not solve the current problem. Founder of analytical philosophy Alfred North Whitehead (1929) famously pronounced, "Fools act on imagination without knowledge; pedants act on knowledge without imagination. The task of a university is to weld together imagination and experience" (p. 93). Being aware of when to use a quick rule and when not to use such a rule is the first step in solving complex problems. Beyond that, learning not only how to focus but on what to focus is the essence of effective problem solving.

Deeper Understanding

Beyond cognitive skills, contemplative and introspective exercises can deepen students' understanding of the material presented. A practice like *lectio divina*, for example, allows students to sink into their experience of reading, a rare opportunity given the amount of reading they are assigned daily. In chemistry courses, Michelle Francl at Bryn Mawr allows students an extended time to simply behold figures of electron wave functions before discussing them. They are given the chance to realize the impact of the words or graphs for themselves. Students report that they can see the regular, successive amplitude changes and thus have a deeper, immediate connection to the otherwise abstract Bohr correspondence principle that mathematically defines these changes. From this kind of engagement, students come to a far more direct and complete understanding of what might otherwise be an abstract and complicated set of mathematical relationships. No longer are these texts or figures something abstract or foreign to students; they are allowed the time to discern what they see in them before discussing them.

In his economics classes at Amherst College, I (D.B.) provide students with the opportunity to experience directly the assumptions of the abstract models they are studying. Rather than provide them with the only definition and explanation of the Easterlin paradox or the relative income hypothesis, I give students exercises in which they experience and reflect on their personal reactions to relative gains or losses. While the model suggests that people always compare themselves to others, many students have never considered how they actually select the persons to whom they compare themselves. As a result of this examination, they come to realize the importance of context and choice in matters of positional changes and have a deeper understanding of the theoretical literature. Carefully designed contemplative practices can locate the students directly in their own learning like no other practice can, allowing students direct access to the material and making it more meaningful and understandable.

Connection and Compassion

Contemplative exercises are particularly effective in the areas of emotional regulation and intra- and interpersonal connection. Each student brings her or his own approach to the material, so it is often difficult to discern just how to reach students and how to treat them fairly. In *Frames of Mind* (2004), Howard Gardner goes beyond logical-mathematical and linguistic modes of knowing and discusses others, like spatial, musical, kinesthetic, and interpersonal and intrapersonal intelligences. These last two are essential forms for navigating personal meaning and connection to others. In a related vein, Daniel Goleman, Antonio Damasio, Robert Frank, and R. B. Zajonc have all shown the central aspect of emotion in the process of decision making (Goleman, 2006; Damasio, 2000; Frank, 1988; Zajonc, 1980). Regardless of the nuances among these views, an increasing amount of evidence has shown that emotional awareness and regulation are essential for well-being and positive, even strategic, decision making. A wide range of teaching and learning methods has been developed out of these ideas, designed to work with students' varying abilities. Mary Helen Immordino-Yang of the University of Southern California's Rossier School of Education has shown that contemplative exercises that focus on compassion and social connectivity are especially effective in increasing learning outcomes (Immordino-Yang & Damasio, 2008).

Practical problems and their solutions require personal involvement and what Sternberg calls "action-oriented knowledge, acquired without the direct help from others, that allows individuals to achieve goals they personally value" (Neisser et al., 1996, p. 79). In our experience, contemplative practices can be especially powerful in supporting this sort of inquiry. Students directly engage with the experience of what they are learning through the exercises and thereby gain meaning in a very practical manner. While other kinds of experiential learning have this quality, contemplative exercises have the special attribute that students do not need to leave the classroom to complete them and can replicate them easily on their own. The point here is not whether this is actually a specific form of intelligence but that broad problem solving requires this sort of thinking.

The importance of education in the cultivation of compassion is becoming clearer as we study the nature of compassion more carefully. The Dalai Lama has focused on the importance of education and training in establishing a "secular ethics" based on a foundation of compassion. In *Beyond Religion*, he states:

> It is clear that something is seriously lacking in the way we humans are going about things. . . . The fundamental problem, I believe, is that at every level we are giving too much attention to the external material aspects of life while neglecting moral ethics and inner values.

> Our inner lives are something we ignore at our own peril, and many of
> the greatest problems we face in today's world are the result of such neglect.
> (His Holiness the Dalai Lama, 2011, p. x)

Education and the intentional cultivation of personal inquiry and compassion are at the core of his conception of how this transformation takes place. We strongly believe that contemplative practices provide a powerful means to realize this vision.

Tania Singer, a neuroscientist working in Leipzig, Germany, has highlighted the importance of education in cultivating compassion. She argues that we are coded, that is, wired to have empathy. When someone is harmed, normally a person will have an empathic response, feeling the suffering of another; this is a passive response, much like the mirror neurons that fire, sympathetically, when we see another person moving (Singer, Weng, Klimecki, & Wager, 2011). However, compassion is not a passive response; it includes the desire to relieve the suffering. The rock star of compassion, Matthieu Ricard, has said that "compassion fatigue" is misnamed; it should be called "empathy fatigue," since empathy is limited and reactive, whereas compassion is cultivated and boundless. Practices that can cultivate and support compassion are extremely important, and we need to foster environments in which our students can explore and nurture it. Contemplative practices do exactly that.

Personal Meaning

While these practices can hone attention, stimulate a deeper understanding of the material, and develop social connectivity, they also allow students to explore personal meaning, perhaps the least well-defined yet most important result. As noted in a study on spirituality in higher education by Alexander and Helen Astin at the UCLA Higher Education Research Institute, students yearn for support in their search for personal meaning. More than two-thirds consider it "essential" or "very important" that their college enhance their self-understanding, and a similar proportion rate highly the role they want their college to play in developing their personal values. Nearly half also say it is "essential" or "very important" that colleges encourage their personal expression of spirituality (Astin, Astin, & Lindholm, 2010).

Although our students might call for it, we know that discussions of morality and spirituality in the classroom pose serious potential problems. While we certainly agree that caution is appropriate, we also believe that we can support students in examining these issues for themselves. Because of the deeply personal and private nature of the exercises, they provide a framework for students to begin to open to their own sense of meaning, first to the material being taught in the class and then to a broader and deeper sense of how their learning fits into their lives. Meditation and introspection provide effective means for students to become aware of their emotions and reactions while at the same time helping them clarify what is personally most important. Both of these qualities contribute to effective decision making.

While we provide information and help students modify behavior, higher education has moved largely away from helping students discover and develop their deepest purpose. How can they decide without examining what truly matters to them? It is no wonder that students are calling out for this opportunity, and it does not require much to open this form of inquiry. For example, a simple exercise in which students are asked to focus on their breath can stimulate significant insights. When a student realizes that although *he* is committed to focusing on his breath and yet *he* somehow is also thinking about this or that, he starts to question the nature of his thinking. In what sense are these rising thoughts his? This quite naturally leads students to thinking about their wanting. If their thinking seems to come out of nowhere and does not seem to really be theirs, and desires arise in a similar fashion, are they really their desires? What sense does it make, then, to attempt to satisfy these desires since they arise like the thoughts, seemingly from nowhere? These questions provide an opportunity for students to think about the fundamental premise of economics: that consumers attempt to achieve well-being by satisfying their desires. This inquiry arises from personal insight and so has far greater valence than a prompt from without. We will see that this sort of personal insight can deepen the teaching and learning in disciplines across the curriculum and lead students to discover their values and develop their purpose.

In a course on the history of science at Amherst College, Arthur Zajonc guides his students through the process of discovery that Einstein experienced as he developed his theory of relativity. It was a process very much like the Tibetan tradition of analytical meditation followed by calm abiding that allowed Einstein to make one of the greatest breakthroughs of the twentieth century. Zajonc guides his students through the complex examination of perspective and its impact on measurement. Students are guided to realize for themselves that they can hold contradictory positions in their minds at once:

> As I work through each step inwardly from both points of view—stationary and moving—I encounter a paradox, a contradiction. How can an object have different lengths? How can a clock (including the clock of my bodily processes) run differently when viewed from the two vantage points? How can my "now" be different than yours? All three are implied by Einstein's relativity theory. Surely one set of observations must be the True set. No, each has equal justification, no vantage point is privileged. Then I remember that I am assuming the universe looks like something without me or anyone around. I presume that it looks like something unto itself. This is not so. All of its attributes, even the most fundamental ones like extension and duration, are attributes as noted by an observer, real or imagined. We and the world are knit together by Einstein's thinking in ways that astonish me. It is so difficult not to reify the world, and instead to recognize that I am implicated everywhere and in every impression. The careful reasoning that leads us to this conclusion is Einstein's gift, the fruit of his analytic meditation. (Zajonc, 2011)

As students follow along, they rediscover the theory of relativity. As Zajonc continues the journey with his students, he recounts the dramatic insight that Einstein achieved only after he had worked through the analytics and then given up trying to control the process. It was only after he let go of the conscious striving that the insight came to him. This dramatic example of the symbiosis of analytical thought and insight can be reexperienced by the students, an amazing contemporary journey into the intellectual history of science.

CAUTIONARY TALES

While contemplative pedagogies are powerful practices, they do come with challenges. As has been widely noted, William James (1890) recognized both the appeal and problem of an integrated, contemplative pedagogy: "Whether the attention come by grace of genius or by dint of will, the longer one does attend to a topic the more mastery of it one has. And the faculty of voluntarily bringing back a wandering attention, over and over again, is the very root of judgment, character and will. No one is *compos sui* if he has it not. An education which should improve this faculty would be the education *par excellence*" (p. 424). James focuses here on only on "attention," describing its benefits as making us perceive, conceive, distinguish, remember, and react better than we would otherwise. Because of this, James has been seen as a champion of the use of contemplative practices. However, James was always a careful thinker and cautions against excessive optimism. He continues: "But it is easier to define this ideal than to give practical directions for bring it about." He does not see introspection as a panacea, and neither do we. James continues to caution against the idea that focused awareness and introspection can cure problems in observation and insight:

> But, since the rest of this volume will be little more than a collection of illustrations of the difficulty of discovering by direct introspection exactly what our feelings and their relations are, we need not anticipate our own future details, but just state our general conclusion that *introspection is difficult and fallible; and that the difficulty is simply that of all observation of whatever kind* [italics in original]. (James, 1890, p. 424)

While contemplative exercises provide a means for students to explore within themselves and the subject matter, they are not intended to replace other effective means of learning. Rather, they are powerful complements for instruction across the curriculum.

Because of the subtle nature of these practices, teachers must have personal experience with them and with the cultivation of their own awareness. These are not modes that can be taught in a single workshop or described in a set of fixed protocols. Without a committed understanding of what it is like to engage in these exercises, teachers cannot guide students or respond meaningfully to them. The practices require a strong connection with the students; they should be thought of as structured improvisations rather than following rigid, fixed scripts.

Students come to our classrooms from many backgrounds. It is important that the practices be framed so that we foster inclusion. For example, students who have felt silenced in their lives might bristle at the instruction to close their eyes and be silent; for such students, it is important to introduce silence by explaining how the exercise helps them hear their own voices and allows more of themselves and their voices to be present in the classroom. Learning about our students' backgrounds is important as we introduce the practices; we can easily alienate students without any intention or awareness of doing so.

CONCLUSION

Contemplative and introspective modes of learning are an exciting pedagogical development. Placing students at the heart of their education fosters a rich environment for learning and provides the opportunity for students to cultivate attention, deepen their understanding of their studies, engender richer relationships with themselves and others, and stimulate profound inquiries into the nature of themselves and the world around them.

Current Research on Contemplative Practice

There are many kinds of contemplative practices, and they are used to achieve many different outcomes. The word *contemplation* derives from *contemplari*, to "gaze attentively," but the word was originally linked to the act of cutting out or creating a space, as in "to mark out a space for observation." The word *temple* comes from this definition: a place reserved or cut out for observance. In many ways, the practices we are discussing provide this space for students to allow them to observe and gain insight. Introspection is inward (*intro*) looking (*specere*)—the mental act of attending carefully to what is occurring within, often in response to an activity, theory, or text.

Although we might have chosen other frames, we focus on two traditions in discussing contemplative practices: meditation and introspection. No single understanding of meditation practice or of a formal model of mind is required to undertake these practices. However, before introducing them to students, it is important to have some sense of their development and the findings from researchers who have studied them.

Meditative practices are most often associated with Buddhism. However, contemplative practices exist within many religious, spiritual, and secular traditions. No specific faith is required to conduct or follow these practices; all that is demanded is that the student enter with an engaged and open mind—the same orientation as in approaching any other intellectual endeavor. The same is true for introspective practices: no specific philosophy of mind or notion of cognition is required to examine one's experience and thoughts. In many ways, introspection has always been one of the hallmarks of deep learning and is a practice encouraged throughout higher education.

Most of the practices don't fall neatly into one category or the other, but these two modes provide a good framework to set the context for their use.

MEDITATION

From the Stoic practices of *meletai*, and the prophetic Kabbalah practices of Abraham ben Samuel Abulafia, to the "noble connection" of Sufi practice through the *Exercitia spiritualia* of Ignatius of Loyola right up to modern programs of mindfulness-based stress reduction, internal reflection and the cultivation of awareness have been important aspects of both religious and secular attempts to deepen and enrich experience and meaning. Although the specific practices are very different in the various traditions, two aspects of meditation are common among them: a deep focus and the intention of developing insight. These can be accomplished in many ways, and in later chapters we outline some of these practices. Because many of these practices are grounded within rich traditions, we must ensure that we are both respectful of those traditions and aware of the implications of the practices in which we ask students to participate.

As meditation has become more prevalent in the West, researchers have become more interested in its impact. The research discoveries can help in selecting practices for the classroom in that they outline the expected results from different types of practices. Generally two types of studies are conducted on the impact of meditation. In one, long-term meditators (monks, for example, with thousands of hours of experience) are studied as they are exposed to different stimuli or asked to achieve certain mind states. While these studies are very interesting and important, their limitation is that the monks are not randomly selected people. It may be that monks become monks and meditate for thousands of hours because of powerful, preexisting conditions that in fact affect the findings of the neuroscientists. In addition, while it certainly is interesting to see the amazing outcomes of these master meditators (neuroscientist Richard

Davidson at the University of Wisconsin calls these monks "Olympic-caliber meditators"), few of us or our students will ever reach the experiences of these monks in this lifetime, so it is not clear how we should interpret their outcomes within our own lives. Although studies of these exceptional meditators are very interesting, we also focus here on studies of more typical students and teachers. These studies have shown significant gains in attention and self-regulation even after short periods (as few as five days) of meditation experience (Tang et al., 2007). This is especially good news since the opportunity to work with our students for thirty years of intense training is limited to only a very few of us.

We can categorize the results of these practices into five broad groups. Throughout the book, we examine how contemplative practices provide support for each. With regard to the scientific research done on meditation, these categories are

- Increased concentration and attention
- Increased mental health and psychological well-being
- Increased connection, generosity, and loving kindness
- Deepened understanding of the course material
- Increased creativity and insight

All academic study requires focused attention. Developing this skill, especially in areas of study that are difficult and required, can be quite challenging. Many contemplative practices foster the cultivation of student attention and concentration. Emotional regulation and positive affect have also been shown to be important in learning. As everyone in higher education knows, universities and colleges can be very stressful places. More and more, teachers are seeking ways to focus on the whole student, and not simply the student in the classroom. Contemplative practices have been shown to profoundly improve health and reduce stress, increase positive affect, and even increase natural immunity. In addition to personal gains, these practices also reveal our connection to others, and many practices are focused on the development of empathy and compassion. Self-inquiry has proven to be a powerful means for students both to understand material more fully and find their own lives in it, increasing their creativity and insight. Contemplative exercises can deepen students' understanding of the material and make it more relevant to their own experience, allowing them to think more broadly.

Of course, the exercises do not need to be limited to just one of the categories listed above but can combine two or more of them or include other aspects. Whatever the goal, when you design and implement exercises, keeping the intention of the exercise in mind is also important. This supports the students in understanding the process and provides a frame for the pedagogical goals of the course. If you are unclear about the purpose of an exercise, it will also be unclear to the students and could cause them more confusion than clarity.

We review the research on meditation using the framework described. In research on novices or meditators with some experience, subjects are examined before and after meditation training, sometimes after eight-week mindfulness-based stress reduction (MBSR) programs and sometimes after weeks of experience with just one to two hours of meditation practice per week. The experimental design of these studies ranges from very well-constructed, randomized tests to rather casual observations of treatment effects. While granting that there are significant issues in the findings of many of these studies, we provide an overview of those major findings relevant to the goals of contemplative pedagogy.

Attention, Concentration, and Brain States

Most meditation practices in the beginning stages focus on attention. It is not surprising, then, that research has focused on attention and shown that meditation develops increased levels of attentive capacities. However, the results are stronger than this. Research has shown that meditation seems to support changes in brain activity that were previously thought to be hardwired in humans and thus unchangeable.

Following on the work of the brilliant economist Herbert Simon, researchers have developed the idea of bounded awareness—the limited ability of our focus to be aware of all the stimuli around us. Studies of "inattentional" and "change" blindness and focusing illusions all can be thought of as our inability to process all the available information, especially when we do not believe or understand the salience of the information (Chugh & Bazerman, 2007). Although we can affect our ability to attend to details in our life, it has long been believed that these abilities are limited by our hardwiring.

For example, a seminal experiment conducted by Helen Slagter and colleagues in 2007 demonstrated that the attentional blink, thought to be part of human consciousness, can be reduced through intensive meditative practice. To demonstrate this, Slagter and her colleagues showed participants a string of letters and numbers one by one on a screen, flashed only for about one-tenth of a second. Most of the time a letter was shown, but occasionally a number would appear. The participants were asked about the numbers. Researchers took baseline values prior to the experiment and found that once the participant noticed a number, their attention fell and another number shown within half a second from the first was not detected—hence the term *attentional blink*. Slagter showed, however, that participants who had completed a three-month insight meditation retreat were often able to discern the second number; these participants had significantly reduced their attentional blinking, something that was not thought possible. Other studies have found even more efficient attentional processing and brain function with meditation (van den Hurk, Giommi, Gielen, Speckens, & Barendregt, 2010; Lutz et al., 2009).

Training can improve the efficiency of our mind, freeing up extra space for increased attention and introspection. In an extensive experiment, the Shamatha Project, Clifford Saron, Katherine MacLean, and colleagues at the University of California, Davis, studied the many impacts on cognition, behavior, and physiology of three months of intensive training in meditation and showed that intensive meditation training improved perceptual sensitivity and vigilance during sustained visual attention. Participants meditated about five hours each day for three months. Researchers took pre- and postmeasures from two randomly assigned groups: a group of thirty who went through the first program and a wait-list group who went through a second program, serving as controls. The findings were robust over both groups, strongly indicating the impact of the training on the attentional efficiency of the groups. MacLean et al. (2010) conclude, "These results suggest that perceptual improvements can reduce the resource demand imposed by target discrimination and thus make it easier to sustain voluntary attention" (p. 829).

Focused concentration has proved to be remarkably powerful. For years, athletes have known the power of visualizing prior to action. In *Golf My Way* (2005), Jack Nicklaus wrote, "I never hit a shot, not even in practice, without having a very sharp, in-focus picture of it in my head. First I see the ball where I want it to finish, nice and white and sitting up high on the bright green grass. Then the scene quickly changes, and I see the ball going there; its path, trajectory, and shape, even its behavior on landing. Then there is a sort of fade-out, and the next scene shows me making the kind of swing that will turn the previous images into reality" (p. 79).

Mental attention has been shown to directly affect the physiological pathways that determine action. In a study on the effects of visualization, Alvaro Pascual-Leone and colleagues showed that subjects undergoing daily physical exercises had similar gains in their ability to perform five-finger piano exercises as subjects who merely visualized these exercises with no physical activity (Pascual-Leone, Amedi, Fregni, & Merabet, 2005). In addition, researchers have begun to examine the reverse implication of focused attention: how the brain itself seems to be affected by meditation. In a remarkable study, neuroscientist Sara Lazar and colleagues at Massachusetts General Hospital demonstrated that relative to a control group, subjects with extensive insight meditation experience showed thicker brain regions (prefrontal cortex and right anterior insula) associated with attention, interoception, and sensory processing. And in good news for aging meditators, the thickness was more pronounced in older participants with extensive experience, suggesting that meditation might overcome the tendency for regions of the brain to become thinner (Lazar et al., 2005).

We are becoming aware of serious barriers to focused attention in student populations. Disorders like attention deficit disorder and attention deficit hyperactivity disorder (ADHD) are more common and debilitating than in previous years. In addition, students have more at their fingertips that provide powerful distractions: smart phones, laptops, tablets, and more. Young and old alike are finding that these conditions can increase stress and depressive or anxiety symptoms, especially in high-intensity environments that demand focused attention, like higher education. Although a number of pharmaceutical treatments are being used, researchers at UCLA have found that meditation can favorably affect both adults and adolescents with ADHD. Lidia Zylowska and colleagues conducted a feasibility study of the impact of meditation on twenty-four adults and eight adolescents with ADHD. Their results show that meditation is a "feasible intervention" in treating ADHD in both adults and adolescents; it can result in measured improvements even among those already on medication and have positive impacts on anxiety and depressive symptoms (Zylowska et al., 2008).

Many mental disciplines increase the ability to focus. We are not suggesting here that meditation is the only or even the most effective manner in which attentive capacities are increased. However, these practices do seem to increase focus, essential for academic study. What we will see later is that while other practices can stimulate attentive capacities, only meditation seems to do this while increasing mental and physical health.

Health and Psychological Well-Being

Academic environments can be stressful places for students, faculty, and staff. In the past few years, events have tragically highlighted the consequences of students acting violently after experiencing mental breakdowns. While these are extreme cases, they have increased the interest in the whole student, not just the student in the classroom. Indeed, mental health concerns have become even more pressing over time. The great successes in treating depression and other mental and emotional afflictions through medication and therapy have meant that a large number of students once unable to cope with the pressures of higher education can now manage quite well. This has been a wonderful change for thousands of students, but it has also meant that institutions have had to expand support services in order to help students continue to thrive. Research is showing that rates of depression and anxiety among students remain disturbingly high, and institutions are looking for new ways to address these issues (Dyrbye, Thomas, & Shanafelt, 2006). One of the means with exciting results is meditation practice. Meditation is being used to great effect in lowering levels of depression, obsessive rumination and anxiety, and raising levels of positive affect while increasing students' immune systems and general physical health.

In a series of carefully constructed experiments, Shauna Shapiro and colleagues have shown that students exposed to eight to ten weeks of meditation practices significantly decreased their levels of anxiety and depression (even during especially stressful finals periods) compared to carefully selected control groups. In a 1998 study, from a list of potential participants, they randomly selected one group, leaving the others on a wait list as the control group. After the full trial, the findings were replicated with the wait-list group, and again the results showed significant reductions in measured anxiety and depression (Shapiro, Schwartz, & Bonner, 1998). In a more recent 2007 study, they matched a treatment group of graduate counseling psychology students taking a ten-week meditation course with a control cohort taking didactic courses. Once again those exposed to the meditation training exhibited significant pre-post declines in negative affect, stress, and state and trait anxiety while demonstrating significant increases in positive affect (Shapiro, Brown, & Biegel, 2007).

Another interesting avenue of research is showing how strongly meditation can support students' ability to regulate and process emotional responses. In a fascinating study, Heather Wadlinger and Derek Isaacowitz (2011) show that one of the important elements in learning to regulate emotion is, not surprisingly, the extent of developed selective attention. Increased attention and focus are critical components of emotional regulatory processes. We saw earlier that long-time meditators had increased this ability, quickly stabilizing their emotional reactions to disturbing images, for example. The ability to recognize and regulate emotions has also been shown to be more pronounced among long-term meditators. In a 2006 study, Lis Nielsen and Alan Kaszniak (2006) showed that meditators with more than ten years of experience demonstrated more clarity of even subtle emotional changes, yielding lower emotional arousal and more regulation of the emotion process. These increased abilities are required to maintain well-being in response to difficult circumstances and stress.

Newer studies on emotional regulation have been conducted on relative novices. Relative to other forms of either relaxation practices or concentration practices like studying music or dance, these studies find that the students undergoing meditation training have a greater ability to recover from negative mood states and have reduced distractive and ruminative thoughts.

Willoughby Britton and colleagues have shown that students who are learning to play musical instruments or to dance have increases in concentration and attention equal to those of students who practiced meditation. However, she shows that these three groups of students differ significantly in emotional regulation: only the meditators show any pre- and postchanges with respect to emotional regulation (Roberts-Wolfe, Sacchet, & Britton, 2009). Shamini Jain and others have found similar results for meditation compared to other types of "relaxation training" (Jain et al., 2007). These responses make sense, given the special attention many meditation practices give to noting and examining emotions or thoughts as they arise while not becoming lost or indulging in them.

In another study from the Shamatha Project, meditation affected participants even on the most elemental level. In a 2010 study, meditation was shown to affect psychological health and thus improve longevity through the increase of the cellular enzyme telomerase (Jacobs et al., 2011). The enzyme strengthens and increases the length of the telomere, the sequence at the end of a chromosome that protects it from deteriorating. Many health risks and diseases are linked to the shortening of telomeres. The researchers found that the most important psychological result of the meditation was an increased sense of control and decreased neuroticism. The increased sense of purpose in life rather than measures of increased mindfulness made the biggest impact on changes in telomerase levels. So how could focusing on your thoughts have such impressive physical effects? The assumption that meditation simply induces a state of relaxation is "dead wrong," says Tonya Jacobs (Jacobs et al., 2011). Brain-imaging studies suggest that it triggers active processes within the brain and can cause physical changes to the structure of regions important to learning, memory, emotion regulation, and cognitive processing.

These findings have also been shown to be robust in other populations. In an experiment conducted by Richard Davidson and colleagues in 2003, workers at a biotech company were trained in MBSR. Compared to the wait-listed control group, those who completed the program had lower levels of reported anxiety and higher levels of positive affect measured by functional magnetic resonance imaging (fMRI), and, perhaps most interesting, they produced more antibodies after receiving a flu shot (Davidson et al., 2003).

Gratitude, Loving Kindness, and Social Connection

In his important study of the breakdown of social connection, *Bowling Alone* (2000), Robert Putnam outlines the negative consequences of increasingly isolated lifestyles. Indeed, John Heiliwell has shown that increases in general social capital, giving, and overall social connection significantly create and sustain individuals' well-being (Heiliwell & Putnam, 2004). Cooperation and connection are also increasingly important in an ever more integrated world. As the problems we face become more complex—global warming, international economic inequality, and mass extinctions, for example—we will increasingly need to work together. Indeed, even the idea of the nation-state is less and less meaningful. Consider for example the ubiquitous iPod. It is an American product, right? Well, as Greg Linden, Kenneth Kraemer, and Jason Dedrick have shown, its parts are produced by US, Japanese, and Korean producers that in turn subcontract production in China and the Philippines (Linden, Kraemer, & Dedrick, 2009).

If we don't develop our recognition and appreciation for our interconnectedness, we will repeat the errors of our past and fail in effectively addressing the most pressing issues. Many meditation practices focus on developing and deepening the realization of our connection to others. One of the best known of these practices is built on examining and cultivating *metta*, most often translated as loving kindness. This is a practice in well-wishing to ourselves and to those we are close to, indifferent to, and in conflict with. In other words, it develops well-wishing for all beings. In later chapters, we have more to say about this practice, but here we look at the experimental evidence of the consequences of this practice.

The best-known studies in this area were done in Richard Davidson's lab at the University of Wisconsin at Madison. He has demonstrated remarkable results with a group of experienced meditators. Davidson's subjects are Tibetan Buddhist monks, each with over ten thousand hours of meditation practice. Davidson and his colleagues showed that monks were able to generate the highest levels of gamma waves ever recorded in healthy subjects. These levels indicate a heightened sense of consciousness and intellectual acuity. Davidson concluded:

> To summarize, our study of compassion meditation found activation in brain regions thought to be responsible for monitoring one's feeling state, planning of movements and positive emotions. This pattern was robustly modulated by the degree of expertise. These data suggest that emotional and empathic processes are flexible skills that can be trained and that such training is accompanied by demonstrable neural changes. (Lutz, Dunne, & Davidson, 2007, p. 543)

In another study with these very experienced meditators, Antoine Lutz and colleagues showed that they had actually changed the extent of their neural circuitry dealing with emotion, enabling them to have a more profound connected and empathic response to others. In response to controlled sounds of distress, for example, Lutz found that long-time meditators' neural activation in areas of emotional processing (e.g., the amygdala) were greater than in control groups. This research seems to show that their mental expertise enabled these experienced meditators to increase empathy and positive emotions in response to emotional stimuli (Lutz, Brefczynski-Lewis, Johnstone, & Davidson, 2008).

Researchers have used compassion meditation and brain activity to examine other physiological responses as well. In a 2009 study, Thaddeus Pace and his research team found that training in compassion meditation lowered stress responses after standard laboratory stressor tests. At the beginning of the experiment, sixty-one healthy adults were randomly assigned to either six weeks of training in compassion meditation or participation in a health discussion control group. Those who had received the meditation training maintained their immune system strength and did not suffer physiologically as much from the induced stressors (Pace et al., 2009). These results indicate that reducing reactivity to stress has profound impacts on our immune systems and our ability to cope with internal responses, so that we can extend our attention to others, increasing our capacity for social connection and empathy. In a study on the link between loving kindness meditation and social connection, Cendri Hutcherson and colleagues found that even just a few minutes of loving kindness increased feelings of social connection and general positivity toward strangers. Subjects were randomly assigned to groups that received either loving kindness meditation instructions or neutral imagery instruction. (In the latter, participants were asked to imagine two little-known acquaintances and focus on their physical appearance.) The findings show that the short intervention of the loving kindness meditation affected the automatic responses to others. The researchers showed that these responses was not due to feeling better in general; rather, meditation directly increased the responses of the participants to others (Hutcherson, Seppala, & Gross, 2008).

These practices not only have impacts on our relationships to others; they also stimulate self-compassion, which has a profound impact on disorders like anxiety and depression. Self-compassion has three fundamental features: kindness and understanding toward oneself rather than self-criticism and judgment, holding oneself as connected rather than separate and isolated, and sustaining balance with thoughts and feelings and not overidentifying with negative thoughts (Neff, 2003). Each of these is naturally supported by mindfulness practices, and so it is not surprising that increases in self-compassion have been found with the practice of mindfulness. For example, exploring the benefits of MBSR, Kathryn Birnie and colleagues showed that MSBR participants "had a greater ability to adopt others' perspectives, experienced reduced distress . . . and were increasingly spiritual and compassionate toward themselves" (Birnie, Speca, & Carlson, 2010).

In a 2011 study, Nicholas Van Dam and colleagues showed that increased measures of self-compassion as measured by the Self-Compassion Scale had a far greater impact on recorded measures of anxiety and depression than mindfulness alone as measured by the Mindful Attention Awareness Scale (Van Dam, Sheppard, Forsyth, & Earleywine, 2011). This doesn't imply that mindfulness is not a powerful means to affect internal states; their studies were not on compassion meditation itself. Rather, these findings remind us that we should be aware of the personal potential of these practices, realizing that compassion meditation can change our relationships not only with others but also with ourselves. They also underscore the importance of supporting students in developing their compassion and the vital role higher education can play in that process.

Researchers investigating this connection between contemplative practice and personal insight found that one of the ways in which meditation affects our worldview is through changing our perspective on the self, that is, on how we identify and conceive of ourselves (Hölzel et al., 2011).

Positive feeling and compassion have also been found to stimulate and increase learning. In a series of interesting studies, Mary Helen Immordino-Yang of University of Southern California's Rossier School of Education documented the role of emotions and compassion in the learning process. In "We Feel, Therefore We Learn: The Relevance of Affective and Social Neuroscience to Education" and other articles, she and colleagues explored the central role of emotions and social connection in decision making and learning. Her research suggests that we should redesign learning environments and pedagogy to reap the benefits of greater self-awareness and social connection (Immordino-Yang & Damasio, 2008).

INTROSPECTION

A second mode of contemplative practice is introspection—the careful examination by students of their internal processes, thoughts, and feelings in order to gain deeper insight into themselves and the material of the course. However, it is not enough for students to analyze themselves in any fashion. The teacher needs to be aware of the limitations and problems within introspection to be able to lead students through meaningful inquiries. A brief history of introspection in modern psychology will help frame how to use introspective exercises effectively.

In the contemplative traditions of Buddhism, Judaism, Islam, and Christianity, introspection has been a major source of insight into both the nature of the world around us and the nature of ourselves. In the Western tradition of psychology and pedagogy, introspection once had a vibrant tradition. In fact, psychology as a discipline came out of an attempt to gather first-person data so that theories of mind and consciousness could be moved from the realm of speculation to a more data-driven, scientific methodology. Although William James saw its overall limitations, he went so far as to proclaim in his grand opus, *The Principles of Psychology* (1890), "*introspective observation is what we have to rely on first and foremost always*" (emphasis in the original text; p. 185).

At the turn of the nineteenth century, Pierre Maine de Biran recognized the benefit of what we could call introspection, and later in the century, Franz Brentano, Wilhelm Wundt, and William James all saw what James had declared. There began a research program carried out in both Europe (in Paris under Alfred Binet and in Germany by the Wurtzburg School headed by Oswald Külpe) and the United States (centered at Cornell University under Edward B. Titchener). These research programs were based on the idea that the gathered first-person accounts provided rigorous, primary data on which the science of behavior and mind, psychology, could be developed. Common to all these approaches was the idea that the subjects had to be trained, in the fineness of the awareness of their perception and its careful articulation by the researcher, or "mediator." However, these cautions have been forgotten over time, and the critiques of introspective research often do not undertake research with subjects with any training. This is not to suggest that our students be forced through rigorous training; rather, it states that the results of casual studies with participants without any training are very different from what Wundt and his colleagues were suggesting.

Very soon these research programs were attacked. The initial critic was the French philosopher Auguste Comte. His classic attack was two-pronged: (1) introspection itself was internally contradictory, and (2) even if we set aside this foundational issue, introspection cannot generate reliable and consistent data. Comte believed it was ridiculous that the subject be asked to perceive what was happening and examine at the same time, from an objective viewpoint, the process and implications of his or her perception. That would be to ask the subject to split himself into two parts.

The modern version of this argument is well articulated by philosopher of mind John Searle. In his *Rediscovery of the Mind* (1992), Searle argues strongly against any special facility of introspection: "Where conscious subjectivity is concerned, there is no distinction between the observation and the thing observed, between the perception and the object perceived." And, he continues, "any introspection I have of my own conscious state is itself that conscious state" (pp. 143–144). While Searle readily admits that we might quite easily think about our own mental states, he objects to the idea that this sort of thinking has any special ability to look within (*spect intro*). In other words, while we might for practical reasons examine the content or extent of our thoughts, we should not believe that we could learn anything special about the nature of our minds with a method known as introspection. "The idea that there might be a special method of investigating consciousness, namely 'introspection,' which is supposed to be a kind of inner observation, was doomed to failure from the start, and it is not surprising that introspective psychology proved bankrupt" (p. 97).

This is not the place to enter this debate, but we should note that even in the most modern, sophisticated fMRI studies, the only way to interpret and map the areas of the brain that are lighting up with increased blood flow is by interviewing the subject in real time, for example, asking the person if she or he is happy when the left medial, prefrontal lobe is activated. In a series of experiments, Morten Overgaard and Thomas Sørensen (2004) show that introspection is distinct from first-order experience so that we can have access to our conscious states "in such a way that makes us able to recognize and think about the state as being conscious" (p. 79). The only way we know that "happiness" or feelings of well-being are happening is through interviewing the subject and asking him or her. Without this, we have only an image of where blood flow is especially high. Recall too that the type of introspection we are encouraging through these exercises is closer to the type that Searle acknowledges; we are most often asking our students to reflect and deeply inquire into their thoughts. As they do this, they will most likely become interested in the underlying nature of thought, and this can be a powerful investigation, especially as they are forming their sense of self.

However, as much attention as his first critique received, Comte's second, empirical objection has been more influential. The second objection was extended through the twentieth century and made especially powerful by studies in cognitive science showing that subjects are often unable to describe the conditions under which they make decisions. This type of research broadly falls under the heading of "subliminal perception," and much work has been done to show that stimuli for which a subject has no awareness can have important impacts on responses and even higher-order decisions.

The classic description of this critique is Richard Nisbett and Timothy Wilson's "Telling More Than We Can Know: Verbal Reports on Mental Processes" (1977). Though this paper was published more than thirty-five years ago, it is still cited as providing strong evidence that introspection has no place in research. In the paper, they review a series of studies describing subjects who cannot describe the higher-order decision making that they are engaged in. Instead of describing internal operations, they claim that the subjects' reports are rather "based on *a priori* implicit causal theories, or judgments about the extent to which a particular stimulus is a plausible cause of a given response" (p. 231).

For example, a test group and a control group were asked to give answers to prompts like, "Please name a brand of laundry detergent." The test group was asked to memorize pairs of words like "moon and ocean." The test group members disproportionately provide the brand "Tide," suggested by the association of words like "moon" and "ocean." When asked why they selected that brand, they answered with explanations like, "My mom always used Tide," or "I like the color of the Tide bottle." Even when asked whether they thought the word pair might have influenced their decision, they most often denied the possibility. This type of study has been used to suggest that subjects cannot properly discern their mental operations and are surprised to hear that they might have been influenced by the structure of the experiment or outright deny that it had an effect on them.

Other studies done on preferences have shown similar results. Basic hedonic responses have been shown to be influenced directly by subliminal cues. In a study in 2005, Piotr Winkielman, K. C. Kent Berridge, and Julia Wilbarger showed that subjects' preferences and consumption behavior were directly altered by subliminal exposure to happy or angry facial expressions, even though they did not express an overall affect change and were not aware that they had been exposed to an image of a happy or angry face (Winkielman, Berridge, & Wilbarger, 2005). In a now classic study, Timothy Wilson and Jonathan Schooler (2008) did a blink-like study in which they had two groups of college students taste different brands of strawberry jam and judge college courses, one group "analyzing" why they felt as they did and the other not. Those who did not go through an analytical appraisal were more likely to agree with "experts" than those who did. In related studies, it has been shown that thinking about the reasons for our choices can actually lower our satisfaction and well-being with them (Wilson, Lisle, Schooler, & Hodges, 1993). Simply allowing an introspective moment certainly does not guarantee insights into behavior or ensure outcomes more consistent with one's values or wishes.

While these studies provide a good sense of caution in drawing conclusions from students' reports, they do not mean that these reports are worthless. As Pierre Vermersch points out, "What is wrong about this line of reasoning is that it moves from the premise that there are facts which are inaccessible to consciousness to the conclusion that even what is accessible to consciousness is uninteresting or non-scientific, and this *a priori*, which is not only absurd but wholly unjustified" (Vermersch, 1999, p. 28).

In fact, I would argue that as we witness students being unconscious of their priors, we should not throw our hands up and say they are inherently incapable of self-knowledge, as Nisbett and Wilson seem to do. Rather, we can address this directly and develop the means for them to uncover their implicit heuristics. It requires establishing the prerequisites for deep and sustained introspection. While increased awareness has advantages, sometimes it seems that a lack of awareness can result in the best outcomes. For example, in his work on flow, Mihaly Csikszentmihalyi notes the paradoxical result that though people seem to generally experience maximum pleasure when they are engaged in flow experiences, they spend most of their leisure time in passive activities, like watching television, that do not produce flow states. Csikszentmihalyi and Judith LeFevre speculate that the reason for this is that people lack the meta-awareness of the positive nature of these states because during them they are too rapt in the experience to actively note "pleasure." "We have, then, the paradoxical situation of people having many more positive feelings at work than in leisure, yet saying that they 'wish to be doing something else' when they are at work, not when they are at leisure . . . Needless to say, such a blindness to the real state of affairs is likely to have unfortunate consequences for individual well-being and the health of society" (Csikszentmihalyi & LeFevre, 1989, pp. 820–821). Their conclusion is that people should become more aware of their inner states; by doing so, they will better allocate their time and achieve higher states of sustained well-being.

This, of course, takes training. As B. Alan Wallace (2007) states, "A simple fact that is hardly acknowledged by either cognitive scientists or philosophers of mind is that mental events *can* be observed directly." However, the careful discernment of these requires training and guidance. He continues, "Crucial to making rigorous observations of mental phenomena is the cultivation of sustained, vivid, high-resolution attention" (p. 15). If we examine the research program of Wilhelm Wundt, for example, we find that he and his students (like Titchener) had clear guidelines for both the subjects and the researchers using introspection. Titchener's description of the proper training of subjects is elaborately detailed in his four-volume, sixteen-hundred-page lab manual (1901).

The studies required systematically training subjects to report subtly and carefully what they perceived. Vermersch (1999) believes that in order to practice deep introspection, we "need to form 'observers,' to subject them to a long training until they become reliable in regard to what they describe." In fact, "for certain research themes it might be necessary to count on the expertise of such subjects to the extent that they would be the only ones capable of gaining access to certain objects of research, for example, those of short duration or which require high levels of discrimination" (p. 35). Using this approach, one cannot simply randomly select students for a study or work closely with subjects who had no training in discerning the variety of their responses. Titchener in his lab notes states that "the average student, on entering the laboratory, is simply not competent to participate as an introspective observer" (Schwitzgebel, 2004, p. 61). On the flip side, the mediator/teacher cannot simply adopt these techniques as one might use a PowerPoint display. Training and attention are also required to facilitate and guide students through any meaningful process of introspection. Our focus should be on both ourselves and our students as we prepare and introduce these techniques.

As B. Alan Wallace (1999) writes, "Just as unaided human vision was found to be an inadequate instrument for examining the moon, planets and stars, Buddhists regard the undisciplined mind as an unreliable instrument for examining mental objects, processes, and the nature of consciousness" (p. 176). How do we encourage the sort of stability that is the ground for meaningful introspection?

The neurologist Richard Cytowic (2002) has written about the use of first-person accounts and how they led him to new discoveries of the neuropsychology of synesthesia. His method is to recognize that "part of the problem is that patients frequently *interpret* events instead of *reporting* them straightforwardly as one would wish ideally" (Cytowic, 2003, p. 158). Just like our students, his patients, while trying to report, were actually slipping into metaphor or interpretation. This requires the clinician, Cytowic continues, to listen carefully and help the patient return to description. It requires that the bias in the patients is discerned by the clinician so that the patient can begin to report without embellishment. This process requires both a "training of the subjects" and careful listening and responses from the clinician, or, in our case, the teacher (2003, p. 159).

CONCLUSION

In the rest of the book, we examine the qualitative benefits of contemplative practices in the academic setting. Many of the significant benefits have yet to be studied by cognitive scientists, but the scientific studies that have been conducted demonstrate many gains in attention and awareness, health and well-being, self-understanding and compassion, and increased and deepened connection with others. The growing literature has only begun to show what those of us who have practiced already know: these contemplative methods are powerful means for a deeper engagement with life and greater insight into ourselves and others. The amazing opportunity to share this with our students is what we explore in the rest of the book.

Contemplative Pedagogy in Practice

Two Experiences

Contemplative practices and introspective exercises have been introduced in every academic discipline from poetry to physics to law. Some teachers have found that just a few minutes of silence at the beginning of class make a big difference in students' ability to be present and learn. Others have integrated practices more fully, adapting them to the needs and context of their course. In this chapter, we provide examples of two quite different courses using contemplative practices. They demonstrate how diverse approaches in integrating the practices and exercises can increase students' discernment and attentive capacity, deepen their understanding of the material of the course, and enrich their relationships with themselves, each other, and the world.

Caring, Listening, and Resilience:
Building Professional Skills for Social Work Students
Mirabai Bush

One afternoon in a third-floor room with no windows, a group of social work students faced each other in two rows, silently repeating phrases about the person across from each of them: "Just like me, this person has known physical pain. Just like me, this person has done things she regrets.

Just like me, this person wants to be happy . . ." They were doing a compassion practice designed to shift their perspectives and deepen their understanding that we human beings are similar in important ways, no matter how vast our differences are. We all need food, and shelter, and love. We crave attention, recognition, affection, and, above all, happiness. Resentments, disagreements, and estrangements hurt all parties because they reinforce feelings of separation. And that separation is true only at one level. This activity was helping them remember how we are connected by our humanity.

When asked to bring others to mind and to add more personal phrases, students said, "My partner is stubborn, just like me." "My client holds grudges, just like me." And for positive connections, they said, for example, "He is generous with his time, just like me." "She is creative, just like me." The exercise ended with wishes for well-being sent to their partners in the opposite row and then to others who were not there: may you be free from pain and suffering, may you live with ease in the world, may you be happy.

This class was at the Smith College School for Social Work, part of the Contemplative Clinical Practice Advanced Certificate Program directed by Dean Carolyn Jacobs. I teach contemplative practices as part of the curriculum to improve students' critical professional skills of listening and communication and increase their personal resilience in a very demanding profession. The program, which is grounded in theory, based in the clinical relationship, and responsive to cultural and spiritual contexts, considers the clinical relationship as a potential locus of the sacred. Compassion and other contemplative practices give clinicians a method for being present in that sacred space. For the program, spirituality is defined as "the aspect of humanity that refers to the way individuals seek and express meaning and purpose and the way they experience their connectedness to the moment, to self, to others in nature, and to the significant or sacred."

Choosing Relevant Practices for Social Work Caregivers

When Carolyn first asked me to teach, I knew I'd have to reflect quietly for some time on what would be the most appropriate practices and the best way to frame them. All forms of spirituality and contemplation had been absent from social work training until very recently, when she and a few other colleagues had introduced them into the curriculum. I wanted to support her bold leadership in developing this program, and I knew that the practices would be effective only if they made sense to the students and connected with their needs and the needs of their clients. In my work at the Center for Contemplative Mind in Society, I'd been teaching contemplative practices to many people—lawyers, judges, journalists, scientists, social justice activists, engineers—but I hadn't taught college or university students in a long time. I started thinking about that.

My first glimpse that contemplative experience can be a way in which we construct knowledge and meaning was during the late 1960s when I was teaching in the English Department at SUNY Buffalo. The department faculty was full of prestigious, creative, and brilliant minds, including John Barth, Bob Creeley, Bob Haas, and Angus Fletcher. Reading, writing, and discussing went on all day and into the nights. And in the background, something else was happening. In 1968 Martin Luther King Jr. was killed, and the New York State legislature ruled that beginning in 1969, the university enrollment would match the demographics of the state: 10 percent of students would be black and Native American. In 1968, the number was less than 1 percent, so the freshman class in the fall was largely students of color. And they all had to take Freshman English.

Most of these students were from the Buffalo public schools, and most were poorly prepared to be in college. Most, in fact, had never dreamed of going to college. In my class, these students didn't have the language skills to construct a well-designed essay, and they didn't have the confidence to trust their own ideas. The traditional approaches to writing didn't work.

But we had to start somewhere. It seemed unfair to bring them onto campus, pay their tuition, and then just let them fail. What would be least threatening, most interesting to them? Influenced as a good literature student was in the late 1960s by phenomenology, existentialism, and Gestalt psychology, I designed a practice called here and now. I asked them to just write what was happening here and now, paying attention to what they were seeing, hearing, touching, and thinking, and letting go of any other ideas or memories. At first they were to begin each sentence, and later each paragraph, with "Here and now." And they were to keep writing until the time was up. I had not heard of freewriting then, but here it was, giving students permission to write what they knew in the moment. The results were sometimes mundane, sometimes astonishing. It wasn't so hard after all. I didn't call this mindful writing, but of course it was: being in the moment, paying attention to one thing at a time, not judging. And they loved doing it. They could write! From here they came (more or less) to appreciate why grammar and structure were important in expressing ideas. And I had discovered my first contemplative practice.

That period was not only an important time in the civil rights movement, when many of us fed breakfast to children in the community with the Black Panthers and protested for more black faculty, but also a brutal time in the antiwar movement on campus, leading to the US invasion of Cambodia and students being shot and killed at Kent State. As well as my English classes, I was teaching a course in film, filling in for faculty who had gone with the Venceremos Brigade to Cuba to help the revolutionaries harvest sugar (times were different). Once a week, we'd watch a film and then discuss it around a seminar table. One night, the film was *The Battle of Algiers*, a story about the anticolonial guerrilla movement in Algeria and the methods the French used to annihilate it. The film evoked much of what was happening in Vietnam, and as I watched it, I felt sadness, anger, frustration, guilt, and fear.

When we returned to the seminar room, it seemed that the students were also powerfully moved. They took their seats around the table and waited for me to open the discussion. Nothing that came to me seemed right. Words seemed to trivialize what we had just experienced, and the quieter we became, the more I could hear. So I didn't speak. *Fine*, I thought, *I can't do it, so one of the students will open the conversation.* No one did. We sat there in silence. Time passed, and passed. When the hour was over, we got up and walked out in silence. On the evaluations at the end of the semester, every student said that this had been the most powerful class: by not speaking and just experiencing their own thoughts and emotions, they had learned so much about the film and themselves.

I didn't think I should use silent classes as a practice at Smith (what a thought!), but seeing what could happen in silence, long before I had ever meditated or done anything "contemplative," taught me that there is a place for silence in teaching and learning. Chaim Potok, whom I was reading at the time, wrote: "I've begun to realize that you can listen to silence and learn from it. It has a quality and a dimension all its own" (Potok, 1967, p. 48).

Since I had learned then to let the methods emerge from the context and in the interim had learned many contemplative practices, it was time to think about the social work students. Who are they? I started reading their applications. They are credentialed social workers returning to Smith for an advanced certificate. They had diverse spiritual, contemplative, and religious backgrounds and some had been through AA. They would want to know that these practices were compatible with their own paths.

The students also wanted many things from this program: to find hope, peace, and purpose; to enhance clinical practice and to help others; to practice balance; to learn how to deal with ethical issues around spirituality; to have a more disciplined daily practice; to be able to listen not only to their clients' words "but their souls"; to feel more comfortable with spirituality in order to assist others with their explorations; to be better prepared to create an outreach program for survivors of trauma with an ecumenical approach; and to protect themselves from the burnout and compassion fatigue associated with their profession.

The center had done a survey of the benefits of meditation for caregivers, so I had been thinking about that. We found that burnout, commonly experienced as a consequence of increased workload and institutional stress, is characterized by depersonalization, emotional exhaustion, and a sense of low personal accomplishment. Many students, not just social work students, experience these symptoms. "Compassion fatigue" is different: it contains an element of trauma as well, common among caregivers in extreme crisis situations, who are vulnerable to vicarious traumatization. The symptoms are both psychological and physical. They include anxiety, depression, heightened irritability, hopelessness, anger, exhaustion, hypertension, gastrointestinal complaints, insomnia, and headaches.

Clearly, if contemplative practices could help social work students in their studies and their clinical practice avoid or recover from these symptoms, we should start offering them immediately. What the center found was that several meta-analytic reviews of nearly three decades of research provide significant evidence that meditative and contemplative practices can help physical and psychological health (Shapiro, Brown, & Astin, 2008). Much of this research has focused on mindfulness-based stress reduction (MBSR), but there are also indications that other forms of contemplative practice can be applied with positive results to a wide range of clinical problems.

After studying the survey, reading the students' applications, and talking to Carolyn about the program, which included a four-day session in the fall and one in the spring, I thought that these social work students could benefit from contemplative practices in three principal ways. First, practice could increase their resilience through self-awareness, self-care, and self-compassion. Like many other caregivers, they experience vicarious trauma from being with people who are suffering. In one seminar session, a student told us that a twenty-one-year-old colleague had committed suicide the day before. A volunteer firefighter, he hung himself with a fire hose in the station. Practice could help this student become calmer and clearer, be more aware of what is arising in his grief, and send loving energy to his friend. It could give him the stability of attention to learn from this experience and deepen his compassion as a caregiver.

Second, mindful listening practice and compassion practices could help them in their relationships with their clients and colleagues. A student told about being with a woman in hospice care who had no one—no friends or family members. "I didn't know what to do for her, so I just breathed with her. I sang to her, a childhood lullaby." It was a good choice.

Loving kindness practice, wishing well to self and others, is helpful in dealing with difficult people. Given their challenging circumstances, clients are often emotional—sad, angry, defeated. Practice can help a caregiver appreciate clients, remembering that they are struggling human beings just like the caregiver and want to be happy.

And third, some of these practices, especially mindfulness of the breath or walking meditation, might be helpful to share with the clients themselves. Practice could also increase their sense of meaning in their lives and work.

The students came from diverse spiritual, religious, and cultural backgrounds, including some who thought that life itself was so astonishing that they didn't need religion. Therefore, the practices had to be secular so they would work for everyone. I would also have to acknowledge that many students had existing practices and explain that we'd chosen secular practices that we could do together as a class, honoring that they would continue their own practices at home. I reread and was inspired by words that an army chaplain, a caregiver, had sent me:

> Time and time again while deployed to a combat environment, I reflected on a phrase from Psalm 46, "Be still and know that I am God." There is great spiritual power in quietness and stillness, and throughout the centuries many spiritual leaders have developed contemplative practices to experience this power. I am a Christian and cannot disassociate the focus or content of my contemplation from my practice, but I recognize that I can learn methods from other sources that can deepen my own practice.
>
> If we are truly God's creation, then there must be a part of us that God built for connecting and communicating with our creator. It is this part that lies at the core of contemplative and mindfulness practices. These practices form a discipline that allows us to communicate and connect even though we may not agree theologically.

Introducing the Practices

Carolyn had created a meditation room from a third-floor conference room, and we did most of the practices there, although we also did a silent walk one Sunday morning on campus, an eating meditation in the dining room, and a closing ritual in the meeting room. When I led case consultations in small groups, I always started with a few minutes of silence.

The schedule was designed to give students opportunities to practice together first thing in the morning, and again in the afternoon and at the end of the day. During the rest of the day, they had case consultations and seminar-style classes, including Introduction to Spiritual Traditions, Death and Dying, Narrative Approaches to Spirituality, and Cross-Cultural Issues and the Significance of Difference. Contemplative perspective and tone marked all the classes, as well as the practice sessions. In the class on death and dying, for example, the students wrote their own elegies and talked about organizing a celebration of life for a patient before the person dies.

The first morning, we gathered in the meditation room. I had brought a flower from my garden, and I lit a votive candle as a reminder that we were creating a sacred space. Sometimes the intention reflected in a simple object can transform a classroom or a bare room into a place of practice. Some people sat on meditation cushions, others on chairs. I began with a welcome, noting what a precious opportunity we had to practice together and learn together. I talked about how I thought practice can be helpful in social work. Then we talked about varieties of practice, the importance of establishing and renewing intention, the importance of self-care through a daily practice. "You wouldn't not eat or brush your teeth," I said. "Practice will become as second nature as that after a while if you are faithful to it. We practice to be present for what arises," I told them. "You never know."

We started with mindfulness and in the following days did a number of other practices: just like me (described in the opening paragraphs), mindful sitting, mindful eating, mindful listening, loving kindness, beholding a painting, and giving and taking (adapted from the Tibetan Buddhist practice called *tonglen*).

Mindfulness

I introduced basic mindful sitting practice to establish stability and focus, on which all other practice rests (see chapter 5 for instructions). Mindfulness brings self-awareness and can alter how we interact with others, so it could help these students know themselves and interact with clients. I gave instructions, and we sat for twenty minutes:

> Bring your awareness to your breath, breathing in and out, noticing everything about the breath. When your mind wanders away, gently return to the breath, again and again. No judgment. Notice the thoughts and emotions, but let them go and return to your breath.

John Cage once said about opinions and thought, "Regard it as something seen momentarily, as though from a window when traveling . . . at any instant, one may leave it, and whenever one wishes, one may return to it. Or you may leave it forever and never return to it, for we possess nothing . . . Anything therefore is a delight (since we do not possess it) and we thus need not fear its loss" (Cage, 1961, p. 110).

After the practice, there were questions: How do I keep from falling asleep? Will my mind ever be still? I am worried about my husband who is home alone—what should I do? We talked until there were no more comments and questions, and then we left the room.

Mindful Eating

Before lunch, we sat together in silence for a few minutes and then did an eating meditation. This brings meditation into the ordinary actions of the day and can be especially revealing to students, who most often eat in a rush amid a clamor of voices, music, and other sounds. We began by remembering those who are hungry and the farmworkers who grew and harvested the food. I taught them mindful eating practice with a raisin: bringing awareness to the color, shape, smell, texture of the raisin in your hand; then putting it into your mouth, not chewing yet, noticing taste, noticing your body respond, noticing your thoughts and emotions, your desire to chew, to swallow; then chewing, swallowing, and noticing all the sensations. At the end we reflected on the earth. Earth brings us into life and nourishes us. Earth takes us back again. We are born and we die with every breath. We tried to keep that awareness as we ate sandwiches and salads in the student center.

Mindful Listening

Most students benefit from learning to listen well; for social workers, it is a critical skill. The program assumes a mastery of basic social work practice skills, including listening, but through the practices we introduce, we invite them to go more deeply into the transformative power of contemplative listening and knowing. That afternoon, I introduced mindful listening (instructions are in chapter 7). Present-moment orientation helps us be aware of what is going on around us and within us. We often realize that our inner voices are not always truthful or helpful to us, so they may not be helpful to the client either. Social workers, like all the rest of us, are often judging others and jumping to conclusions instead of relaxing into what the client is saying and listening with care and attention. They are often composing what they are going to say next, which keeps them from fully hearing the client. In a discussion on aging and dying, students said that just listening was often the best thing they could offer—listening, encouraging reminiscences, helping clients reframe the past. Being heard helps a client find meaning in his or her life.

In our listening exercise, each speaker began with the phrase, "In my work, I am hoping that contemplative practice can help me with . . ." This allowed the students to get to know each other's concerns, and articulating those concerns clarified them. How do I think this will help me anyhow? They became very engaged in both the speaking and the listening. In their work, they listen all day long, but they are rarely listened *to* with full attention. They loved it. They concluded only when I rang the bell; had I not, they might still be talking and listening even today. They returned to the full circle and shared what they learned.

Beholding

At the center, we have often integrated contemplative arts into our work. At a retreat for environmental leaders, Paul Winter played the saxophone accompanied by a recording of the sounds of wolves who had recently been reintroduced into Yellowstone. Aaron Shragge played the shakuhachi (a Japanese end-blown flute) at an academic retreat session on listening. Performance artist Akim Funk Buddha once did a hip-hop tea ceremony at a summer curriculum session. And Carrie Bergman often leads contemplative drawing and collage sessions at academic gatherings. So I wanted to include art in this course.

We decided to take advantage of the Smith College Museum of Art to practice contemplative seeing, or beholding (see chapter 7 for instructions). Art museums, along with gardens, wilderness areas, and some churches, are among the few public contemplative spaces in the United States. For the beholding practice, Carolyn chose *La Bendición en el Día de la Boda* (The Blessing on Wedding Day), a painting by Carmen Lomas Garza, a Chicana narrative artist who creates images about the everyday events in the lives of Mexican Americans based on her memories and experiences in Texas and California. We gathered around the painting, first sitting quietly doing a short mindfulness practice, then looking at the painting silently in small groups for fifteen minutes each, allowing the painting to speak to each of us and being with what it said. While looking, the students reflected on questions like these: What do you see? What are you bringing to what you see? They looked and looked again and continued to look at the painting. Carolyn encouraged them to suspend what they know of colors, medium, history, and culture and "allow the essence of knowing to flow from beyond the boundaries of disciplinary knowledge to an intuitive presence from within." When everyone had had time with the painting, we sat together again around it and discussed our reactions and the process of letting go and looking again and again.

The responses were quite varied. Was the grandmother happy or sad? Were those suitcases about leaving the family and its culture? Why was the sister looking away? They disagreed about interpretations: "I think it is full of happiness." "No, I see grief there." It had become personal. Everyone saw the same painting, but they all saw something slightly different. Beholding the painting instead of looking for a moment and walking by allowed the students to be intimate with the painting, to know it in a contemplative way. They could now take that way of looking home with them.

Compassion: Giving and Taking.
In a session on collective trauma, which considered events like Hurricane Katrina, Carolyn had talked about how we have separated the mind/body/spirit of the individual from the collective. The giving and taking practice (*tonglen* in Tibetan) reveals our interconnection with the collective, with the world, and with each other (instructions are in chapter 9). A powerful method, it is sometimes used in environmental classes to illustrate ecological awareness or in political science to demonstrate the nature of strong community. It is a process of breathing in, allowing ourselves to be open to things we want to avoid, and breathing out, letting go and sharing what we want to keep for ourselves.

Tonglen cultivates compassion, a sense of caring about another's pain and wanting to relieve it. It is a fundamental part of a strong and mature heart and mind and a principal skill of caregiving. Compassion for others is built on compassion for ourselves and on the understanding that if we can't care for ourselves, we cannot care about others. Self-care in our culture has come to seem selfish, egoistic, a process of withdrawal, antithetical to good service; the caregiver or activist or teacher is often the last to receive care for herself. But the importance of self-care has been known since ancient times as the foundation for knowing oneself— the purpose of education and the path to becoming fully human. Socrates would stop young men on the street and say, "You must care for yourselves." It remained a fundamental principle for knowing oneself through the Greek, Hellenistic, and Roman cultures and philosophy. Michel Foucault, in a brilliant analysis of the modern Western mind, wrote that it was the "Cartesian moment" ("I think, therefore I am") that devalued self-care by making thinking into a "fundamental means of access to truth." Descartes believed that knowledge and knowledge alone gives access to truth. Spirituality that posits that the person must undergo a transformation (through practices and self-care) in order to know the truth is discredited. There was a break between "on the one hand, the principle of an access to truth accomplished in terms of the knowing subject alone and, on the other hand, the spiritual necessity of the subject's work on himself, of his self-transformation and expectation of enlightenment and transfiguration from the truth" (Foucault, 1988, p. 26). We are left with the results of that break—the belief that truth is known through knowledge alone rather than wisdom; the reemergence of contemplative practices is a response to that belief.

Students and social workers also often have a hard time accepting the full catastrophe of their own lives or those of their clients, and they often take on too much work or responsibility. They need to let go of some of it, but letting go is not easy. I once had the insight that even letting go of things you don't want isn't easy. I once realized that even "losing" weight is a loss. We don't like loss. We resist it. But once we understand how less is more, then the lightness of being that replaces what we lose will open up our lives. Then it's okay. That is what this practice reveals.

Although it is often easy to feel compassion for others who are sick or troubled, it can be harder to feel it for people who are threatening or problematic. In the practice, you can bring one of these persons to mind, breathing in and out, feeling connected. Breathe in what you want to avoid, imagining it as heavy, thick, and hot. Breathe out to the other whatever you want to keep for yourself—happiness, joy, ease, peace, and imagining it as light, bright, and cool. The practice helps us grow larger hearts, and it opens our minds. One student said that it is like being an air-conditioner, taking in hot, humid air and giving out cool, dry, comforting air.

Walking Meditation

The last practice we did was walking meditation (see chapter 8 for instructions). Students walk frequently at most institutions; walking meditation is a way for them to center, clear their minds, and experience calm and ease between demanding classes, whether they are walking through a city or on wooded college grounds. It was a beautiful morning, and Smith has an extraordinary campus, designed in the nineteenth century by Frederick Law Olmsted, who also designed Central Park and many other American public spaces. The entire campus is an arboretum; there are curving drives and walkways, open spaces with specimen trees, and vistas over Paradise Pond through wooded groves. The many gardens include the Japanese Garden for Reflection and Contemplation, which incorporates elements of traditional Japanese design adapted to the context of a New England setting.

Each person chose a place to walk and a type of walking meditation from the several I demonstrated. They walked for thirty minutes and returned to share their experiences. "The trees were shimmering." "I began to notice the space between things more than the things themselves." "I kept letting go of my thoughts and stayed with the sensations in my feet. My mind became really clear." "I used the verse, 'I have arrived, I am home,' with each two steps. And I actually felt like I was home, in the middle of Smith!"

Closing Ritual

At the end of the last session, Carolyn led a ritual in which students read their original intentions, which they had written on cards on the first day. Some felt they had moved toward their goals; others found that their goals had changed. They all expressed deep appreciation for the course and predicted that their work would be quite different now. The practices they learned in this class can be adapted in many academic classes, as the rest of this book demonstrates. These practices worked for this spiritually, professionally, and ethically diverse group because they are not esoteric rituals but simple practices that helped them become better caregivers and lifelong students, knowing better what it is to be fully human.

Friends or Foes? The Use of Contemplative Practice in Economics
Daniel Barbezat

Love and kindness are the very basis of society. If we lose those feelings, society will face tremendous difficulties; the survival of humanity will be endangered.
—Dalai Lama, *A Policy of Kindness*

Economic Well-Being

Although economics is associated with consumer welfare and utility, it is a social science most associated with trade-offs, opportunity costs, and constraints; little wonder it is known as the "dismal science." I was not surprised, therefore, to find that a search for "happiness" over the period 1946 to 1990 using the economic literature database EconLit yielded just nineteen results. In the past twenty years, though, economists have become increasingly interested in well-being and even happiness itself. In a search for the keyword *happiness* over the period 1991 to 2013, I found 1,704 results. In about half the time, the increase was nearly ninety-fold. This incredible change has come about with the heightened attention to ideas of the quality of life and life satisfaction, along with the growing interest in more subtle and robust ways to think about worldwide development and economic well-being. Survey data on well-being have been used to test both micro- and macroeconomic theories and to estimate the impact of public policies.

Upon learning about this vast literature, I wanted to explore it and teach a class that examined it. After all, economics is the study of the interaction of supply and demand—supply being the resources and production that exist and demand the expression of preferences—that yields economic welfare. Fundamentally economics is the study of how we attain and sustain well-being through our market interactions. The study of well-being—its definition, measurement, and attainment—is central to all economic analysis.

In order to explore this issue and the literature generated about it, I thought that first-person, experiential, contemplative exercises would be a powerful way for students to engage with the material and understand it more deeply. Through exercises designed to illustrate aspects of the readings and lectures, students would come to find themselves in the center of their own education while deepening their understanding of the material, themselves, and others. Instead of lecturing about positional concerns and assigning readings in the literature, I had students think about their own experience with comparing themselves to others, so that they could see that rather than a mechanical relationship, they created and largely controlled the ways in which they related to others. Once the students had discovered their own experience of comparing themselves to others and helping others, they were ready to explore the economic theories known as the Easterlin paradox and the relative income hypothesis.

Student Agency, Contemplative Exercises, and Learning

Before turning to the example, let's review the intention and gains from contemplative exercises so that we can see how they are applied to this example from economics.

Creating cooperative environments in which students have more voice than is typical in their own learning is a common and powerful theme in modern pedagogy. Teachers have used many formats, methods, and theories to attempt this; however, these attempts are often rather forced and awkward as teachers grapple with their role in guiding and evaluating students. Teachers can easily become frustrated as they attempt to negotiate inclusion and control, yet see themselves as betraying students by inviting them to participate equally yet submit to evaluation. Although finding the appropriate level of authority and cooperation is challenging, creating an environment in which students have more direct control over their learning and experience, and more voice and agency, is worth the effort. As Pablo Freire has challenged, "Education must begin with the solution of the teacher-student contradiction, by reconciling the poles of the contradiction so that both are simultaneously students and teachers" (1970, p. 172). Contemplative pedagogy is one way to respond to this challenge, especially in a field like economics that is essentially about choice under constraints.

One area in which students have undisputed authority is their awareness of their own experience and their reactions and relationships to the material presented by the teacher. This is what makes contemplative practice such a fertile method for both enriching students' understanding of the material and elevating the role of students from passive learners to active, reflective responders to their own learning. Through introspection and guided contemplative practices, students can be powerful, first-person sources in their learning. In order for this to be meaningful, however, they must develop the ability to be keenly aware of their own reactions and sustain careful examination of them in light of the material of the course. For this process, the basic tools of mindfulness are extremely useful.

I am not addressing the broad epistemological questions of learning from experience here or the ideas developed under those of a contemplative science, like those of B. Alan Wallace or Evan Thompson; rather, I am focusing on the use of contemplative and introspective exercises to allow students to be at the center of their own learning. Through this sort of attention and inquiry, students can develop different strengths. The contemplative exercise examined here stresses four main goals:

1. To engage students in their own learning and enable them to generate their own data in a context where they are the authority, thereby coming to a deeper understanding of the material, themselves, and others
2. To stimulate students' broader introspection so they can learn about themselves and their economic environment, thereby increasing their sense of connection and compassion
3. To increase and sharpen their focus and attention, thereby enabling them to perceive and retain more of what they are experiencing and learning
4. To initiate an inquiry into their role in the world and an examination of their personal sense of meaning

These exercises place the students at the heart of their own education and validate their responses to abstract, conceptual material by integrating those experiences directly into the classroom. This process extends far beyond the material covered in the course, stimulating an examination of their lives in terms of the concepts of the course, as well as more broadly in terms of their values and aims. How can our students live lives of deep, personal meaning when they are not supported in deeply examining the implications of what we teach them? These exercises directly support sustained inquiry into the material of the courses and validate our students' responses to them. I draw this example from my course Consumption and the Pursuit of Happiness taught at Amherst College. I hope that this will show how complex, abstract theories can be directly meaningful and clear through the use of contemplative practices.

The Easterlin Paradox and the Relative Income Hypothesis

Richard Easterlin famously noted in a paper in 1974 (and refined in later papers) that while the incomes of developed economies have risen quite markedly over the past fifty years, the average levels of self-reported well-being have remained relatively flat. Since that initial paper, there have been many responses and reestimations. Google Scholar shows 1,146 direct citations and 2,610 associated hits. Betsy Stevenson and Justin Wolfers (2008) have reanalyzed the extensive global data Easterlin used and have shown that over time and in cross-section, higher incomes are associated with higher well-being. They examine cross-sections of international data and look keenly at time-series data for the United States, Europe, and Japan. Their analysis of the Japanese data is especially interesting; they show that over time, the characterizations of well-being had been changed in the data, something others had not recognized. More recently, Daniel Kahneman and Angus Deaton (2010) have questioned this idea and have shown that higher and increasing incomes are in fact associated with higher reported well-being but that these results are sensitive to the measure of well-being. They distinguish between "emotional well-being" and "life evaluation." Figure 3.1 shows that measures of emotional well-being, like "positive affect" and "blue" (mood), are not that sensitive to income, while life evaluation measures like "ladder" (a measure of one's perceived position) are more correlated with income levels. This makes sense since income levels are associated with many more aspects than simply money. Ability to stabilize mood and keep it at a positive level is limited, so while mood generally improves with income up to a certain point, it does not keep improving as incomes rise. This is in contrast to life evaluation measures, far more similar to what economists mean by "utility," which does keep rising as income rises. This is an important finding since it had become a sort of truism that income matters only up to a certain point (usually associated with "basic needs") but flattens out at higher levels.

Measures of Well-Being and Income

In the course, we discuss Easterlin's findings on well-being and income over consumers' life cycles within the United States and across other nations, as well as the responses to his findings, developing over several weeks the complicated relationship between income and well-being found in the literature. One of the mechanisms that explains the relationship of rising incomes and well-being is the notion that our utility from income is gauged relative to others: essentially, other things equal, our

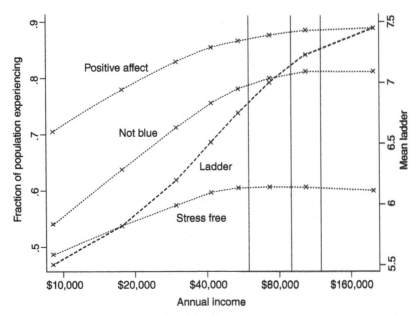

Figure 3.1 Positive Affect, Blue Affect, Stress, and Life Evaluation in Relation to Household Income

Note: Positive affect: The average of the fractions of the population reporting happiness, smiling, and enjoyment. Not blue: 1 minus the average of the fractions of the population reporting worry and sadness. Stress free: The fraction of the population who did not report stress for the previous day. These three measures are marked on the left-hand scale. The ladder is the average reported number on a scale of 0 to 10 on the right-hand scale.

Source: Reprinted with permission from D. Kahneman and A. Deaton, "High Income Improves Evaluation of Life But Not Emotional Well-Being." *PNAS* 107 (2010): 6489–6493.

assumed utility is lowered by the gains of others. So in an economy where average income is rising, individuals do not perceive rising income as an overall gain. The basic idea is that while our own income is rising, the incomes of others in society are rising too, leaving us with no relative gains.

As other people's incomes rise and the average rises, one's own income looks smaller by comparison. Easterlin quotes Karl Marx and Fredrich Engels to illustrate this: "A house may be large or small as long as the surrounding houses are equally small . . . If a palace rises beside the little house, the little house shrinks to a hut." Marx and Engels continue, "However high it may shoot up in the course of civilization, if the neighboring palace rises in equal or even in greater measure, the occupant of the relatively little house will always find himself more uncomfortable, more dissatisfied, more cramped within his four walls" (Marx & Engels, 1902, p. 42). The theory presupposes that there is an antagonistic relationship between the gains of others and ourselves. Easterlin goes on:

> Put generally, happiness, or subjective well-being, varies directly with one's own income and inversely with the incomes of others. Raising the incomes of all does not increase the happiness of all, because the positive effect of higher income on subjective well-being is offset by the negative effect of higher living level norms brought about by the growth in incomes generally. (Easterlin, 1995, p. 36)

Fundamental to this view is the idea that the gains of others detract from our own happiness. This might seem odd, but imagine this: you go to a lecture or attend a meeting for which you expected no direct payment. Suppose the convener said, "Thank you all for coming. I would like to give you a token of my appreciation. I will give each of you fifty dollars, except you; you will get ten dollars." You anticipated getting nothing, and now you have ten dollars. That should be great, right? However, many people would feel upset at receiving only ten dollars while others received fifty dollars. Even though in absolute terms you are better off (even better than you had expected), there appears to be a problem in relative terms.

This idea of the antagonistic relationship between the gains of others and our own well-being is developed in a number of studies. Whereas sometimes it is rather clear why we would be concerned about the gains of others, other times we would welcome these relative changes or find them irrelevant. Just as one might expect, the evidence is mixed as to what extent our own well-being is hostage to that of others. The first question is how we choose the "others." Who are the "Joneses" we compare ourselves to? This is a complicated issue and is one that students find interesting to examine (see, for example, Falk & Knell, 2004). Most studies use some group in direct proximity as the reference group and compare that to results of broad averages, as in the case with Easterlin's explanation. Because the reference group is not clearly theoretically defined, there is not a clear consensus on the evidence from the literature. For example, in an article entitled "Neighbors and Negatives: Relative Earnings and Well-Being" (2005), Enzo Luttmer uses detailed panel data and finds that after controlling for a variety of personal factors, higher earnings of nearby neighbors are associated with lower levels of overall well-being and higher levels of depression; he even finds that the frequency of disagreements within families concerning money is positively correlated with gains of others, while more private matters (like care of children, household tasks) are not. While Luttmer finds this negative impact of the gains of others, Peter Kuhn and colleagues find that there are no clear negative effects from relative gains drawn from the evidence of winners in the Dutch postal code lottery; in fact, after six months, winning the lottery does not make households happier, nor do a neighbor's winnings reduce happiness (Kuhn, Kooreman, Soetevent, & Kapteyn, 2011). Using a detailed data set from China, John Knight, Lina Song, and Ramani Gunatilaka (2009) show that, controlling for personal and village income levels, respondents who say their income was above village average report higher happiness than those below the average. In fact, perceived relative income was the most important factor in explaining differences in reported happiness.

Mechanisms of Selfishness, Kindness, and Compassion
The literature on both the impact of income and relative incomes presents contradictory results. In order to explore these results, we need to unpack the underlying mechanisms that lead to either positive or negative relationships between the variables. I focus here on relative income and the interaction of status and positional concerns and well-being. So that students develop a clear understanding and examination of these underlying mechanisms, I present them with both abstract, conceptual approaches and first-person contemplative exercises.

In a famous study on cooperation, Robert Axelrod (1988) showed that a strategy of simply responding in-kind (tit-for-tat) to others most easily supports cooperation. So if someone cooperates with you, you cooperate in return; however, if someone defects from that cooperation, you immediately respond to the "uncalled-for" defection. In fact, Axelrod argues, "The longer defections are allowed to go unchallenged, the more likely it is that the other player will draw the conclusion that defection can pay" (p. 191). Clearly, this functions only if the interactions are repeated; in fact, if the contact is only once, then there is no reason to cooperate. This is an example of the impact of reciprocity. Axelrod claims that this is effective because it encourages connection. He asks, "But why does this work?" and answers, "It succeeds by eliciting cooperation from others, not by defeating them" (p. 191). Notice, however, that the cooperation really has nothing to do with kindness and connection to others; the only reason that the other continues to cooperate is that the other party has a credible means of punishing defection. In this relationship, the parties are simply connected as a manner of convenience, not out of any sense of compassion or deep connection. Any group that cannot retaliate has no means of securing cooperation, and other groups will prey on them. This illustrates the importance of reciprocity in explaining giving in the context of self-gain and is the cornerstone of the work on the evolutionary explanations for altruistic behavior. Notions of "kin altruism" and "reciprocal altruism" are built on these ideas (Hamilton, 1964; Trivers, 1971). In this view, people are self-interested and will either make personal sacrifices for the benefit of their broader genetic pool (kin altruism) or make sacrifices that will directly benefit them later in future contact. Personal sacrifice, as in the act of giving, is done only with an underlying calculus of personal benefit. Michael Ghiselin (1974) states this view starkly: "No hint of genuine charity ameliorates our vision of society, once sentimentalism has been laid aside. What passes for cooperation turns out to be a mixture of opportunism and exploitation" (p. 247).

And yet, data and experience do suggest that people make intended sacrifices with no clear, direct intention of possible personal gain. Even the strongest believers in the inherent selfish nature of human beings place faith in education. Richard Dawkins, in the introduction to *The Selfish Gene* (1989), states,

> My own feeling is that a human society based simply on the gene's law of universal ruthless selfishness would be a very nasty society in which to live. But unfortunately, however much we may deplore something, it does not stop it being true . . . Be warned that if you wish, as I do, to build a society in which individuals cooperate generously and unselfishly towards a common good, you can expect little help from biological nature. Let us try to *teach* generosity and altruism, because we are born selfish. Let us understand what our own selfish genes are up to because we may then at least have the chance to upset their designs, something that no other species has ever aspired to [italics in original]. (p. 3)

Interestingly, this emphasis on education and the cultivation of compassion is stressed by thinkers from very different views on the nature of human being. The Dalai Lama, for example, has stressed the importance of developing unconditional, open compassion through secular education as well as through religious practices. Generosity and compassion are opened and sustained through training and the application of intelligence and awareness. Contemplative and introspective practices in the classroom are well suited to do this.

While the deepening and support of compassion and generosity can come through education, a great deal of experimental data robustly records behavior that does not fit the notion of narrow self-interest. In experiments analyzing the ultimatum game, the public goods game, and contract enforcement, generosity and cooperation levels were higher than predicted under standard models of narrowly self-interested actors. In a series of papers Herbert Gintis, Samuel Bowles, and others have explained these results by what they call "strong reciprocity"—the idea that humans have developed norms and institutions that punish and reward even though those carrying out the responses are not likely to benefit from the actions (Gintis, Bowles, Bowd, & Fehr, 2003). From this perspective, even in single interactions, the demands of reciprocity and cooperation hold. They demonstrate how this strong form of reciprocity might have uniquely developed in human evolution, still linking our behavior toward others to our genetic makeup and the Darwinian process that selected our genes and therefore disposition and behavior. This sort of evolutionary explanation for altruism and generosity is further developed in the work of Stanford biologist Joan Roughgarden. In her *Genial Gene: Deconstructing Darwinian Selfishness* (2009), Roughgarden demonstrates the extent and complexity of cooperation in successful species throughout the animal kingdom.

The literature covered demonstrates many views. About our concerns of relative gains, we've seen that some claim we view others as foes: when others experience a relative gain, we suffer a welfare loss. Others, though, see relative gains as either neutral of actually supporting our well-being. On the underlying mechanism of human behavior, researchers also reach opposite conclusions: some claim we are inherently heartless and selfish, while others that we are kind and cooperative. As the debate rages, we can provide students an opportunity to examine their own experience with these issues and use this experience to inform their understanding of the underlying features of the competing theories. Their experience will not provide hard proof for or against certain views, but it will stimulate and guide their inquiry into these complex ideas.

Exploratory Exercises
While the literature on how other people's gains and losses affect our own well-being is extensive, it does not resolve the issue or address some of the central questions concerning it. When are we most likely to be affected by others? Is our relationship to others fixed, or is it highly affected by context? These and other questions like them are best explored directly through exercises that allow students to experience how they relate to others and examine what might affect those relationships. In this way,

students come to a new perspective on the controversies in the literature and can form a deeper, keener understanding of the mechanisms that explain these relationships.

To help students discover their own attitudes toward relative outcomes and relate these to the literature just summarized, I ask them to do a mental experiment prior to studying the literature outlined above. I want their reactions to the exercise to be their own, without their getting caught up in second-guessing their responses to the theories. So without any introduction or explanation of the purpose of the exercise, after students have taken their seats, I ask them to play a sort of "dictator" game, where they choose between two ways of dividing money among the class. The only instruction is this: "On the sheet that I'm passing out, I have provided four scenarios, each with two options. Please select an option in each scenario and predict the percentage of the class that would select the first option." I ask them not to think about where the money being distributed comes from or any external effects of distributing the money. (I don't want the students worrying about the relative opportunity costs of the two options.) I simply ask students to decide between two distribution options.

Each of the scenarios confronts the student with a choice of what they might receive and what others might. I also tell the students that they make these choices in private. Finally, on the back of the sheet of their answers to the scenarios, the students fill out a well-being survey so that I could see how levels of well-being corresponded to the selection of the different options. This connection between well-being and generosity relates to several other papers that we read in class.

So, let's go through the scenarios. Assume thirty students in the class.

Scenario 1: Choose between Two Alternatives
A: One person in the class is selected at random and given $30.
B: You get $2 and no other money is distributed.

Which do you choose? _____
What percentage of the class will select A? _____

Students in this course would be familiar with the concept of the expected value of a risk. In this case, since there are thirty students, a student has a one in thirty chance to be selected in option A. Since the prize is $30, if the scenario were played over and over again, the student could expect to win one in every thirty times. This means that the most she or he would be willing to pay to play this sort of game in order to break even would be $1. The expected value of option A would be $1. (The expected value is simply the Pr (A) × (payment of A); here, that is (1/30) × ($30) = $1.) In this scenario, option B gives the student $1 more than the expected value of option A; in other words, since winning $30 is possible with the rather low probability of 1/30, the student might select a direct $2 payment. However, giving up this $1 allows the student to gamble on winning the $30 or allowing someone else in the class the opportunity to win $30. When we did this in class, 43 percent selected option A, whereas the prediction was that only 31 percent would select A. Students were either risk averse or were not willing to provide the opportunity for someone (including themselves) to win the $30.

Scenario 2 raises the stakes:

Scenario 2: Choose between Two Alternatives
A: The class is divided into ten groups of three people, and one group, selected at random, gets $3,000 to divide among themselves equally. Each of the three people gets $1,000.
B: You get $200, and no other money is distributed.

Which do you choose? ____
What percentage of the class will select A? ____

This scenario is just like the first, really, except that the amount at stake is now much larger. Here, option B has an expected value $100 greater than the expected value of option A. Since there are now 10 groups, the probability that one will be chosen is 1/10, and each student in the winning group will get $1,000; the expected value of the option is $100. Given that option B now has a certain value of $200, students would be gambling $100 to select option A. With this disparity, only 18 percent selected option A; the class predicted that 23 percent would select A. With each of these scenarios, we cannot tell whether the students are simply risk averse or risk taking or whether they are being "generous" and allowing for the opportunity of others to gain.

The third scenario removes all the personal gain from option A:

Scenario 3: Choose between Two Alternatives
A: One person among twenty-nine is selected at random and given $30, but you are excluded.
B: You get $2, and no other money is distributed.

Which do you choose? ____
What percentage of the class selects A? ____

Note here that the expected value of option A is zero to the student but the student can give up $2 to watch someone else in the class get $30. In this case, we have removed any risk-taking behavior. Only 25 percent of the class was willing to give up the $2; far fewer students selected option A, suggesting that the distribution of scenario 1 was actually risk aversion rather than generosity. The class prediction was that 19 percent would select option A.

In the last scenario, relative gain is directly tested:

Scenario 4: Choose between Two Alternatives
A: The class is randomly divided into two groups, 1 and 2. You are a member of group 1. All members of groups 1 and 2 get $100 each.
B: The class is randomly divided into two groups, 1 and 2. You are a member of group 1. Members of group 1 get $100 and members of group 2 get $200.

Which do you choose? _____
What percentage of the class selects A? _____

Note that in either case, everyone in group 1 gets $100; in option B, though, members of group 2 get an extra $100. I tell the students, as in all the cases, that group 2 does not know the options that are being considered. Here we have a striking opportunity to see how students respond. The direct monetary cost of providing the members of group 2 with the extra $100 is zero. (Remember I have asked them not to consider any impact of where the money comes from; it is simple "helicopter money.") Given this, one might predict that almost everyone would select option B. However, when I have done this in my class and with other groups, between 40 and 60 percent say that they would select option A, and students generally predict that less than 40 percent of the students would select A.

These distributions accord rather well with the idea of securing even small personal gains over the gains of others, even if the potential gain to others is much larger. Students were largely unwilling to give up even $2 to see someone win $30 in their class, and about half the class was not willing to see the other half of their class get $100 more than they did, even if it did not directly cost them anything. Tying these results to the levels of reported well-being of the students has shown mixed results. In one trial, those who selected option A, the even split, rather than the other group getting an extra $100 had a significantly lower level of reported general well-being. This is similar to the results James Konow and Joseph Earley (2008) found, suggesting that while giving perhaps lowers well-being in the instant, it supports and sustains well-being over the medium and long terms.

In order to give the students some sense of how their decisions could be affected by context, several weeks later I returned to this exercise, this time with a twist. In this class exercise, I first asked students (without any other introduction) to write down some things for which they are grateful. I didn't specify any more than that. After they've written some items down, I told them to ask themselves, "What else am I grateful for?" After repeating this process a few times, I found that the students loosened up a little and that the number of items they wrote down rose. We do not often have the opportunity to sit and open to our gratitude; I allowed them some time to develop theirs. After they had thought and written for a bit, I asked them to put down their pens and allow their minds to rest, noticing what arises and allowing it to pass away. After a short time, I asked them to recall one of their "gratitudes" that involved a person. Once they had one, I asked them to imagine that person. I then guided them through a *metta*-like (without mentioning *metta* or loving kindness) meditation, with the recipient of the well-wishing being the person for whom the student felt gratitude.

I asked the students to remain with their person, wishing him or her well. I asked them to notice what they were feeling. After a moment, I asked the students to recall the distribution game we had played earlier in the semester. I ask them to recall the fourth scenario, where they were to decide whether members of the other group received $100 or $200. I ask them to imagine that all of the group 2 members are the people for whom students in the class felt gratitude. I asked them to think of *their* person and remember their gratitude. Next, I asked them to imagine that next to their person someone else is standing, and that stranger there, next to their person, is someone to whom one of their classmates feels grateful. Then I asked them to imagine that they can see everyone in group 2 and that each of them has someone who feels gratitude for them. Now, with this in mind, I asked them to make a decision: "Would you select option A, giving everyone $100, or option B, giving members of Group 2 an extra $100?" I ended the exercise and gave them a moment to write down anything that they noticed. We then discussed the articles that I had assigned.

A week or so later, I asked them to shut their eyes and respond: "How many of you, after the gratitude exercise, selected option B, giving the other group an extra $100?" Almost all of them had. Only one or two students said that they selected option A. (I have replicated this exercise several times, each time with very similar results.)

When the context of the giving changed, students radically changed their decisions. Even students who thought of this as a stilted example were compelled to offer the other group the $200. One student in a discussion forum said, "Even though I know that it was a trick, I still had to switch from what I had said before and offer the other group the greater amount." Being with gratitude and changing the frame of the decision greatly altered their response. It provides a powerful example of how their relationship to others and their relative gains is contextual. Students came to realize that they select those whom they enjoy witnessing benefiting; they came to realize that they select their "Joneses." This startling revelation embarks students on an inquiry into whom they feel antagonistic toward and to whom they feel sympathetic joy. Once they start to examine this, they easily move to asking whether it is possible to cultivate the joy in seeing others benefit from consuming. This is a radical step and brings into question fundamental relationships within economics. If I can benefit from your consumption of a good, then the whole idea of rivalry and cooperation in markets comes into question and the notion of trade-offs across consumers breaks down.

Similar to the conjecture by Bowles and Gintis, the students freely gave to those who had given, even if no specific benefit was to be received. But was this an example of the kind of evolutionary behavior discussed by them, or was it a shift in generosity brought on by an overall sense of gratitude? To push this a bit further, I asked students to silently wish well for someone they did not know—strangers they saw while traveling—and themselves. As with the other exercises, this elicited a variety of responses. Students were surprised to realize that wishing well for someone felt good, as did the idea that someone might be wishing them well. They reported feeling warmer and more open from being generous. They tried to explain this feeling in a variety of ways, linked to the kinds of literature above, but more often than not, they were simply moved by the experience. Almost uniformly, though, the act of wishing themselves well was odd for them. While they were able to feel the response of wishing someone else well and not fully understand it, they seemed far less willing to sit with the discomfort of wishing themselves well. Students complained about their focus on themselves: "Wishing myself well was less tangible, and thus less rewarding." They reported that it would have no external effects and therefore was less valuable. Teachers of Buddhist loving kindness have reported that this has been very common among Western students. I believe that kindness toward oneself is an important aspect of our students' well-being. Supporting them in cultivating a warm heart for themselves is essential if we want them to extend kindness to others. Perhaps with increased attention and effort, we can expect to see more of what one student reported: "Wishing myself well also had positive effects. I recall that I had been having a bad day earlier, and giving myself explicitly positive thoughts for my well-being made me feel more lighthearted."

Conclusion

Whatever our evolutionary predisposition for kindness or selfishness, it is critical that we explore how we can learn about and support the growth and expansion of compassion and loving kindness in our students and ourselves. By encouraging the students to inquire into their own experience, they developed a deeper, more nuanced understanding of this important literature. These exercises required extended and subtle concentration, allowing students to practice and increase their powers of attention, a skill they require whatever their course of study. Through their experience, they engaged with the abstract and conceptual material on a direct personal level, deepening their interest and understanding of the models examined. Furthermore, and ultimately most important, these inquiries stimulated reflection on their relationships with others. Why was it so easy to decide to give the other group the additional $100? Is an act of kindness simply a change in the frame of how we hold others? Once we realize that we are all connected, can we really hold ourselves apart? These exercises stimulate a deep inquiry into the nature of giving, kindness, and compassion, an essential place to begin thinking about ourselves and our role in society. These practices relate the abstract, conceptual material to the meaning and direction of the students' own lives, affecting how they act and live.

The manner in which we relate to others is the basis of all civil society. It is only through a deep examination of our relationships with others— in markets, at home, in our workplace, on the street—that we can come to understand our selfishness, kindness, and compassion. In these exercises, the students explored their own relation to others and how their own sense of connection and gratitude affects their decisions. Students experienced their focus on themselves and on others; they experienced, rather than simply heard, that humans are both self-centered and socially oriented; with that insight, they could more thoroughly explore these underlying propensities.

The students' responses provide a living test of the notion put forward by Easterlin and others that we have an antagonistic relationship to the gains of others; they demonstrated that how we relate to others is complex and subject to change. The nature of our preferences speaks to a complicated and mutable set of preferences, not to an independent and fixed function that can be held independent of context. This has important implications for the nature of education and for our interaction with others. Although these exercises do not prove anything about the nature of our preferences, they stimulate deeper inquiry. Through the use of introspective exercises, students can directly experience their own personal sense of how they compare themselves to others, placing the sometimes abstract material of models like the relative income hypothesis at the heart of their education. From here, they can inquire more deeply into the nature of their relationship to others, examine the theories directly in the context of their own lives, and build a society in which both Richard Dawkins and the Dalai Lama would rejoice, providing them with far more than knowledge: an inquiry into how they want to relate to others and live their lives.

Teacher Preparation and Classroom Challenges

Academics are an especially careful group. We are deeply skeptical of most change and are trained to analyze carefully even the smallest alterations. Contemplative and introspective practices appear as no small deviation from traditional methods, and a good deal of skepticism and concern about their use exists. While we believe that their incorporation enriches the classroom, we also recognize that skeptics and critics have concerns that should be addressed. The contemplative practices used in the classroom certainly provide many challenges. In this chapter, we first address some major critiques and then discuss problems that we have faced. We hope that this discussion will help you as challenges arise in your own teaching and guide you to the preparation and attention that these methods require.

A PRACTICE OF ONE'S OWN

There is no effective way to teach contemplative practices without practicing them yourself. While many of the practices in this book are rather simple, they all require the awareness that comes with committed practice, including the experience of their varied consequences. As we have seen, few hard and fixed rules exist concerning the integration of contemplative and introspective practices; however, you need a deep familiarity with the practices before introducing them so that you can guide students through them and help them process their experience afterward. Consider an instruction like, "Focus on your breath." This is a simple instruction yet very difficult to do. Without a sense of this paradox and the experience of the instability of attention when leading the practice, it will be difficult to guide a student's personal discovery. In addition, the potential insights and concerns about personal agency (Whose thoughts are these? What control do I actually have? Who/what am I?) stimulated by this simple practice can easily be missed, leading to lost opportunities or even harm to students who are already struggling with an undeveloped sense of themselves.

Guiding students from many backgrounds within the context of your own discipline is no easy task. Implementing these practices is often more like a structured improvisation than following a script. This means that you need an especially keen relationship with your students, and even this is not enough to lead the practices. Without a solid grounding in your own practice, you may not be able to respond in ways that help students learn.

ESTABLISHING CONTEXT

While your own preparation is essential, acknowledging your students' backgrounds is important too. Many students do not have any experience with formal meditation or guided introspection and so approach these exercises with curiosity, openness, or skepticism. Moreover, students have often been led to avoid and deny their personal responses to class material, adopting instead an abstract and more objective attitude. For these reasons, it can seem rather frivolous (some claim the exercises seem "new agey") or even risky for them to attend to their own experience. The best response to this sort of resistance is to be aware of it, listen to it, and adapt exercises so that you lead students only as far as they are willing to go.

Knowing the extent of the students' reticence or resistance is important for two reasons:

1. Students must be able to follow the instructions of the guided exercise; if they are too apprehensive, they will not gain from the exercises.

2. If you ignore the context for the students, they may not trust that their experience actually does matter and may not believe the stated intention of the exercises. Recall that the motivation for the exercise is for the students to assert their agency along with the material in a meaningful way; students will quickly perceive a structure that contradicts the basic intent.

Even when students are willing participants in contemplative exercises, having a sense of how students are feeling (focused, sleepy, something else) is extremely helpful so that you can adapt the exercises to the situation. A surefire way to have these exercises fall flat is to attempt them at the wrong time or place; what might work for one group of students might not at all for another. For example, when Arthur Zajonc, professor of physics at Amherst College, introduces practices to his Introduction to Physics students, he prefaces them with scientific data and conducts them in a straightforward, instrumental manner appropriate for science students accustomed to developing meaning from research and data. Since many of his students are also pre-med, he introduces meditation with data on the impact of meditation on the reported stress levels of medical school students and the positive impacts of mindfulness-based stress reduction on a variety of subjects. This is the sort of information that these students can most easily hear; your students might need other sorts of introductions. The best way to develop awareness of your students' needs is through the practice of cultivating attention yourself. Students also need to see you model the attention and discernment that you are asking from them.

Although the use of these practices needs to be supported by a dedicated personal practice, it is important that in framing them for the students, you remember that to conduct in a spirit of inquiry rather than faith, even if your own practice is part of a spiritual path.

RESPECT FOR TRADITIONS

Even after you establish a clear context for the exercises, important issues remain. Many contemplative exercises come from elaborate and long traditions. Whether they are from the desert fathers of the Catholic faith, the Theravada, Mahayana, or Vajrayana traditions in Buddhism, or even the more clinical protocols of stress reduction, we often present students with practices out of their original context. This is not a simple issue to address. Often, describing or introducing the complete context of these practices could confuse or potentially alienate students. This matter has to be handled subtly: whereas, on the one hand, it is appropriate and respectful to acknowledge the origin of the practices, it is not necessary or advisable that students be asked to adopt any particular tradition or belief to undertake the exercises. Respect for students' beliefs (or lack of them) is essential. The long and difficult process of academic departments of religion to shed specific religious affiliations and gain respect as secular, academic disciplines provides an informative example; it has created an important intellectual discipline, but its turbulent and bitter history has affected the ability of professors of religion to conduct first-person practices that do not require any particular faith. This issue has been fruitfully addressed by the Contemplative Studies Consultation group of the American Academy of Religion, cochaired by Louis Komjathy (University of San Diego) and Anne Klein (Rice University). (See their website: http://www.sandiego.edu/cas/contemplative studies/aar.php.)

Increased contact with and interest in global cultures has blurred the line between "domestic" and "foreign" in the economic, social, and cultural realms. Increased contact has deepened understanding of our own humanity as ideas and worldviews have been increasingly shared. However, the cultural contexts of rituals and objects, like *mporo* marriage beads or *didjeridus*, and practices, like yoga or meditation, have sometimes been ignored in their appropriation for other purposes—for example, the impact of Western commodification on cultural items like Samburu heirlooms (Straight, 2002) or *didjeridus* (Welch, 2002). Both mporo marriage beads and *didjeridus* are appropriated without any sense of their original intent or even name. Mporo beads have become collectors' items and worn for fashion, both the actual beads and facsimile, without any regard for their original meaning and intent. The long tube instrument made from a termite-hollowed branch or tree trunk often referred to as a *didjeridu*, or sometimes *didgeridoo*, is an integral part of ceremonial dance music of Australia's aboriginal people. The traditional name for the instrument is *yidaki*; the term *didgeridoo* is a made-up name by white settlers. This issue is especially relevant to many of the contemplative practices adapted to the classroom. While we certainly believe we all have much to learn from each other, we also believe that we should adopt practices only with a careful awareness and attention to their recontextualization.

When a practice is introduced from another cultural tradition, we must consider the appropriate level of context to provide for students. Traditions are complex and tend to be difficult to encapsulate in a brief introduction. At the same time, not providing students any context for the practices wastes a great educational opportunity and may prevent the students' full participation in the exercises. So rather than trying to establish a strict, fixed overall strategy, the best approach is to design an introduction appropriate for your students, the nature of the class, and the type of practice used. And no practice should require a religious belief or faith stance that is not their own. For example, a prayer to a particular deity or a faith-based ritual might be a topic of study, but it should not be used as a personal, spiritual, or introspective guide.

The exercises used should be conducted in the spirit of personal experimentation in an open laboratory of exploration. Harold Roth at Brown University has pioneered the use of contemplative lab sessions for his courses in which students develop critical first-person methods to explore and more deeply understand the texts they are studying (Roth, 2008, p. 21). Although they are explicitly studying religious texts, Roth and his students complement their understanding by direct experience of described practices done in the spirit of discovery, requiring no appropriation of belief.

Each instructor using contemplative and introspective practices will have to grapple with how much or how little context to provide. The real issue is that the question of appropriate use is kept alive so that we remain respectful and authentic as we adapt practices for our classrooms. Judith Simmer-Brown of Naropa University, for example, believes it is imperative that we "bring forward our third-person perspectives as scholars and train our students accordingly." She argues that the first step is that those who are introducing practices—hatha yoga (the series of postures known popularly as yoga), for example—need to be aware of the philosophical, cultural, and religious roots of these practices before they use them in the classroom.

In addition, knowing the background of the practices enables us to better respond to potential student reactions, like anxiety arising during mindfulness or energy pulses occurring in practices that focus on awakening somatic energies. We are not saying that you should interpret students' reactions for them but that you should have some sense of the potential of these practices so you can be ready to help students find support if such responses arise.

INTENTIONS AND OUTCOMES

Students who trust their teachers are willing to take risks. Trust deepens for the students when they understand why they are being asked to do something, especially if it is outside their comfort zone. To establish this, clearly explain the intention of the exercise. Starting with relatively simple exercises at the beginning of the course and then proceeding to those that are more demanding and complex can allow the students to adapt and manage the practices better. Many of the exercises in economics courses require students to observe themselves making decisions, so the purpose of the exercise cannot be stated at the outset without affecting their participation.

On the first day of my (D.B.) Consumption and the Pursuit of Happiness course, I ask students to look over the syllabus and imagine themselves throughout the semester. I then ask them to write down on their syllabus what percent of the reading they want to complete over the semester. After a short time of sitting quietly, I ask them how much of the assigned texts they are willing to commit right now to reading. After a bit, I ask them to think about their past semesters and how much they think (really) they will read this semester. After speaking for a bit, I ask them to write down the three numbers on a piece of paper without their names. This exercise does not take much time or much special effort on their part. The students are simply answering questions; however, they are already playing with how their own mental framing affects their predictions. Many students are stunned to see that they *want* different amounts than they are willing to commit to and, at virtually the same time, think that they will actually read! It is a simple illustration of their wanting and their actions not lining up, even with a statement of commitment. Students even have to reassess what they mean by *commit* when they see that they committed to, say, 85 percent of the reading and at virtually the same time believed they would actually read only 65 percent. When I talk with students after collecting their responses, they immediately see that paying attention to their decision making can be surprisingly fruitful.

Examples like this, which demonstrate to students that more is operating within them than they are conscious of, allows for their participation in more complex and challenging exercises later in the semester. They become more willing to engage in exercises that involve far more introspection, time, and vulnerability. This exercise was designed for economics students; you might start with a different introduction for students studying different material.

INCLUSION AND VARIATION

One of the great advances in higher education over the past fifty years has been the increase in variation among students, faculty, administration, and staff. This has deepened the learning within classrooms, greatly enriched both our institutions and our society, and given opportunities to a far greater number of people than ever before. We believe it is important to stress "variation" rather than "diversity" because as difference (diversity) rises, we need to keep a focus on our common connection (variation). We acknowledge difference and also hold our commonality. To deny differences is to remove an important aspect of self-determination. Yet to frame difference as defect or fault can be harmful. Of course, denying difference can be harmful too. Claims of color blindness can be alienating. Experiments have shown that ignoring race in order to be politically correct stunts communication and connection (Apfelbaum, Norton, & Sommers, 2012) and that attempting to ignore race actually deepens racial inequality (Bonilla-Silva, 2006). We are all variations on a theme: in the context of contemplative practices, while contemplation and introspection is common to us all, we come to these practices from various contexts and understandings, and ignoring differences will not bring us together.

While the significant achievement of increasing variation in our institutions has made our teaching and research far richer, it has also brought new and complicated challenges. Just as in other parts of the curriculum, practitioners of contemplative practices must learn about and adapt to the new conditions. The dimensions of difference are far too varied to chronicle here, but we can suggest some approaches through the use of examples.

Like almost every other aspect of this type of work, the first step is deep awareness of oneself and of the students being addressed. This seems simple, but without careful inquiry, we can easily miss important aspects of our students' lives and the opportunity for helping them to engage with our courses more deeply. An example of this is the use of silence in the class during an exercise. This seems like a positive and simple act, especially in lives that are bombarded with distractions. However, students who have felt traditionally silenced by formal education may meet the command to be silent with tension and resentment. This can be easily addressed without making any assumptions about who these students might be by establishing at the outset of the exercises that the silence is an opportunity for an internal experience that will result in more participation and involvement rather than less. This sounds like a simple setting of the context, but it is now mindful of the potential differences in responses to the request for silence, and it benefits all students with an increased sense of the motivation for the exercises.

Another example of what might seem simple is for students to close their eyes to focus within. For some students, this is a path for potential demonic possession. (In "Christians and Demon Possession: Can a Christian Be Demon Possessed?" Timothy Morton lists meditation as one of the five paths toward demon oppression and possession: http://www.biblebelievers.com/morton _demon.html.) For others who have suffered trauma and do not feel safe closing their eyes in a group, this is potentially a disturbing situation. Clearly you do not have to engage with students at their level of belief about demonic possession or their past trauma; you can simply invite students to close their eyes or to leave them open in soft focus at a point about six feet away. This avoids discussion of the particulars of what students bring to class yet allows them to choose a safe way to relate to the exercise. Becoming more aware of the contexts that students bring with them allows us to foster safer, more inclusive environments for all students.

Researchers and teachers are devoting increasing attention to the implications of race, class, and sexual orientation for the practice of meditation. While contemplative and introspective exercises are not all meditation, we can learn from studies focused on the outcomes of meditative practice. The aim of this inquiry should be to come to understand difference so that the exercises are broadly inclusive, not distorted by our preconceptions of difference. We recognize that while we are looking at the implications of difference, we cannot prejudge the nature of an individual by his or her class, race, or sexual orientation. The presumption that a particular group needs a particular form of practice can be as alienating as giving no thought to difference. The real point here is that we want to establish a frame in which students from the widest range of backgrounds feel welcome and safe.

The critical first step in this process is to confront your own preexisting beliefs and biases. Many of these operate below the conscious level and can be unpleasant to examine. This requires time and attention because most of us have convinced ourselves that we do not discriminate against others, even mentally. While most of us do embrace principles of equality and social justice, cultural norms we have learned through years of exposure and countless heuristics render these principles tenuous, especially since most of what we are doing requires a quick reaction. We are beings designed to use perceptual data very quickly to make judgments. Indeed, many times these skills are essential. Since most of our responses operate below the level of conscious choice, we often create environments or react to situations that preclude establishing contexts for all students to participate. We need to become aware of our underlying beliefs and make sure that we are choosing our responses rather than simply following old and potentially inappropriate heuristics.

A large literature has developed on this subject of implicit beliefs and attitudes. Behavioral studies as well as neuroscientific studies have focused on the nature and influence of our implicit assumption and attitudes (Greenwald & Banaji, 1995; Stanley, Phelps, & Banaji, 2008). You can even start to explore your own implicit attitudes at the Project Implicit website: https://implicit.harvard.edu /implicit/demo/. A deep and sustained inquiry into the nature of your own biases is the best way to ensure that you will cultivate an open environment accessible to the greatest number of students.

TEACHER INTENTION AND STUDENT MOTIVATION

Colleges and universities are stressful places. In any assignment given, students engage more fully when they understand how the work they are doing affects their understanding and, even better, their lives. With contemplative practices, it is even more important. For many students, these practices will be far outside the norm (students often refer to our exercises as "out there"). Unfamiliar practices can add uncertainty and easily overwhelm students. They may be unwilling to participate before the exercises begin. For this reason, it is especially important that you carefully explain the specific goals of the exercises: the more specific you can be with students, the more likely they will be to learn from the exercises. This requires attention to your pedagogical intentions for using specific practices.

The purpose can be stated before or after the exercises. For many exercises designed to have students discover how they personally react to situations, the explanation or intent of the practice is described only after the students have completed them, because too much prompting would bias the students' experiences. In fact, prior to talking about the exercises with them, giving students five or ten minutes to write about their own reactions and talk with another student about what they noticed can provide them a good anchor. This combination of self-reflection and talking to others helps ground their experience, so when they discuss the exercises, they have a better basis for applying their experience to the material they are studying. In addition, this written record can be primary source material for their final papers.

Allowing them to have their own, unique experience and then helping them make sense of it in terms of the material they are studying helps them integrate their experience and allows them to trust processes that will arise in the future. Even the simplest exercise can lead to important insights. Asking students to focus on their breath and then to follow the rising and falling of their breath can be simple to describe. As they begin to wander into thoughts and body sensations, you can help them see the nature of their minds: even though they have decided to focus on their breath, it is difficult to focus on it. In economics courses, for example, we discuss that and relate it to decision making; students quickly recognize the importance of attention and their lack of practice with it. This motivates them to explore their own level of concentration and develop it further.

Once that is established, you can gently ask them to inquire into what is happening as their minds wander. They have decided to focus on their breathing, yet thoughts and sensations somehow arise, and their attention is drawn away. They quickly realize that these interventions were not of their choosing. From where did they arise? In an economics course, we quickly move to consider our wants. Is our wanting like these thoughts—simply arising unchosen? This simple inquiry shakes up students and forces them to consider their agency, a central concern in any study of decision making. This whole process can be done rather quickly and without much drama; however, without proper questioning, students might not inquire very deeply into their frustration, boredom, or interest in response to a simple exercise of following the breath.

EVALUATION

Clearly no one will want to grade students narrowly for the depth of their meditation or the extensiveness of their introspection. This does not mean that these practices cannot be incorporated into the students' evaluations. As with other forms of participation, like asking questions and attending class, students can be credited for their level of engagement. For basic concentration practices or other daily practices, attendance logs or some basic record of whether the student is making an effort can mirror the ways in which we traditionally assess class participation.

Beyond this level, the exercises can form significant parts of more elaborate assignments; this is especially true as the exercises are more closely tailored to the subject matter of the course. For example, Professor Judith Simmer-Brown at Naropa University assigns a paper in her courses in which students combine their experience and the material for the course: "They may begin with anecdotes, but I guide them to reflect, in the present moment, on their insights rather than turning to plotlines to explain their views. Eventually they draw richly from the depths of their reflections, improving their ability to engage in first-person investigation and to trust themselves as participants in their own education" (Simmer-Brown, 2011, p. 116).

A paper in which students consider their own experience as a meaningful source for understanding the material of the course seems an excellent way to integrate exercises while providing a method for evaluating performance. In my Consumption and the Pursuit of Happiness course, I have adopted a version of this assignment. In the syllabus and early in the course, I make it clear to students that the final paper of the course will be an opportunity for them to integrate their experiences with the required readings. After each exercise, I give them time to write down brief notes about their experiences and insights during the exercises and create an online discussion forum for them to share their reactions, insights, and observations.

Assigned papers can require them to integrate their firsthand experience and their understanding of the reading, providing a deeper analysis of the material in the course. Asking them to relate their own experience in at least one of the exercises to the readings in the course validates their own experience while allowing them to discover deeper understandings of the material. Through this process, it is obvious to them that their own experience matters: it constitutes a vital primary source that they can cite and discuss. Coming at the end of the course, this also functions as a way for them to reflect on the exercises from a new, more sophisticated perspective. The assignment validates the attention to their own experience while demonstrating that their education can expand their understanding of themselves. Thus, the relevance of otherwise complex and abstract research becomes evident, and questions like, "What good is this all in the *real world*?" are far less likely to arise. While all of this is happening for the students, the assignment is also a natural way for me to assess their understanding of the material I am presenting. The assessment is based not only on their participation in the exercises but also on their ability to examine and reflect on their experience, deepening their understanding of the course material.

HIDING RELIGION IN THE TROJAN HORSE AND GURUISM

In formal, secular education, religious beliefs have been held separate. This is essential to academic freedom. We might discuss religious views, but in the manner in which we would any other position. In secular institutions, it is unacceptable to require students to have a particular spiritual belief or to proselytize a religious view. Because many contemplative practices have roots in religious traditions, we need to be especially careful not to impose religious views on students. This does not mean, however, that we must avoid all spiritual aspects of the exercises; rather, we must accept what arises while respecting students' views and experiences.

As we have seen robustly in survey data, many students yearn for spiritual guidance. We can see this in the extensive surveys conducted at UCLA by the Higher Education Research Institute (for the full discussion, see Astin, Astin, & Lindholm, 2010). We do not have to deny this aspect of our students or ourselves, yet we must strike a delicate balance between this acknowledgment and the openness and tolerance of differing views. In addition, since students find little of this sort of support in their formal education, they often look to those who are comfortable with these issues. This can be a powerful connection with students, but it can also lead to inappropriate leadership in what should be private aspects of our students' lives. Embodying respect and openness while being sought as a spiritual teacher can be quite difficult, but it is imperative; we have to maintain a healthy relationship with our students while supporting them in their journeys.

One of the fiercest critiques of contemplative practices in the classroom is that religious views are being rolled in within the Trojan horse of secular ideas of "attention" and "mindfulness." We understand this concern, but the practices we are suggesting require no particular belief by the participants; they are intended to allow students to experience, for themselves, their own inner processes. Practices give students the opportunity to make sense of their own experience for themselves. We cannot stress this point enough. As Harold Roth (2008) has explained, "The understanding that contemplative experiences are not confined exclusively to religion" (p. 20) is central to any contemplative pedagogy.

This need for students to have the freedom of their own beliefs is such an important issue that we discuss it further. In order to make sure that we do not force any particular views on our students we can do the following:

- Construct our practices so that no element requires the adoption or even role playing of a particular religious view.

- Become aware of our language so that we do not use a particular vernacular that implies particular religious worldviews.

- Allow our students to use their own language to express and understand their experiences while supporting them in being respectful of others.

- Include practices from a variety of backgrounds so that students do not perceive an underlying bias.

- Ground clearly in our own practice so that we are capable of mindful listening.

- Open fully and be aware of our judgments as they arise, letting them go in order to listen and connect deeply.

If students wish to explore various religious traditions, they certainly should do so. Our role is not providing religious rituals or practices for students. Traditional prayers or rituals should not be adapted for use without great thought about how students from other traditions or from within the borrowed tradition would view the practice. Being asked to repeat a prayer in a language that they do not know in an exercise can be disturbing to students. Even though a student is told to think of the prayer in any personal manner, if he does not fully understand what is being said or is not able to relate to the ancient context of the actual prayer, he may be put in a very awkward position.

This leads to issues of language and appropriation. We need to develop a language of pluralism that does not lead to students' forgoing their own views. In her essay "Training the Heart Responsibly: Ethical Considerations in Contemplative Teaching" (2011), Judith Simmer-Brown presents Diana Eck's views as most helpful. Professor Eck heads the Pluralism Project at Harvard University. She advocates for people to hold their own views while connecting and listening to others. In her essay "The Challenge of Pluralism" (1993), she writes:

> Pluralism is not simply relativism, but makes room for real commitment. In the public square or in the interfaith council, commitments are not left at the door. On the contrary, the encounter of a multicultural society must be the encounter of commitments, the encounter of each other with all our particularities and angularities. This is a critical point to see plainly, because through a cynical intellectual sleight of hand, some critics have linked pluralism with a valueless relativism—an undiscriminating twilight in which "all cats are gray," all perspectives equally viable, and as a result, equally uncompelling.

Thus, she argues that we must cultivate our own perspective and practice in order to stand firm in our experience; while we are so grounded, we need to engage with others in listening to them:

> The encounter of a pluralistic society is not premised on achieving agreement, but achieving relationship. *Unum* does not mean uniformity. Perhaps the most valuable thing we have in common is commitment to a society based on the give and take of civil dialogue at a common table. Dialogue does not mean we will like what everyone at the table says. The process of public discussion will inevitably reveal much that various participants do not like. But it is a commitment to being at the table—with one's commitments. (Eck, 1993)

In addition to embracing and including other views, we also must be careful not to overstep our bounds as teachers. Since contemplative exercises require first-person reflection and attention, students are likely to uncover aspects of their experience that are uncomfortable for them and possibly frightening. While we need to prepare for this and be ready to support our students, we also should recognize that most of us are not trained therapists or counselors. Each situation must be handled uniquely, but we should be ready to help students in ways in which we might not be accustomed. In addition, you might fancy yourself as an expert in some areas. For example, you might not be certified to teach yoga in any tradition, but if you introduce some poses into a class, the students may think of you as a yoga instructor. The same could be true of meditation or other forms of contemplative practice. This is again why it is important to develop deep practices before bringing them to the classroom. Anyone with a developed practice has a good idea of the appropriate bounds of his or her teaching. In addition, this background helps to keep us aware if the desire to be the authority or guru arises. Knowing one's own limits and the other resources available for students is essential for using these practices. For example, many schools have spiritual and religious advisors for students. Given the particular kind of authority a professor has over his or her students, maintaining an appropriate relationship in private matters is essential; we must guard against inappropriately influencing students.

Many of the practices are evocative, and students sometimes want to delve further into them. Without any context other than the classroom, students can be left confused or see their instructors as the only means to pursue their self-discovery. It is quite natural for the student to see the professor who introduced these practices as having special understanding of their implications. But while an instructor certainly can be a mentor in many ways to a student, he or she should not attempt any inappropriate role in the spiritual direction of the student. Before incorporating contemplative practices into your courses, you should work out your appropriate role in students' lives and then continue to examine that role during the course. This can be challenging. We are used to working with students on rather abstract levels; these practices are designed for far more personal engagement. Learning to manage interactions with students is an important part of their proper implementation. One helpful way to deal with this is to demonstrate to students that you have the same sorts of questions and curiosities as they do.

THE ROLE OF LANGUAGE

Most contemplative exercises are introduced through verbal guidance, so the way in which they are framed by language is important. This does not mean that you should use a special jargon or set of buzzwords; quite the contrary, the clearer and more familiar the language is that you use, the better. The focus should be on giving clear guidance while allowing the students' experiences to arise naturally, with minimal shaping by the manner in which you are directing them. Examples abound on how language can create a frame that influences students. One famous frame was created by Daniel Kahneman and Amos Tversky (1984) in which physicians were asked which policies they would prefer, given a scenario in which a disease is expected to kill six hundred people. Participants were first asked which they would choose: program A, which will certainly save two hundred people, or program B, which will save all six hundred people with a probability of one-third. Not surprisingly, the majority of physicians, 72 percent, selected the more certain outcome of program A. Some minutes later, they were asked about another version: program C, which will result in four hundred people certainly dying, or program D with six hundred people dying with a two-thirds probability. Even though option C is equivalent to option A (in both cases, two hundred survive and four hundred die) and D is equivalent to B (both have an expected value of two hundred surviving and four hundred dying), this time 78 percent preferred program D over C. Even when the two options were given just minutes apart, the same respondent switched his or her preference with the change of frame. This striking example illustrates how important our descriptions and use of language can be. Being keenly aware of how we frame our exercises is critical in order to allow students to have their own responses rather than those that we imposed, even subtly.

One of the ways in which we can explore the power of language in cognition and response is to study the attention on language by relational frame theory and by therapists using mindfulness-based approaches, such as acceptance and commitment therapy, dialectic therapy, and mindful-based cognitive therapy. All have carefully attended to the manner in which language frames reaction and behavior. Relational frame theory (RFT) is a framework for understanding human language and cognition—how relational frames are created to form reactions in response to words and how words themselves comprise active cognition (Hayes, Barnes-Holmes, & Roche, 2001). It is a form of behaviorism, linking language cues to learned and conditioned responses. What is helpful about this somewhat abstract approach is that it can easily be translated into an awareness of how words can form triggers for various groups and the need to become aware of how our different students have learned to associate words with certain reactions and thoughts. The therapeutic application of RFT is acceptance and commitment therapy, which advocates the awareness and acceptance of the frames that arise from stimuli. What is so useful for our context, the use of contemplative practices in class settings, is that this structure can help us understand not only how we might attend to the language we are using but also how we respond to our students' reactions to the frames we are using with them. Other therapies incorporating mindfulness have also paid special attention to how the therapist describes and introduces the work, leading the participant to his or her own experience most openly. This is not to imply that the work done in the classroom is a form of therapy: rather, it suggests that using the careful work done by therapists with respect to their use of language can help us become aware of the subtle and powerful ways in which we influence our students.

COMPLEMENTARITY

Contemplative and introspective methods are complements to traditional teaching methods. Contemplative pedagogy offers a range of extensions and even transformations for traditional lecture and discussion formats. Rather than abandoning or rejecting abstract, analytical thought, contemplative modes can help students more deeply understand material and can integrate third-person views better into their own lives through the examination of their own experience of the material. They should be used only with a clear pedagogic intention.

For example, Beth Berlia, director of women's studies at St. Cloud University, noted with some concern that

> my feminist students can be politically aware of issues and have "mastered" feminist theory, but nevertheless struggle with eating disorders, low self-esteem, poor body image, and abusive relationships. What is worse, they often think they "should know better," and so use feminism to beat themselves up for "succumbing" to those cultural pressures. I began to wonder what was missing—what Women's Studies, and higher education as a whole, needed to do differently in order to extend the intellectual empowerment students feel through feminism to deeper, more integrated level. (Berlia, 2012, p. 2)

By directly experiencing their own engagement with the ideas of the course, Berlia's students will have both a deeper understanding of the material and a vehicle to apply it directly to their lives. This can be deeply moving to students and can provide a new and more intense motivation to learn since the context of the material is no longer at arm's length. It can also be deeply, personally challenging.

In addition to developing an experiential sense of the material, contemplative and introspective methods can hone analytical thinking. As we have seen, these methods heighten attention and focus, but far more can be developed. Many practices deepen and extend analytical thinking. Perhaps the best developed is the analytical meditation of the Tibetan tradition. The Dalai Lama has explained, "In analytic meditation, one brings about inner change through systematic investigation and analysis. In this way we can properly use our human intelligence, our capacity for reason and analysis, to contribute to our happiness and satisfaction" (Cutler, 2009). This is an important insight; contemplative pedagogy does not supplant or detract from rigorous analytical inquiry. On the contrary, contemplative and introspective modes can heighten and place in context what might otherwise be drier, less accessible modes of learning. They are not broad substitutes for other modes of thinking; rather, they can augment and enhance, and even transform, traditional modes of teaching and learning.

CONCLUSION

These practices, as beneficial as they can be in the right environment, are not for everyone to introduce and are not appropriate for all situations. Like other classroom methods, they have limitations, pitfalls, and dangerous currents. In this chapter we have recommended that practitioners cultivate the following:

- A committed practice of their own, which allows them to plan their timing, adapt practices as needed, and process the students' experiences afterward
- Attention to and knowledge of the context from which the practices arise and the appropriate incorporation of the tradition into the classroom
- Freedom for students to maintain their own beliefs while not requiring them to believe anything specific in order to engage in the exercises
- Humility and clarity so that students new to these practices do not identify them exclusively with the teacher
- Awareness of the different backgrounds of the students so that practices can be introduced in the most open and accessible manner

- Recognition that these practices are powerful complements to other forms of teaching and learning

While developing the contemplative methods most likely to be effective, we should also engage others who are not as open to these practices. Rather than deny or fight against skeptics, we should learn to listen to the critiques of these methods so we can strengthen and improve them.

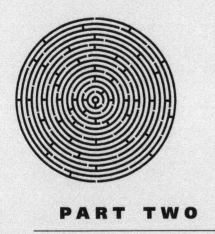

A Guide to Contemplative Practices

PART TWO

A Guide to
Contemplative Practices

Introduction to the Practices

The chapters in part 2 present examples of contemplative practices being used in higher education classrooms. Many of the courses were taught by the Center for Contemplative Mind in Society's contemplative practice fellows; we drew from their insightful fellowship reports and presentations. Only teachers in four-year institutions were eligible for the fellowships, so we do not have examples of contemplative courses in community colleges. Excellent courses in community colleges do exist; some are discussed in *Contemplative Teaching and Learning* (2010), edited by Keith Kroll, first published as a special issue of New Directions for Community Colleges. We also haven't presented examples of every practice, but we hope that those we do discuss will provide an overview and stimulate creative new methods for your courses.

INTRODUCING PRACTICE IN THE CLASSROOM

Contemplative practices, though quite varied, have much in common. They all cultivate greater focus; some lead to insight, wisdom, and compassion. Although here we stress the specific, instrumental use of these practices in courses, we recognize their potential for profound transformation in ourselves and our students. They are vehicles for students to gain insight and wisdom far beyond what they learn in our courses. When we teach these practices, we are planting seeds; we can trust that they will grow and flourish long after students leave the academy.

The following guidelines may be useful for those who are designing and teaching a contemplative course:

- Plan the structure of the exercise but hold it lightly, more like a structured improvisation, so that you can be present in the moment with student responses.

- Frame the exercises skillfully. Choose appropriate language, timing, context, and other factors so that students are open to learn and have the space to discover their own responses.

- Have a clear pedagogical purpose for the practice, so that you can lead the session toward the goal and properly assess its impact.

- Provide an opportunity for students to opt out during any exercise so that they feel safe in exploring it.

- Allow students time after the exercise to reflect on and write about their experience.

- Explain the purpose of the practice in the course so that students understand how it is affecting their learning.

Along with these reminders for facilitating the practices, Professor Gurleen Grewal of the University of San Francisco has offered some helpful suggestions for conducting practices in the classroom to support and increase the efficacy of the many practices:

- After a long period of discussion, provide the opportunity for some mindful movement. Have students get up and stretch or walk quietly around the room.

- Appreciate gaps during discussions. As you and others speak, allow spaces and gaps to occur. Notice any anxiety, impatience, or tension that arises during these open moments—or feelings of competition or irritation with others.

- Appreciate the interplay of serious logical exchange with spontaneous playfulness and humor.

- Practice holding the questions posed by others or yourself without needing to supply an immediate response.

- Allow room for different textures in discussions: cool, careful, fiery, tender, intimate, bold, expansive. Think of diversity in discussion styles as analogous to biodiversity in a healthy ecosystem.

- Trust disagreement and doubt. Do not artificially work for agreement, but value nonaggressive differences and direct feedback.

- Let go of preconceived outcomes for the discussion or for your contribution. Notice your resistance to dissolving preconceived goals. Allow the discussion to emerge in ways that are original, creative, surprising, and adventurous.

- If you are generally vocal in class, allow space for those who are silent to speak. Practice courtesy and compassion as well as directness.

We hope that these guidelines and suggestions will help in designing your course, whether you use the practices that follow or create your own.

PERSONAL PRACTICE

The heart of the contemplative course is practice. Like any other skill or subject matter, we have to know it well before we can teach it to others. With contemplative practices, it is even more important to be soundly grounded in the practice, since practice affects not only how students inquire and learn but also how teachers teach and how they act in the world. We practice to be fully present in the moment, listen deeply, refrain from judgment while exercising discernment, and act from our deepest source of knowing. The teacher's presence is the heart of teaching.

We can encourage students to strengthen their attention, sustain their commitment, cultivate equanimity and openness, realize insights, and appreciate interconnection only if we are on that path of awakening ourselves. Students have excellent radar. They will be listening for the humility, clarity, and calm that are integral to contemplative awareness. They notice the quality of our interactions. If we are not embodying contemplative qualities, why should they practice?

In contemplative teaching, the principles of contemplative practice guide the pedagogy: seeing things as they are, being open to new ideas, appreciating the contribution of silence to learning, valuing each human voice, honoring the constantly changing nature of ideas. To design a contemplative course, you need these capacities. You will cultivate them through practice.

Your experience will also guide you when students encounter difficulties with practice—the usual struggles with distraction, doubt, sleepiness, and lack of motivation, as well as the uncovering of repressed memories and ideas.

This is not to say that you need to be enlightened or be a saint to introduce practice into your course, but that you need to have a practice that is fairly well grounded and to be committed to making it an important part of your life.

Beginning and Cultivating a Practice

Choose the practice that seems right for you, whatever it might be. You may focus on one or include several techniques, combining yoga with meditation or contemplative reading with walking the labyrinth. You might start with a book of instructions or an audio series, but eventually most people need a teacher to guide them past the beginning stages. If you are interested in introducing yoga postures in your classroom, it is very important to have studied with a mature yoga teacher and have learned the potential dangers of postures not performed correctly.

Try to commit to regular, perhaps daily, practice sessions. If you cannot sustain a regular schedule, persevere as best you can. As with most other activities that have not yet become familiar and routine, it's common to postpone engagement with contemplative practice because circumstances are not perfect. It's easy to make excuses about lacking materials, supplies, or adequate time and space ("If only I had a nice meditation cushion or a dedicated yoga room and an hour free after work—then I could really do this"). If your mind sounds like this, try to use the situation as an opportunity to face your discomfort. Begin your practice. Really, you probably already have everything you need!

You can make things easier for yourself by committing to brief but regular sessions. For example, if you decide to take up a silent meditation practice, it is perfectly fine to begin with just a few minutes per session. After you've become accustomed to your short sitting periods, honestly and gently assess how that amount of time is serving you, and increase your practice time if it feels right to do so.

Feeling twinges of guilt or self-indulgence when you're beginning a practice is common. For many of us, time is precious, and we face many demands from family, friends, and work. In those moments when you question your priorities, remember that contemplative practices are not distractions or diversions from daily activities but opportunities to get in touch with what is deeply meaningful to us. Have we lost the ability to be at peace in our moments of rest? Cluttered schedules not only constrict the time we have, but also manipulate our understanding of value and worth. It is crucial to remember the simple value and beauty of life as it is, not as it is used. The simple awareness cultivated by contemplative practices can bring us back in touch with this beauty, enriching our interactions with others.

Here are some suggestions for supporting a regular practice:

- Find a space for practice, however small, in your home or office, where you can reflect, be quiet, go inside, and get centered. Identify it as a place of inspiration with a flower, a candle, a photo, or any other object sacred to you. Over time, the space will support your practice. When you sit or do yoga there, you will be supported by your intention and reminded of other times you have practiced.

- Keep a "practice journal" of your thoughts, experiences, and questions. If you attend workshops or retreats, take notes on what is said; if you read a good book, write down what moves you. Then, when you feel bored or discouraged, reread your journal to connect to your practice and your intentions for undertaking it in the first place.

- Join a local community of practitioners at a studio, meditation center, house of worship, or your university. Regular meetings with others help keep practice consistent in your daily life.

- Spend time outdoors. Slowing down to observe the natural world can help order your priorities and is an easy way to reengage your senses.

- If you are able to get away, a retreat can invigorate your practice or deepen an already strong one. Retreat centers are usually simple places with few distractions. You can also "retreat" at home, which will present you with the interesting challenge of focusing on your practice while being surrounded by familiar distractions.

Guidance

Contemplative practices are not always peaceful and stress free. In fact, while some may be more gentle and others more rigorous, all practices are intended to be somewhat challenging. Learning often happens through coping with difficulties, and the contemplative path can be intense, radically transforming your sense of self and identity. While this could be a largely peaceful and pleasant process, it is quite common to experience ups and downs, and most contemplative traditions recognize that difficult periods may need to be worked through. In such times, the guidance of a teacher, spiritual director, counselor or other guide can be very helpful.

Resources

The following resources combined with those at the end of each practice chapter are a place to begin:

William J. Broad, *The Science of Yoga: the Risks and the Rewards* (New York: Simon & Schuster, 2012).

Norman Fischer, *Training in Compassion* (Boston: Shambhala, 2012).

Daniel Goleman, *The Meditative Mind: The Varieties of Meditative Experience* (New York: Tarcher, 1996).

Thich Nhat Hanh, *The Miracle of Mindfulness* (Boston: Beacon Press, 1999).

B.K.S. Iyengar, *Light on Yoga* (Berlin, Germany: Schocken Press, 1995).

Jon Kabat-Zinn, *Mindfulness for Beginners* (New York: Sounds True, 2011).

Thomas Keating, *Open Mind, Open Heart* (New York: Continuum, 1994).

Jack Kornfield, *Meditation for Beginners* (New York: Sounds True, 2008).

Marcia Z. Nelson and Wayne Teasdale, *Come and Sit: A Week inside Meditation Centers* (New York: Skylight Paths Publishing, 2001).

Mary Rose O'Reilley, *Radical Presence: Teaching as Contemplative Practice* (Portsmouth, NH: Boynton/Cook, 1998).

Sharon Salzberg, *Real Happiness: The Power of Meditation* (New York: Workman, 2010).

Susan L. Smalley and Diana Winston, *Fully Present: The Science, Art, and Practice of Meditation* (Cambridge, MA: Da Capo Press, 2010).

Mindfulness

In Chinese, the word for mindfulness is a composite:
the character for now is drawn atop
the character for heart/mind.

Calligraphy by Kazuaki Tanahashi.

Mindfulness is both a process (mindfulness practice) and an outcome (mindful awareness). It begins with the simple act of paying attention with care and respect. Mindfulness practices are found in many traditions around the world. The word *mindfulness* can mean something particular in each of these traditions, so as a shorthand definition, many academics use the one inspired by Jon Kabat Zinn, founder of the Center for Mindfulness in Medicine, Health Care, and Society and mindfulness-based stress reduction (MBSR): the awareness that arises by paying attention on purpose in the present moment nonjudgmentally. Other definitions of *mindfulness* are discussed by Georges Dreyfus (2013), a Buddhist scholar at Williams College.

Mindfulness is a way of being in which one is highly aware (of what is inside yourself and outside yourself in the environment) and focused on the reality of the present moment, accepting and acknowledging it without getting caught up in thoughts about the situation or emotional reactions to the situation. It is a capability we can all cultivate. Mindful awareness allows us to observe our mental states without overidentifying with them, creating an attitude of acceptance that can lead to greater curiosity and better self-understanding.

In "Buddha Shoveling Snow" poet Billy Collins (1998) gives us a portrait of utterly mindful activity, one shovelful at a time. The Buddha in the form of a friend or teacher is shoveling snow "inside his generous pocket of silence." Working all morning long until the snow is piled high, the Buddha has thrown himself into shoveling snow "as if it were the purpose of existence" (p. 104).

When we are fully in the moment of shoveling or reading a text or observing an experiment in the lab, we disengage from our habitual patterns of reactivity and come closer to clear comprehension of any situation, "as if it were the purpose of existence." When introduced in an academic setting, mindfulness has yet another cognitive advantage: it develops the capacity to retain and make sense of information learned while mindfully paying attention, abilities closely associated with working memory. Professors find that not only are students better able to be present in the moment with the subject matter and each other, but they are better able to hold on to what they are learning over time and integrate it into meaningful patterns. So when architecture students mindfully watch the light through a tree branch change over the course of a day at a building site, they remember those changes and can use that new information to design a building that makes best use of natural light. Professors across disciplines report transformative changes after integrating mindfulness into their classes: increased concentration, greater capacity for synthetic thinking, conceptual flexibility, and an appreciation for a different type of intellectual process, distinct from the linear, analytical, and product-oriented processes so often valued in contemporary education. Many examples follow in this chapter.

Mindfulness as taught in the classroom is a secular activity. It is a basic human capacity. But it was also developed as a sacred practice in religious and spiritual traditions, like mindful walking in Christian monasteries, the mindful illumination of the Bible, or the contemplative exercises of St. Ignatius. An example in the Jewish tradition is the Talmud scholarship of Maimonides and the contemplative approaches in his *Guide for the Perplexed.* In Islam, the three fundamental modes of prayer are contemplations: *dhikr* ("remembrance," the repeating of holy phrases), *muraqabah* (the contemplation of scripture), and *tafakkur* (the contemplation of nature). The Buddhist practice of mindfulness adapts well to the multicultural secular classroom, since the original Buddha wanted his students to become autonomous in their understanding of the truth and not to become dependent on him or any other authority figure or system. "Be a lamp unto yourself," he told them. Pay attention. (See "Mindfulness Instructions" for basic instructions.)

Mindfulness Instructions

Instructions

Begin by sitting in a chair or on a cushion on the floor, with your back straight. Either close your eyes or rest them with a soft gaze on a point nearby. Relax into your sitting posture with a few deep breaths. Allow the body and mind to become utterly relaxed while remaining very alert. Sweep your awareness through your body, feeling the sensations with no agenda, no goal, just staying mindful of these sensations.

After some time, shift your awareness to the sounds that you hear. Be aware of both the pure sound vibration and the space or silence between the sounds. As with body sensations, incline your awareness away from the definition of the sound, or thoughts about the sound, and simply attune to the sound just as it is.

After some minutes of awareness of body and sounds, bring your attention to your natural breathing process. Locate the area where the breath is most clear, and let awareness lightly rest there. For some, it is the sensation of the rising and falling of the abdomen. For others, it may be the sensations experienced at the nostrils with the inhalation and exhalation.

Let the breath breathe itself without control, direction, or force. Feel the full breath cycle from the beginning through the middle to the end.

The awareness is a combination of receptivity, like listening, and alert, attentive presence. Let go of everything else, or let it be in the background. Just let the breathing breathe itself. As soon as you notice the mind wandering off, lost in thought, be aware of that without judging, and gently return again to your breath.

Short Instruction

Breathe normally. Pay attention to the breath as it enters through your nostrils and fills your lungs and then flows back out of your body. When thoughts or emotions or sensations arise and you lose awareness of your breath, bring your awareness gently back to the breath and begin again.

The definitions of the terms *mindful learning* and *mindful teaching* are evolving as educators gain experience. Mindful learning, according to Ellen Langer (1997) at Harvard, has three characteristics: the continuous creation of new categories, openness to new information, and an implicit awareness of more than one perspective. She states that the essence of mindfulness is flexible thinking. Dan Siegel, in *The Mindful Brain* (2007), identifies the essential dimensions of mindful learning as openness to novelty, alertness to distinction, context sensitivity, multiple perspectives, and present orientation. He calls reflection "the fourth R of education," the skill that embeds self-knowing and empathy in the curriculum. Mary Rose O'Reilley (1998) from the University of St. Thomas says in a report to the Center for Contemplative Mind in Society that mindfulness has to do with "being awake, being there, being present, listening, creating a space for learning and for developing an inner life by your very attention to the moment."

CLASSROOM APPLICATIONS

Mindfulness is being aware in the present moment, not judging but accepting things as they are—everything that arises: the sound of voices outside the window, the text that seemed so dense when you first read it, the blank page waiting for your paintbrush. You still have discriminating awareness, you can still notice whether, for example, a poetic metaphor in your assigned novel wakes up your senses or is a tired cliché. In fact, your discrimination is more refined because you are not bringing a prejudgment to the situation. This way of being, and it does become a way of being and thinking and acting, allows every moment to be fresh—a moment we can learn and grow from. Mindfulness opens the mind and gives space for new understanding. It is the essential contemplative practice for the academy and, not surprisingly, the practice most widely incorporated into higher education.

Witnessing and Welcoming: Being Present with Difficult Issues

Think about how overwhelming environmental issues like climate change and shrinking water supplies are to young college students looking at the future. Many just want to look away. At American University, in a course on practical environmentalism, Paul Wapner added mindfulness and other contemplative practices to help students deal with the difficulties of environmental political action, where there are few victories in a battle against immense odds. "They called my course Introduction to Doom," he says. Mindfulness became a way for his students to be able to deal with all this bad news. The mindfulness reduced their stress by allowing the students to be more fully present in the moment, learning to respect and pay close attention to this important but difficult information. "Mindfulness looks at what is. In politics, we are often looking away. Mindfulness turns discomfort into inquiry. It makes us more human, opens up a new part of us not available before." Now, he says, students understand that "climate change is a great path to inner growth, and working on our inner growth is a terrific path to dealing with environmental issues."

After teaching Cultivating Mindfulness and Human Rights, a course in the Humanities at the University of North Carolina, Alexandra Schultheis and Gregory Grieve wrote that mindfulness practices worked with the course materials

> not in a simplistic way to cheer for humanitarianism, but to expand the range of responses possible to human rights violations (including acknowledging a space for silence claimed by sufferers of rights violations, learning to read forms of storytelling that don't conform to expected patterns, cultivating a compassion that clearly acknowledges power imbalances and privilege, and critical thinking about humanitarianism itself). We were perhaps most pleased about the ways in which contemplative practices allowed the students to delve deeply into the intellectual core of the course, and then to translate that core into their own terms.

Addressing the difficulty of the subjects that arise in her courses on sociology, women's studies, and Latin American/Latina studies at Vassar, Light Carruyo introduced mindfulness to help students confront the hard issues that inevitably engage their experience as social and emotional beings. In teaching courses in the past, she had found that disregarding the personal and focusing on the text was "infinitely more manageable" but limited the extent of the learning, so she was interested in the effects of mindfulness as part of a "healing form of critical inquiry." The mindfulness did increase awareness of emotion, which is not always easy for students but helps them understand the issues more viscerally, and the discussions led to a dialogue on the connection between personal transformation and the transformation of the structures of inequality, a dialogue that is alive and well in the civil society activist community. These practices also help students develop their emotional regulation, something especially important in courses with such difficult themes.

Gurleen Grewal taught mindfulness in a women's studies course at the University of South Florida: "In each class we have silent sittings, quieting the mind via the breath, with basic instructions to observe the flow of thoughts/reactions from a nonjudgmental space—a practice crucial in developing acceptance, tolerance, and compassion for oneself and others. I like to begin class with five to ten minutes of mindfulness that very gradually increases as the semester proceeds." These are her instructions:

- Sitting in your chairs, body relaxed and spine erect, eyes closed, follow the sound of the gong or singing bowl as it reverberates and hums in space.
- Follow the ebbing of the sound into silence.
- Rest in that silence.
- If thoughts arise, simply observe them.
- Do the same for any bodily sensations or emotions: simply witness them.
- If you find yourself getting caught up in your thoughts, return to the awareness of your breath. Anchoring your attention in your breath breaks the compulsiveness of thought.
- Return to rest in silence.
- Witness and welcome, without getting caught in whatever arises.
- Simply notice the mental chatter, the resistance to what is.
- The meditation ends with the sound of the gong or the bowl. Gradually open your eyes.

Shape Shifting: A Mindful Look at Personal Identity

"Trying to define yourself," said Alan Watts, "is like trying to bite your own teeth." Nevertheless, readings ranging from the ancients to contemporary psychology demonstrate that humans have always tried to do it. But Allen Stairs, teaching philosophy at the University of Maryland, wanted to go more deeply into questions like, How do we define happiness? How do we define well-being? What constitutes personal identity? The course he developed, Contemplation, Well-Being, and Personal Identity, gives students a chance to explore these philosophical questions through contemplative practice. Early in the course, he provides his students basic instruction in mindfulness, which is followed by more extensive instruction from a senior teacher at the Insight Meditation Community of Washington, DC. In addition to practicing in class, students are required to meditate on their own at least three times a week and keep a journal in which they report and reflect on their practice. They also study mindfulness from a more empirical perspective through assigned texts and guest lecturers who speak to what is known about the neurological, psychological, and medical effects of mindfulness meditation.

With this grounding, students explore the connections between mindfulness and self-identity. In particular, the class examines how the Buddhist notion of identity—that identity is a construct and that there is no such thing as an enduring self—might both complement and complicate Western notions of identity. They explored the theme that "however valuable the perspective recommended by mindfulness, it needs to be enriched by ways of looking at ourselves that *do not* rest in the here and now." They also discussed whether our tendency to see ourselves in narrative terms makes a genuine contribution to our flourishing, even if the narratives are not true at the deeper level of metaphysics.

Hey Man, Slow Down: Mindfulness and the Arts

At Syracuse University, Anne Beffel teaches mindfulness in her Contemplative Arts and Society course, which attracts students who aspire to cultivate creativity, well-being, and compassionate connections. They practice what they call paying attention and opening awareness to their connections with their surroundings and each other. They developed the sitting still contemplative video project, which includes exercises designed specifically for developing close observation. As part of the Art in Odd Places festival in New York, the City Meditation Crew in white uniforms took their "hey man, slow down" philosophy to Union Square, where they slowly constructed a giant mandala from discarded gum wrappers (in honor of Gandhi's birthday, October 2).

Because many art and design students are particularly hard on themselves and tend to be perfectionists, Beffel stresses the nonjudging that is cultivated through mindfulness, using Pema Chodron's phrase, being "unconditionally friendly to oneself." One student wrote:

> Before this class, I found myself often judging my work while I was creating. I had a hard time staying in the present moment and allowing myself to relax and enjoy the process. I worried about what others would think about my art. In this course, I realized that I have gotten away from what I believe to be true art: art that completes me as an artist. I wanted to get back to the stage where I didn't notice the judgmental opinions of others and simply did art for myself—connected and accepting.

And others did as well:

> To me, awareness is the feeling of seeing everything as though it were the first time and the last time, at the same time.

> The acts of slowing down, looking around you, listening to someone, tasting a raisin, all these things are alternatives to violence . . . Even though you might not necessarily be thinking "this is non-violent," you are acting in that way and it gives you an alternative.

Amy Cheng, professor of studio art at State University of New York at New Paltz, sees the inherent connection between the arts and mindfulness: "Our ultimate goal in my course is to find the writing strategies that, like meditation, help us to tap the intuitive creative functions of the right brain: to think in complex images rather than in sequential order, to see the whole as well as the parts, to grasp interconnections, correspondences, resemblances, and nuances rather than the bits and pieces and linear, logical patterns." Her students looked at three aspects of creativity in a meditative context:

- Making something new, original, or unexpected
- Renewing or sustaining what already exists
- Healing and making things whole

Mindfulness as Self-Management

Jeremy Hunter, who teaches at the Peter F. Drucker and Masatoshi Ito Graduate School of Management at Claremont Graduate University, believes mindfulness should be at the center of teaching in business schools. That, he argues, is because it improves the quality of attention, and in the modern workplace, attention is key. It also makes us more aware of emotions, which play an important role in business relationships. "To me, it's fundamental to how work gets done these days," he said. Hunter's work is based on many years of meditation study and the work of Peter Drucker, the founder of the discipline of modern management. Drucker recognized that knowledge workers were the key to economic survival for the developed economies. He also recognized that although knowledge workers use their minds to make a living, they are rarely taught to use their minds more effectively. In a series of four seven-week executive education classes, and a separate course for MBA students, Hunter teaches what he calls self-management—"managing your insides so you can deal with your outsides better." He often starts class with a mindfulness meditation and covers topics like managing emotional reactions and dealing with change. His graduate students are working in management jobs, so he gives them exercises to apply at work and at home. One mindful exercise is to look at a very familiar place or person as if it were the first time, mindfully noting every detail. This practice usually generates astonishment among students at what they no longer see of the familiar.

During a conversation about the difficulty of being mindful while multitasking, one student reportedly became frustrated with a weekly work meeting where staff seemed more focused on their cellphones than on the discussion. When he returned to the office and insisted that everyone put their phones in a box before starting, his colleagues initially responded with irritation, but the weekly gathering soon became so much more efficient that it was cut to an hour from ninety minutes.

Looking, Listening, Remembering: The Education of Reflective Scientists

Science courses reveal the investigative nature of mindfulness practices. Arthur Zajonc, teaching physics and the history of science at Amherst College, asks his students to bring their mindfulness to natural and man-made objects:

> First study the physical object carefully: its shape, color, size, structural components, etc. If you have selected a paper clip, observe its shiny surface, the thickness of the wire of which it is made, its peculiar shape, and so on. Then close your eyes and imagine it before yourself in detail. Can you call to mind the exact shape of the paper clip? If not, go back to the physical object again and make further observations, repeating this until you have a clear mental picture of the whole object.

After students have engaged with this exercise, they see common objects differently. They suddenly realize the brilliant design and execution of a paper clip, an object that they have looked at thousands of times before but never actually *seen*. This enables the students to radically change their approach to the world around them.

Al Kaszniak teaches psychology at the University of Arizona. In 2010, he taught The Psychology of Empathy and Compassion: Contemplative and Scientific Perspectives, which included breath-focused mindful attention, mindful listening, and reflective journaling. The reflective journaling is actually a mindfulness exercise:

- Before reading, do 10 minutes of breath-focused mindful attention.
- Don't think about the reading—try to stay fully attentive to the breath.
- Allow this mindful attitude to remain as you read.
- After the reading and another breath-focused practice of 10 minutes, write no more than one page describing how the reading relates to your personal experience. Be specific.
- Describe anything you noticed about your experience during the reading.

As he proceeds through the semester, teaching about empathy and compassion from the perspective of both scientific and contemplative traditions, he introduces practices relevant to the session: mindful breathing when he teaches about attention, loving kindness when he teaches the neuroscience of empathy. The final session met in a contemplative garden, where they practiced mindful attention and discussed the difference between their meditation in the garden and meditation in other environments, noticing how natural and built environments relate to the expression or inhibition of empathy and compassion.

Many educators are concerned about the effects of technology and multitasking on their students. At the University of Washington, David Levy uses contemplative practices as a lens to observe and critique information practices and, in particular, investigate problems of information overload, the fragmentation of attention, and the busyness and speed of everyday life. The basic practice of the course is mindfulness: mindful sitting (attention to the breath) and walking (attention to the feet). Students then mindfully observe an information practice like texting or e-mailing, document what they observe, and reflect on what they documented. They discovered, for example, that they tended to check e-mail when they were anxious or bored but that reading e-mail only exacerbated their anxiety. Their practice changed to this one:

- Observe your own patterns of behavior, bringing attention to body, breath, emotions, and so on.
- Decide which dimensions of your experience you want to cultivate or minimize (e.g., clarity of attention, fatigue, anxiety).
- Make conscious choices in order to cultivate some states and minimize others.

FIRST-PERSON STUDY IN THE LAB

The most problematic place in the academy to introduce contemplative practices has been religion departments, where the concern has been that a professor who practices the religion he or she is teaching would not be sufficiently objective. Teaching contemplative practices to students raises a further concern: proselytizing. These concerns go back to the birth of the modern academy, when enlightened thought and scientific method replaced the earlier monastic institutions. Today, however, some professors of religion who think it is important for their students to explore these practices in order to understand the religions they are studying have found ways based on critical inquiry and "first-person study" to engage students in the practices they are studying in their texts.

Harold Roth, a Taoist scholar at Brown University, has established the Contemplative Studies Initiative, a group of Brown faculty with diverse academic specializations who are united around a common interest in the study of contemplative states of mind, including the underlying philosophy, psychology, and phenomenology of human contemplative experience. For Roth, one of the shortcomings of higher education is that it remains heavily biased toward "third-person learning." Students learn how to analyze, memorize, and quantify subjects as objects—as something "out there," separate from themselves. At the same time, the subjectivity of the knower is all but ignored. One of the values of contemplative pedagogy is that it tries to bridge this rift between the knower and the known by bridging the gap between more traditional, objective study and what Roth calls "critical first-person learning." "First person" means that students engage directly with the practices being studied, and "critical" means that students are not asked to believe anything but instead to evaluate their own experience with openness and discernment.

In Introduction to Contemplative Studies, Roth introduces students to a variety of contemplative experiences from the Zen, Taoist, and Vipassana traditions through both study of the texts and practice in what is called a "lab" but looks to other eyes like a meditation hall. Early each day, they transform the dance studio while the dancers are still sleeping and do their first-person lab work, meditation. They read *Embodied Mind* (1991) by Francisco Varela, Evan Thompson, and Eleanor Rosch and the *Anapanasati sutta* (the Buddha's instructions on the mindfulness of breathing), and they practice mindfulness of breath at the tip of the nose and in the diaphragm; then they learn body scan and mindfulness of sensation, feeling, thought, and perception. They discuss their direct experience in relation to what they read in the text.

SEEING FROM MULTIPLE PERSPECTIVES: MINDFULNESS IN LAW SCHOOLS

The Center for Contemplative Mind in Society held three retreats for Yale Law School students led by Joseph Goldstein, founding meditation teacher of Insight Meditation Society. Although the retreats were off campus and did not focus on the law curriculum, they led to an appreciation of the many ways in which mindfulness could benefit law education, including the themes of listening and the relationship between internal and external conflict, separation and connection, winning and nonwinning.

In 1999, Len Riskin, then teaching at the University of Missouri-Columbia Law School, based his course, Understanding Conflict, on these themes and integrating mindfulness with the readings and discussions. They discussed how mindfulness could help lawyers stay present with the suffering of clients, develop compassion and patience, and make better decisions. One student wrote after the course:

> I think the most important thing the practice gives us is deliberation. I find I am less likely to jump to conclusions, the way your law professors try to get you to do. It's harder to push my buttons than it was before I started this practice. I'm cooler-headed and likely to see any issue from more angles, which is the key to solving legal problems.

More recently, at Roger Williams University School of Law, David Zlotnick taught Trial Advocacy: Integrating Mindfulness Theory and Practice. He introduced mindfulness to help students stay in the moment and let go of the illusion of control in order to improve their confidence and skills. He also exposed them to deeper practices of compassion and connectedness to teach them that there is a way to be a compassionate trial lawyer without losing effectiveness in the courtroom. In one interesting practice, students practiced mindfulness of being present. Then, without advance notice, a student was asked to redo a direct examination of a witness while blindfolded, which required the student to put aside his or her notes and listen to the witness. Students found this exercise liberating and helpful. Later, after doing a mindfulness practice that focused on staying present with discomfort and moving through it, they did a simulated trial during which an attorney tried to frustrate the student with repeated objections (which the judge sustained). When the student lawyer began to get angry, a bell was rung with the instruction to try the mindfulness-of-anger practice. Students reported that the practice allowed them to let go of anger and return to the present moment with a clear mind so they could focus on the facts of the case.

In the law, judgment is central. Judges judge. Juries judge. Law professors judge. Lawyers make judgments about the merits of their clients' cases. In *Mindfulness for Law Students*, Scott Rogers invites law students to investigate the judging quality of their own minds. It is important, he says, to distinguish one type of judging from another—"to distinguish King Solomon wisdom from reactionary thoughts that continually arise in the mind and label events, information, and people, as good and bad, right and wrong." He encourages students to explore their own minds through mindfulness practice to see if their thoughts are biased and judgmental, independent of the facts. When thoughts arise in the mind, he says, "Follow them as if you were a private investigator hired to see where they go."

Interest in applying mindfulness to legal studies is rising. For example, in 2011, Charles Halpern, Rhonda Magee, and others at the Berkeley Initiative for Mindfulness in Law hosted a conference devoted to the examination of mindfulness and the law. The meeting drew hundreds of lawyers, judges, law professors, and law students interested in how contemplative approaches can improve legal education and the legal profession. That was followed by a meeting in 2013 for fifty law professors from thirty law schools who are introducing mindfulness into their teaching.

A panel of five students presented their experiences of mindfulness in law school to a large audience. The first speaker said, "We are under a lot of pressure to speak in a lawyerly way, to think like a lawyer, and I feel my compass is gone, my self is gone. The ground seems very shaky, and it's important to be OK with not knowing. Mindfulness has been invaluable; it makes it okay to feel insecure. It helps me forgive myself."

A student on the panel from Northwestern Law School had learned mindfulness in a law class. Her well-organized mind saw these challenges to starting a practice in a law school:

1. Lifestyle. Speed. Do and read as much as you can as fast as you can.

2. Lawyers are trained as skeptics. We don't think it will work.

3. Lots of questions and criticism from peers.

4. Concerns that if you look inside, what are you going to find? "I have a shield for law school; mindfulness might take down the shield."

5. Finding the time ("15 minutes is a big deal for me").

6. Patience ("I want to be right and right away").

7. Exhaustion ("When I do the body scan, I fall asleep").

And then she listed these benefits:

1. Stress reduction ("Helped my stomach and headaches. Friends say I am so much calmer.")

2. More able to pay attention in class.

3. Easier to enjoy other things—music, chocolate cake, and Lake Michigan.

A SENSE OF PERSPECTIVE: MINDFULNESS AND DISABILITIES

"Students with disabilities bring a valuable perspective and accumulated wisdom to the learning environment on campus. But the advantage can be compromised by the significant personal liabilities faced by these students, including increased stress," wrote Dan Holland, who taught an experiential seminar at the University of Arkansas entitled Contemplative Practice, Health Promotion, and Disability on Campus. He taught mindfulness as well as somatic awareness practices: "Through the greater breadth and depth of attention that mindfulness brings, a person can begin to gain a sense of perspective that does not necessarily improve a specific health condition or lessen the sociopolitical obstacles facing people with disabilities but might empower one in relationship to those challenges. This deepened perspective or context is itself a form of improved health." Students reported that mindfulness had caused significant improvement in their ability to cope with daily stressors. And shortly after the end of the course, Dan saw a four-wheel-drive mud-splattered truck on campus "with the exaggerated suspension and big knobby tires that are common in Arkansas." What struck him as interesting about this particular truck was the bumper sticker: "Breathe."

CONCLUSION

These examples suggest that the possibilities for deepening academic inquiry through mindfulness are virtually endless. Stopping, looking, listening, paying attention—it is simple but not easy, and the effects are profound. And they are at the very heart of learning. "If your mind is empty," said Zen teacher Suzuki Roshi to his San Francisco students, "it is always ready for anything; it is open to everything. In the beginner's mind, there are many possibilities, but in the expert's there are few."

Resources

Jack Kornfield, *Meditation for Beginners* (Boulder, CO: Sounds True, 2008).
Thich Nhat Hanh, *The Miracle of Mindfulness* (Boston: Beacon Press, 1975).
Scott L. Rogers, *Mindfulness for Law Students* (Miami: Mindful Living Press, 2009).
Arthur Zajonc, *Meditation as Contemplative Inquiry* (Great Barrington, MA: Lindisfarne Books, 2009).
Jon Kabat Zinn, *Mindfulness for Beginners* (Boulder, CO: Sounds True, 2012).

Contemplative
Approaches to
Reading and Writing

One of the key ways we interact with students is through the reading and writing that we assign. Reading is often the main way we convey information, supplement lectures, and stimulate discussion. The centrality of reading in curriculum begins in the earliest grades and continues, ever more strongly, through postgraduate work. Reading is such a critical resource that we often assign our students so much material that they cannot possibly take the time necessary to reflect on and consider the implications of their assignments.

Writing assignments are the way we ask students to reflect and integrate what they have read and learned. However, often these assignments become perfunctory exercises in which students hastily guess what we might want to hear. It is thrilling to receive a paper that has been composed through deep and sustained reflection. Creating assignments and class-time exercises that allow students to inhabit their writing can help them discover and explore insights into the disciplines and themselves. Contemplative writing practices help reclaim the sacred art of writing, deepening students' understanding and stimulating their insight and creativity.

CONTEMPLATIVE READING

Exercises that require students to slow down and attend carefully to their reading can fundamentally change their relationship to the material and transform their attitude to reading in general.

The Sacred Roots of Reading

Deep, contemplative reading is part of all traditions with written scriptures. In religions with revered texts, reading is a form of devotion. Such reading is the historical background for contemporary contemplative methods of reading.

In the Christian tradition, contemplative reading is known as *lectio divina*. It was adapted from early Judaism as a system for reading and exegesis of the Hebrew Bible. It recognized four levels of meaning: literal, metaphorical or symbolic, moral, and mystical. The levels increase in complexity, from simply paying attention to what is on the page to the inquiry into more complex interpretation and extension. Through the process, the simple words on the page become integrated into the moral and spiritual life of the reader. This process brings greater understanding and connection, often missed in a superficial, quick reading. In the third century, the Christian scholar Origen saw that if you read in the right spirit, you would find the meaning "hidden from most people." In the fourth century, carrying on with this tradition, Augustine created the West's first developed theory of reading, in which reading could cease to be a "wandering" from one literary delight to another and become a "pilgrimage." When Benedict compiled his rules for monasteries in the sixth century, a time when personal reading was still relatively rare, he included reading as an important part of the monk's day. He recognized that this was a way of the monks' being with scripture that called them to study deeply, ponder, listen, and pray. To this day, the Rule of St. Benedict is the most common and influential rule used by monasteries and monks, more than fourteen hundred years after its writing.

Benedict's instructions included, as did the earliest Judaic practice, four levels of meaning and four approaches to the text: *lectio* (reading and then understanding the text), *meditatio* (reflection and contextualizing the meaning), *oratio* (listening within and living the meaning), and *contemplatio* (being still and meeting God in the text). It was a fundamentally contemplative approach: first becoming keenly aware of what was on the page and then successively attending to greater and deeper meaning within, building to the realization of global and divine connection. Through the vehicle of the written word, the reader journeyed deeply within to connect profoundly with the world, and, in Benedict's tradition, the divine.

This connection of the written word to the divine is also central to Islamic beliefs about the Koran. Since it is believed that the words of the holy text were dictated by God to Muhammad after his contemplative retreat in the Cave of Hira, reading or even hearing the words connect the faithful to God. Though even hearing the words without understanding their meanings is a blessing, in a Hadith (wisdom attributed to Muhammad rather than God), Muhammad compares superficial reading to gulping down milk, allowing it to flow over the tongue without any realization or attention. Only through deep attention can words transform the faithful.

There are instructions and stories for contemplative reading in the Eastern traditions as well. In Hinduism, it is said that before one reads the *Ramayana*, the epic story of Lord Rama (one of the most popular Hindu deities, whose life depicts the perfect embodiment of the dharma), his consort Sita, and his great devotee Hanuman, the reader should invoke and worship both the gods and the book's author in order to hear the story with an "enraptured mind." "Taking flowers in the hollow of his or her palms, the reader should meditate on Sri Rama . . . whose charming eyes resemble the petals of a red lotus." Water is sipped and mantras are recited. The right hand is placed over the heart. If read (or, originally, listened to) in this spirit, the story brings joy and blessings and "secures freedom from the bondage of mundane existence." Again, reading must be done as an intentional and attentive act for it to transform the reader.

The great Tibetan Buddhist scholar Naropa was studying one day when a *dakini* (a female embodiment of enlightened energy) appeared and asked if he understood the words of the dharma, the teachings of Buddha. Do you understand the words or the sense? When he said, "the words," she laughed and danced and waved her walking stick. But when he said, "I also understand the sense," she began to weep. He asked her why. She said, "When you said words, I laughed that a great scholar like you would tell the truth. When you said you understood the meaning, I wept that a great scholar would lie." Naropa realized that she was right and that he needed to find a contemplative teacher to help him get beyond the words to achieve full realization.

CONTEMPLATIVE READING IN THE CLASSROOM

Reading in college today is more often a race to finish a text than a search for hidden meaning. Woody Allen captured it well: "I took a speed-reading course and read *War and Peace* in twenty minutes. It involves Russia." Contemplative reading in the classroom is radically different. It slows down the reader and the reading, and that alone changes the student's experience. It is a process of quiet reflection, which requires mindful attentiveness, a letting go of distracting thoughts and opinions to be fully in the moment with the text. It requires patient receptivity and an intention to go further, and it moves the reader into a calm awareness, allowing a more profound experience and understanding. It often involves repeated reading of one passage. Students read and advance, then return and read again. Each time they may hear something new, leading to more connection with the material.

Contemplative reading, which brings together the literal meaning and the meaning discovered through personal reflection, is finding a place in the contemporary classroom as a method for revealing the full meaning of a text. By adapting this ancient practice, teachers are not attempting to elevate academic texts, even literature, to the status of scripture or sacred texts but are seeking to increase students' engagement with and comprehension of their subject, guided by a method that has led monks and others to find the wisdom "hidden from most people." The adaptations described in this chapter are inspired by the formal monastic practice but are not the full religious practice of, for example, *lectio divina*, although most share many elements of the original sacred process.

Lectio Divina

As a professor of literature at Bryn Mawr and a Benedictine nun, Linda Susan Beard is uniquely qualified as one of the first to adapt *lectio divina* for the classroom. In her class on the literature of suffering, Crossing the Threshold of Pain's Legacy, she had found that it was difficult for her students to absorb the painful truths of the Holocaust, slavery, and apartheid that were revealed through the literature. In response, she asked students to explore each of the four stages of *lectio divina* both in and out of the classroom. The assigned texts were used as *lectio*, the reflective work done as a community constituted a shared *meditatio*, the class discussions were used as *oratio*, and the final individual essay was framed as the "rich elixir" made possible by *contemplatio*. The students were able to acknowledge their emotions and painful identifications, share them with each other, and write about them in connection with the literal meaning of the texts. Through this process, they were able to connect their own experience even to these painful and difficult events, allowing them to feel more connected and compassionate.

In Images for the Soul: Vision and Contemplation in Christian History, a class at Colgate University in which much of the reading material was dense and unfamiliar to students, Georgia Frank introduced a type of disciplined, attentive reading that she knew from the Christian contemplative tradition. Each assigned text was explored in a first reading and a second reading. For the first reading, the students read the entire work and a limited selection of background materials. As a class, they worked on interpreting a small portion of the text in order to acquaint themselves with the writer's style and religious sensibilities. "The first reading," she said, "was like walking the students around a neighborhood and the perimeter of a building. We found a few points of entry into that strange building." They used this form of disciplined, attentive reading again for the second reading, which took place five days later at the next class meeting. The students reread the text with the aim of writing about it. Two or three students prepared discussion questions, which provided the basis for the class discussion. The remainder of the students prepared a brief response paper to the same reading. The students arrived with a renewed confidence. This time, "it was the students who showed me new, exciting entrances into the sprawling house." The practice helped students "engage in theological reflection in the context of lived experience." Practicing in the "sterility" of the classroom allowed them to cultivate the "type of dialog, experimentation, and imagination that opened up rich possibilities for the contemplative life of the students."

Departing somewhat more from the traditional form, David G. Haskell, associate professor of biology and environmental science at the University of the South, in his course Food and Hunger: Contemplation and Action, introduced a modification of Basil Pennington's *lectio divina* for reading short essays on hunger and food or, as he said, "*Lectio* without too much *Divina*" and gave these instructions:

- Sit quietly and relax your minds and bodies for one minute.
- Read aloud, slowly, the entire text, each person reading one or two sentences, "passing along" the reading to the left to the next reader.
- One minute of silence and reflection.
- One person reads aloud a short passage that is chosen in advance.
- Another minute of silence and reflection.
- Each person shares a word or short phrase in response to the reading—just giving voice to the word without explanation or discussion.
- Another person reads the short passage again.
- One minute of silence and reflection.
- Each person shares a longer response to the text—a sentence or two. All listen attentively to one another without correcting or disputing.
- Another person reads the short passage one last time, followed by another minute of silence.

This participatory process of reading aloud around the room, he remarks, "immerses students in the text so that they're swimming in it, even putting the snorkel beneath it, rather than speed boating over the surface." In a circle of students, he reminds them that it will be necessary to project their voices and assures them that it is all right to stumble or pass to the next student; in initial stages of group work, it is important that students feel comfortable and know that they can have the freedom to hesitate or even opt out. This provides a sense of freedom that allows them to embrace fear rather than fight it.

Haskell sometimes uses "Zen Wheelbarrows and Collard Greens," a chapter by Dan Barker in *Food and Faith: Justice, Joy, and Daily Bread.* At a meeting of contemplative educators hosted by the center, Haskell led participants slowly and contemplatively through the text, and a deep silence settled over the conference room. During the process of going around the circle, each person read and then spoke, bringing about deep engagement. There was a nearly hypnotic quality to sinking into the text, and Haskell cautioned that one did need to be careful about the choice of text and what values and themes it conveys, because it evokes emotions as well as ideas. "Zen Wheelbarrows" turned out to be an offering rich with earthy details about an activist dedicated to restoring the vitality of the impoverished soil in the slums and the hope of city dwellers in need of sustenance.

Haskell's course connects academic work with social action as well as contemplative practice. Students research the distribution systems for food, visit the colossal storehouses for it, and examine the reality of hunger among rural poor living near their university, some of whom work after hours on campus, cleaning or even, ironically, in dining services. In class, they practice silence, watch their breath, and write in their journals to reflect on these disparities and embedded injustices. These practices provide tools for students to engage with the difficult realizations of the course while enabling them to act on them. Compassionate social action requires this balance between the recognition of suffering and the willingness to act while understanding that change is slow and difficult.

After contemplative reading and discussion, students develop a plan for action, and they prepare, serve, and then sit down to a Thanksgiving meal with eighty guests during the week before Thanksgiving. This last requirement, it turns out, is the most difficult. To engage with people from different classes, races, and life situations, make conversation, and honor them with attention can be a challenge for students. The contemplative practices, including the contemplative reading, helped students look at their thoughts and emotions without judgment and share them thoughtfully with other students.

Shifting Perspectives

Gurleen Grewal, professor of women's studies at the University of South Florida, uses contemplative reading in her classroom because "uncertainty is the ground of life, and contemplative practice helps us face it." In her teaching, she finds that while it's difficult to give up the "fake certainty" of authority to acknowledge that so much is unknown, the conditions that arise from this gesture allow trust to build. Inviting practice into the classroom generates questions, dissonance, and new areas to explore. This requires willingness on the part of the teacher to explore and find new territory; it is not always easy to give up the comfortable control developed over years of teaching. However, allowing students this sort of freedom can initiate discoveries that can vitalize their learning and our teaching.

After teaching women's studies for eleven years, Grewal departed from the established paradigm of feminist inquiry, which has been an issues-based approach that proposes political, social, and economic strategies for addressing injustice. Now she is making use of a contemplative approach that looks more deeply at the roots of violence and power and at how an inward transformation of the relationship between those in different positions makes progress possible. The shift in perspective has given students a new understanding of how change can happen even within intractable situations.

In her course Beyond Victimhood, Grewal uses Adrienne Rich's poem "Diving into the Wreck" as a model for how to explore deeply lodged trauma, using the metaphor of a ladder to symbolize going down to explore the submerged ship-wreck rather than the story that has been told about it. Students read the poem, then reflect on it, read it again, share with a partner what resonates for them, and then sit with it for two minutes before writing or formulating some other response, such as a picture or a gesture to share. The practice demonstrates how an indirect, metaphoric, contemplative approach can reveal the truth about a condition sometimes better than a rational technique.

Ancient Texts in the Present Moment

Contemplative approaches to reading can affect students' ability to engage with action, but they also can create greater connection with material, even when that material is a thousand years old. With the theme of pilgrimage as a guiding thread, Sol Miguel-Prendes's class in Contemplative Practices and Literary Creation in Spain at Wake Forest University explored through critical reading and thinking how the practice of *lectio divina* developed in the Middle Ages and influenced intellectual life and nonreligious literary creation. Then, adopting the theme of "allowing yourself to be spoken to," the students expanded beyond critical reading to engage in contemplative reading and inquiry: "the intimate encounter with the text, the moment of being touched or awakened." Students read texts, including John of the Cross, Jorge Manrique, and Antonio Machado, using both critical and contemplative approaches.

Rather than reading as if these were alien, ancient texts, the students read as if these authors are directly speaking to them. This creates an opportunity for the students to realize that they are actually sharing the thoughts of another person, in this case one now dead for over a thousand years. The magic and power of writing become real for the students.

Reading About Nature

Mary Rose O'Reilley adapted contemplative reading for The Writer in Nature, her course at the University of Saint Thomas. Texts included writing by Shunryu Suzuki, Jane Tompkins, Thomas Merton, and Annie Dillard. "It's hard to be a nature writer," she wrote, "without being also in some sense a contemplative. Nature makes you a contemplative if you stare at any square foot of the planet in a disciplined way." But, she continued, "however obvious this point might be to some of us, when I began to teach The Writer in Nature, I discovered that it is not at all apparent to most active young students who—while perhaps experiencing fleeting bouts of mindfulness now and again—have no name for it, no patience with it, no desire to rest and stay. I felt lucky to get my classes of English majors outside, never mind sitting in meditation, without a tanning agenda."

O'Reilley shifted her students' awareness toward the contemplative with a contemplative reading practice. These are her instructions for the reflective reading or rereading of a short text:

- Center yourself in your mind and body, place and purpose.
- Read the passage reflectively several times.
- Consider the questions: What speaks most profoundly to me here? What does my inner teacher want me to hear?
- Write for five or ten minutes.

And these are her instructions for shared reflective reading or rereading together:

- Keep a few minutes of silence together.
- One person reads the text aloud. All listen.
- Each one speaks to something the reading sparks in him or her.
- If appropriate, general discussion.

Engaged in slow reading for short periods, the students were not forced to endure a concentration exercise for which they had no context. In addition, the shared reading revealed their connection with the material and with the other students.

The Peace of Contemplative Reading

While contemplative reading can connect students to concepts and histories that they have never before experienced, it can also provide surprising results—even a measure of peace where they least expect it or a fresh sense of a word or idea that they've heard many times before. When Kathleen Biddick introduced contemplative reading in Refuge and Refugees: Contemplating Asylum, at Temple University, a student wrote, "I discovered something I didn't expect to find." It was "a small measure of inner peace. I recall the first day that we decided to do a 'word slam.' This entails the reading of a certain passage and then sitting in a small circle with others, each person saying aloud a single word that has meaning for them. Following the reading of a short prayer by the Dalai Lama, I became absorbed in the word 'sanctuary.' What is sanctuary? How do we welcome individuals seeking it? Must we bar people from receiving sanctuary?" At the end of the semester, he wrote, "Everyone should engage in daily contemplative reading because it relaxes the mind and body and can help you consider ideas and concepts with a fresh perspective." Another student wrote that contemplative reading helped him understand the importance of withholding judgment and working to patiently consider the text at hand instead of rushing to conclusions and "slamming down the gavel."

Across the Disciplines

Contemplative reading also found a place in law school. Legal theory and even practice can seem cold, distanced from one's own understanding of right and wrong. In LAW: Love in Action with Wisdom, a course at CUNY Law, Victor Goode and Maria Arias used Martin Luther King Jr.'s "Letter from the Birmingham Jail" as their text. The letter contains powerful sentences like these: "Injustice anywhere is a threat to justice everywhere. We are caught in an inescapable network of mutuality, tied in a single garment of destiny. Whatever affects one directly, affects all indirectly." Students each read one sentence from the letter, which allowed the whole class to participate and reflect on social justice and the meaning of the words while challenging legal precedent. Realizing the impact of a single case in depth, students can better realize the importance of each ruling, each law.

Contemplative reading can be nurtured and introduced in simple ways that allow students to engage with the reading deeply and not experience it as esoteric or rarified. In the syllabus for Animals in US History, at California State University, Northridge, Thomas Andrews used meditation to "set the stage" for contemplative reading. To his students he said: "Think of contemplative practices as an invitation to experiment with silence, to transcend the received ideas and institutions which condition our experience of ourselves and our world—and thus to glimpse with greater clarity and insight *what is*."

At the first class, he passed out copies of nature writer Craig Childs's short nonfiction piece, "Animal," which they read in the round. Each person spoke a sentence and then yielded to the next person. When the story was finished, they sat in silence for a few minutes. Then he asked one student to read a paragraph that was "particularly dense and ripe with meaning." After a few minutes of additional silence, he invited the students to offer a sentence or phrase in response to that text. After everyone had spoken, a few more minutes of silence. Andrews wrote that the students' words and phrases startled him: "Thoughtful, penetrating, direct, and far-ranging, virtually every contribution condensed whole constellations of argument and emotion, folding elaborate truths into microcosmic utterances of surpassing wisdom." By simply reading aloud, listening, sitting silently, and saying what came to mind, his students "limned the contours of a discussion that might have taken us two or three meetings to pursue."

Contemplative reading can also be added to already established practices in a course. Santiago Colas, who teaches comparative literature at the University of Michigan and is working on a book entitled *Reading to Live*, taught Zen practices, including sitting, walking, prostrations, and chanting, and asked his students to bring the awareness developed in those practices to reading. He said that he found the students to be both deeply engaged and frequently profoundly unsettled by the experience of the class. "What pleasantly surprised me, over the course of the semester, was just how powerfully these practices and texts 'seeped' into and disrupted their more comfortable literary reading practices. Where at the beginning of the course, the handful of most-experienced literature students dominated the conversations with well-informed arguments about the meaning of a particular poem, by the end of the course, all students in the seminar were participating equally in discussions that cultivated a rich field of ambiguity and possibility (and uncertainty) in relation to the literary text."

Judith Zimmer Brown often begins her classes at Naropa University this way: "I fold the papers and pass them out, and we sit and do silent breathing practice to just be there." On each paper is a provocative quote from some sacred tradition. Then the students open the paper and read the quote. "Don't try to figure out the meaning," she says, "just stay with words." They read it aloud together and stay with the words for some minutes. Then they turn to a partner and discuss their first sense of what they have read. After the reading and sharing, the focused and deep reading is allowed to percolate and produce associations and insights. They then return to mindfulness practice, followed by freewriting for one page about the meaning. "I encourage them to do this with any of their assignments, to bring personal integration into their writing." The integration of the writing with the careful reading allows students to explore and anchor what they have discovered.

Contemplative Reading and the Web

We are presented with a question and a paradox: Can we use digital media, which have created the hyperbusyness of our relentlessly interconnected lives through the rapid, distracted sampling of bits of information from many sources, to help faculty and students enter a place of spacious awareness, the quiet present mind where we wander free and undistracted and attend fully to whatever arises? Using digital media, which has vastly increased the influence of outer voices telling us what to do and think, can we offer ways to hear that still, small voice within? The nature of the digital world is interconnectedness, but that net exists horizontally, not vertically, and it is spread thin; it dwells in what Nicholas Carr calls "the shallows." Some brave teachers have found ways to take the plunge through the shallows into depth, to truly engage the subject being studied so that we reach a new awareness of its significance. They are seeking to increase attention, contemplation, wisdom, and compassion by using the very digital media that seem to be decreasing these capacities.

Bringing the monastic practice of *lectio divina* fully into this century, Francis J. Ambrosio, associate professor of philosophy at Georgetown University, developed "My Dante," an interactive website of Dante's *Divina Commedia* to "stimulate the students' imaginations to stop, linger, and dwell contemplatively on those elements of the poem which most require and reward focused attention so as to appropriate their meaning on an individual and personal level. Contemplative reading," he says, "is a path of access to the virtual reality of realms of truth contained within the text that only the human imagination can reach."

What are the advantages of digital technology for contemplative reading? The student views the text in both English and Italian—not in an illuminated manuscript but illuminated beautifully by the computer screen. A click away, the reader finds not only literary criticism on Dante but the comments of friends and other students. Ambrosio says it is the "use of a technology of reading that invites us to become aware of and deepen our capacity to be contemplative: to see beyond the surface of things, to recognize and rest in truths that can only be experienced by living them."

How does reading as a contemplative practice work in this course? First, Ambrosio tells his students that one must recognize that just as Dante told his patron, Cangrande della Scala of Verona, there are multiple levels of meaning simultaneously at work in the poem, each of which requires a different kind of understanding. Second, one learns how to move progressively through three levels:

1. *The literal, narrative level,* contained in the story of Dante the pilgrim as his journey begins in the Dark Wood until it ends in the Final Vision. The goal of reading at this first level is clear comprehension of the main characters and events that form the plot of the poem's narrative. In other words, understanding at this level means asking, "Who is Dante the pilgrim?"

2. *The ironic and metaphoric level* contained in and communicated by the artistic choices Dante the poet makes regarding characters, episodes, images, and themes at the narrative level. By recognizing these as choices, the reader becomes aware that, ironically, Dante the pilgrim both is and is not "really" the same person as Dante the poet. Who is Dante the poet? What is he trying so hard to tell me?

3. *The reflective level,* contained in the reader's personal responses to the poet's confession, witness, and testimony, in the form of a kind of dialogue between the poet and the reader. The goal of this level of understanding is personal reflection. The meaning of the poem is not finally understood until reader and poet find themselves standing face-to-face in the presence of all the others who face the same universal human questions of personal identity, freedom, and responsibility. It requires imagining how one's own journey is the same as the poet's, how both are universal, the same for all persons, despite every difference of time, place, and culture, making the poem genuinely one's own by responding to the question, "Who am I?"

CONTEMPLATIVE WRITING

Writers are often alone as they work in silence; they need a quiet, still mind so that the words can fall from the mind to the page. Such acts of writing share much with traditional contemplative practices. Like Zen archery, in writing we are preparing to allow the string, the arrow, the word, the idea, to release itself. It is a process of inquiry that, like meditation, can reveal not only content but both the workings of the mind and the nature of the mind itself. At the same time, it is an acknowledgment of our interconnection: all writers are *giving* something, and they need a reader who will accept their gift. Natalie Goldberg says that when you write, you "reach out of the deep chasm of loneliness and express yourself to another human being." So it has long been a contemplative practice favored by many, including monastics. The Chinese writer Lu Ji said, "The poet knocks on silence to make a sound." In the fourth century, Augustine used contemplative writing to create the first spiritual autobiography in the Christian world. Sixteen centuries later, Thomas Merton shared what it means to be a monk writing about the world both inside and outside the monastery. Writing is a means to share our thoughts, our inner selves, even with those we will never meet.

Writing benefits from the capacities that mindfulness, mindful listening, and other contemplative practices cultivate: seeing and hearing things as they are, bearing witness to life; being in the moment, even when remembering the past or imagining the future; no judging others and oneself yet exercising discriminating wisdom; holding multiple perspectives while being open to the new; and practicing kindness, compassion, and patience. As Gerard Manley Hopkins wrote, mindful awareness helps us see "all things . . . original, spare, strange." Alice Walker, a writer and a meditator, wrote a line that touched all who read it: "I think it pisses God off when you walk by the color purple in a field and don't notice it."

Contemplation is not the opposite of thinking but its complement. It is not the emptying of the mind of thoughts but the cultivation of awareness of thoughts within the mind. Through contemplation, the mind is open to itself. Meditation before, during, and after writing sessions can develop a healthy relationship with thoughts, so that the student becomes aware of a thought rather than identified with it, attached to it. Once identified with the thought ("My thought!"), the student has a hard time letting go of it or modifying it, whereas awareness of thought ("How interesting—a thought is arising") creates space around the thought in which to critique it and then to develop it, use it, or let it go.

A core skill for students in higher education, writing is important in almost every course. Contemplative writing methods will influence a student's education far beyond the single course in which they are taught. Much writing in academic settings, of course, uses mainly analytic capacities and draws solely on ideas of others rather than fresh thought from the student herself. But education can teach the student not only to do rigorous research and appreciate the history of thought but also to make contact with that within herself that is truly original—what poet David Whyte calls "the great shout of joy within everyone waiting to be born." Contemplative techniques like freewriting, journal writing, deep listening, and mindfulness practice give students a way to discover their great shout, which they can then integrate through critical thinking with the wisdom passed on by others. They need the practice, as David Whyte also says, "so you can find/the one line/already written/inside you."

Writing is communication, but contemplative writing as a practice often emphasizes process rather than outcome. Journal writing and freewriting encourage simple noticing what is in the mind and in the world and writing the raw truth as experienced, not crafted for communication until later—what Chogyam Trungpa Rinpoche called "first thought, best thought." The truth is often revealed in the quickness, in not judging, in the safety of knowing no one will read it unless you want them to. The reflection, the editing, comes after the exercise.

Mary Rose O'Reilley, who has been awarded the Walt Whitman Award for her poetry, sees writing exercises as "creating a spacious moment." At the beginning of class, these exercises can help students find their center; in the middle, to brainstorm; and at the end, to reflect. That final period of silence is the most productive, surprising, and moving, she says. Fifteen minutes before the end of class, she asks her students to write for a moment to gather their thoughts on the day's discussion, to come to some experience of closure. Five minutes later, she sometimes asks whether anyone wants to speak out of the silence, to share any final thoughts.

In *Radical Presence*, O'Reilley wrote: "The first time I issued this invitation—and it happened to be in the first week of a freshman course—I expected no takers, an early exit toward lunch. But a young man began, 'I'd like to thank Jennifer for what she said. It took me right to the heart of the poem.' Other students asked questions to be carried over to the next day, meditated on insights that had occurred to them and, again and again, thanked each other. A gentle closing. Students seem to thrive on such islands of quiet" (O'Reilley, 1998, pp. 5–6).

JOURNAL WRITING

Writing in a journal is one of the oldest methods of self-exploration and expression. Although journals usually are not written for publication and often do not last longer than their authors, we do have extraordinary examples of journals from Virginia Woolf, Thomas Merton, May Sarton, and Anne Frank, among others. As these illustrate, a journal can help one cultivate the ability to live in the present, to become deeply aware and appreciative of life. Journal writing is used in many different kinds of courses, from philosophy to law. It is taught in many different ways, but the usual instruction is to write about one's experience in the first person, without thought of a reader other than oneself, even though the professor will usually read it. Students use either paper journals or their computers or tablets.

A journal records the movement of one's inner experience. It differs from a diary, which usually records the unstructured events of a person's life. Journal entries are reflections of the mental, emotional, and imagistic occurrences within the writer. "Journals take for granted that every day in our life there is something new and different," wrote Thomas Merton in *Learning to Love*. The more mindful the writer becomes, the more likely it is that he will capture the essence of each day. By writing close to the time when an event occurred, the writer can capture specific details of his response to it. In *Essentials of Spontaneous Prose*, Jack Kerouac urges the writer to dig deep within his soul and blow, freestyle like a jazz artist, to find his defining rhythm. "Details are the heart of it," he wrote. Some teachers also use the journal for students to reflect on an assigned reading or experience.

Be Brief, Write Frequently

The instructions for journal writing can be as simple as those that Layli Phillips Maparyan gave her students in her Womanist Perspectives in Social Activism course at Georgia State University:

Every time we do a contemplative exercise in class or have a contemplative homework assignment, briefly comment in this journal. It may be handwritten. Please use a campus blue book or other small pamphlet you can hand in at the end of the term. Each entry should be about a paragraph. You should record your feelings, thoughts, sensations, and any related experiences or insights. Do this as soon after the exercise as possible, as you will lose clarity if you wait.

After a session of listening to sound, one student wrote:

> When I focused on sounds outside my body I heard the hum of lights, the heating, people laughing, stomachs growling, people walking by, etc. When I focused on listening inward, I noticed that my stomach was producing gases and I felt a burp wanting to escape because I had just eaten an apple. I enjoyed this exercise and I'm going to do it again because it's easy to forget that things go on inside of our bodies that we never focus on and it's nice to stop and slow life down and appreciate the small things.

This student's reflections also illustrate how these exercises, so seemingly private, result in connection with those around us. Notice how the student first reports hearing other stomachs growling and then notes his or her own stomach. These associations help the students to recognize the connections of their inner and outer worlds.

Not everyone finds it natural to write each day in a journal. Depending on the group, you might need to suggest that resistance can be overcome and that practice does make the process easier over time. Jake Gibbs offered his students some encouragement for the journal writing required for his Crime, Criminal Justice, and Consciousness course at Indiana University of Pennsylvania:

> It is important to write and write frequently. I recommend that you write every day. Try not to fall behind. At first you may find some kinds of entries difficult. But they will get easier as you continue, and you will develop habits and skills that will serve you well the rest of your life. All journal entries will be kept strictly confidential, and I will do my best to be nonjudgmental while reading your journals and responding to you.

Some teachers provide specific guidance for journal writing. Santiago Colas in his University of Michigan comparative literature course required his students to keep a daily journal. Each journal entry followed this structure:

1. Day, Date, and Time of Writing

2. What time did you arise this morning?

3. What formal practice did you do today (sitting, prostrations, walking, chanting, work)?

4. Did you exhale and inhale deeply today?

5. What troubled you most today? Which of your six senses did you have trouble with?

6. What made you happy today?

7. Please respond to the primary text.

8. Anything else you wish to note down?

The directions for the journal reflect the intentions of the course. For example, in contrast to Santiago Colas, SunHee Gertz, who teaches English at Clark University, tells her students:

> The journal should not be viewed as an exercise in recording what you've done, nor should you consider it your intimate diary. Consider it a *conversation partner*, and probe your reactions to our texts, to yoga, to the talks, to the probably somewhat difficult attempt to find the still space in your hopefully enjoyable, but also at times undoubtedly stressful, life as a student.

Reflections on Practice

David Gardiner at Colorado College teaches an upper-level course in Buddhism combining scholarly study with an experiential component to help students gain firsthand experience of the context, traditions, and practice of Buddhism. Students round out their exploration by keeping a journal of their own path, in which they explore the fits and misfits they find between the Buddhism they encounter on the page and the Buddhism they experience on the cushion.

In her poetry writing class at West Point, Marilyn Nelson also used journaling to focus and complement the meditation experience. A regular class session included five minutes of meditation at the beginning of each class meeting, fifteen minutes of daily meditation outside class, and journaling. Nelson sees herself as helping her students find the silence and space into which words and poems can take shape. The creative process takes time; it is an unpredictable, often unruly process. There are no crash courses in the creative process. It can't be crammed for. Inspiration happens on its own time, and it tends to favor spontaneity and serendipity as much as training and discipline. The art of writing, and the art of teaching writing, then, lies in knowing how and when to make the space and time for inspiration and serendipity to happen. Writing in journals along with their meditation practice is a way Nelson opens up this space for her students. She explains:

> I encourage [students] to listen *for* silence and then listen *to* silence, because poetry in my experience is born out of silence and I want them to understand that poetry is an utterance; every poem is an utterance that is defined by the silence around it in the way that a poem on a page . . . is defined by the white space around it . . . It doesn't matter whether you're producing poems or [reading them], I think you have to learn how to take them in; you have to create a sort of space for them, and the space is created by finding your own silence so that there's room for the poem.

Daily writing can also help students attune to aspects of their lives that they might otherwise not notice. Jeanne Moskal, teaching at the University of North Carolina, added a contemplative practice to her course in travel literature. She instructed her students to use their daily commutes as experiments in "passage," that is, mindful travel focused on the material conditions of moving through space rather than focused on destination, reinforced by journal writing. With this assignment, the whole notion of "travel" changed, so that students noted their own movement from place to place and how that related to what they more conventionally thought of as travel.

One of the areas of our lives in which we are so deeply immersed that we rarely notice our activity is our interaction with computers and mobile devices. David Levy, in his information science class at the University of Washington, asked his students to keep a journal in which to keep track of their thoughts and experiences. He asked them to write what happened during meditation as well as what they observed about their information practices (e-mail, texting, social media, and so on). He gave suggestions, like, "Keep a log or journal of your email sessions, noting start and stop times, number of messages dealt with, and comments. Notice how you feel when you read or write email messages, or simply when you see them in your box." This sounds a simple exercise but is a radically different way to interact with these media. We and our students tend to "lose ourselves" in these activities, not even realizing how extensively we engage them throughout the day. Bringing an awareness to our use of technology is a radical transformation. Writing their reactions to what they discover allows students to deepen their realizations and reflect on them, changing the manner in which they act as "digital natives."

Your Curious, Questioning Self on the Page

Sometimes students need direct instruction to pay attention to their process; sometimes they need guidance to be able to discern their own development. Barbara Anderson-Siebert tells her students at Pennsylvania State University, "The journal will be a personal documentation of your process. We will be looking for signs of struggle, of moving beyond what you already know, of deepening the quality of your experience, evidence of work & thought outside of class, new insights & relationships between the course & your life."

In his Animals in US History course, Thomas Andrews used journal writing to deepen students' understanding of past and present relationships between humans and other animals. The students submitted at least twelve journal entries over the course of the semester in response to a set of prompts, which included these:

- Write a letter to an animal whose death you played some part in causing.
- Go horseback riding and write about what you learned about human-animal relationships through your equine encounter.
- Spend a few hours in a vet's waiting room and reflect upon what you saw there.
- Meditate on the decisions you make regarding animals as food.

He added, "You do not need to show me that you have all the answers, but you do need to present your most curious, questioning self on the page."

Where Am I? When Am I?

When Andrew Schelling developed a course at Naropa University titled Poetry, Contemplative Practice, and the Bioregion, he wanted his students to experience poetry as a means of opening themselves up to and engaging more deeply with the local ecology and environment. In an attempt to get students to experience poetry as a means by which we get in touch with our environment rather than simply project ourselves onto it, Schelling often first introduces his students to genres other than poetry, including journaling. He tells his students that journals have historically been used by natural historians, ecologists, and travelers as a way of engaging with their environment by combining close attention and observation with reflection. Unlike many less contingent forms of writing, the journal entry remains grounded in the specific time and place in which it is written. By locating the "I" in a particular time and place, journaling takes some of the pressure off the aspiring poet by bringing him out of his own habitual story and into the present moment and landscape. Thus, as Schelling explains, the great question of Western civilization—"Who am I?"—shifts into "Where am I?" and "When am I?" Journals thus offer a sense of a self that evolves in relation to time and space, a self that is very much in communication with "the forces and dynamics and aspects of the ecosystem, bio-system, or watershed that you're in."

WRITING ABOUT READING

While most of these practices integrate the contemplative into the writing process itself, other contemplative practices prepare students for writing. Rather than the kind of brainstorming that asks students prior to writing to think about all aspects of a piece of reading and what they might say, students in Al Kaszniak's course at the University of Arizona took ten minutes both before and after each reading assignment to practice breath-focused mindful attention. He told them, "Don't actively think about the reading during this time, but rather, try to stay fully attentive to the breath. After the reading and your second breath-focused practice, write no more than one page in your journal, describing how the major points or conclusions of the reading relate to your own personal experience." This encourages insights to arise naturally, unforced by patterned ways of thinking. When students have a time of still, focused practice, they have more mental space to consider the assigned reading.

The Medium and the Message

Students can also be encouraged to supplement their writing with other media. Janet Berlo, at the University of Rochester, in her course, Art and Contemplative Practice: Through the Lens of Gender and Culture, asks students to introduce other elements:

Your principal ongoing assignment in this course will be the active building of a journal/notebook/commonplace book. This book will contain your own reflections/responses to our discussions. These responses should be intellectual and critical as well as affective. I hope that you will also insert other items that you happen upon in your quest: items clipped from magazines or newspapers, visual images that please you, photocopied quotes from diverse sources.

Dan Holland opened up the medium in his course on disability at the University of Arkansas. He left the form of the journal to the students to decrease any barriers posed for students whose disability might make standard written communication a challenge. All but one chose the written form or drew images or a combination of the two. One student recorded his journal on audiotape.

Developing the Skill

While some students have facility with daily, reflective writing, many do not. Students who struggle with writing may need special attention. Despite glorious exceptions like Abraham Verghese, author of *Cutting for Stone*, many doctors and medical students are not natural writers. Anne Hunsaker Hawkins, at Penn State University College of Medicine, says that journaling was an important requirement for her course, as were daily meditative exercises. She met with every student halfway through the course to find out whether they were experiencing difficulties with either journaling or meditation. This proved an important intervention: talking one-on-one seemed to help several students who said they "just didn't seem to be able to get into it." Having students recognize that their lack of ease with the assignment was a fine topic for their writing allowed them greater freedom in the course and allowed them to examine just what was preventing them from engaging.

Maria Arias and Victor Goode assigned their students at CUNY School of Law a weekly journal. Journaling is often used in law school clinics, and several law review articles are available to offer guidance on that practice (Ogilvy, 1996; Katz, 1997). They felt that this combination of active participation and writing would allow them to monitor whether the students were engaging with the assigned readings yet not turn the class into a traditional seminar where a research paper is the focus of the semester's work. To their surprise, journaling turned out to be quite challenging for many students. Arias and Goode learned that journaling is a special skill and that if they use it in the future, they will have to devote classroom time to developing the skill rather than merely assuming that students have the willingness and ability to write in a truly reflective way.

MINDFUL WRITING

Mindfulness enables us to stop and pay attention to what is happening in the moment and creates a space for fresh insights, so many teachers introduce mindfulness practice before, during, and after periods of writing or reading. Mindful writing also helps students discover direct, honest language, without self-conscious cleverness or display of ego, a language that yearns to reveal, to lay bare the truth of the student's insight and the details of his or her unique story.

Writer and translator Stephen Mitchell writes about mindful observation of bamboo:

> Sometimes I have spent hours face to face with a single stalk, watching for its essence, listening, waiting on the sheer edge of attention, until my arm begins to sway in the light wind, and my brush is blown across the page, along the branches, out to the tendrils and leaves, the last spray turns into calligraphy, moves down the lines of verse, and with one final half-dry flourish: signs my name. (Mitchell, 1990, p. 63)

At Naropa University, Allen Ginsberg taught one of the first courses in mindful writing at the Jack Kerouac School of Disembodied Poetics. Here is one of his famous homework exercises:

1. Stop in tracks once a day, take account of sky, ground & self, write 3 verses haiku.

2. Sit 5 minutes a day, & after, re-collect your thoughts.

3. Stop in middle of street or country, turn in 360-degree circle, write what you remember. (Ginsberg, 2001)

In her writing course at West Point, Marilyn Nelson wrote that she hoped that her student cadets will "live the all-but lost values of a nation conceived in the absurd concept of liberty and dedicated to the ridiculous proposition that we are all created equal. I hope," she said, "they will be soldiers who live the humanist values kept alive by the poets, aborigines, and fools who refuse to close the door on our inner wilderness, with its echoing silence." One of those students wrote the following in his journal:

> In class, we had to pick a couple of verbs from poems that we wrote and make sentences. Kevin made one that I loved: "Swim through a heartbeat of clouds." Anyway, while I meditated, I thought about swimming through clouds. It was incredible. And over and over in my head, I said the sentence. I don't know if that was meditation or not, but I got up and felt so wonderfully relaxed. It was like I had been swimming in clouds.

So what is it like "in the moment"? Marilyn Krysl and Marcia Westkott, teaching Contemplation, Ecstatic Poetry, and Ideas of Self at the University of Colorado, asked students to describe in either poetry or prose at least one "moment" during each week when they had been focused and present. Students generally liked the assignment. Many noted that they appreciated the chance to write creatively and "freely," since writing in most of their courses follows a traditional format.

FREEWRITING

Many teachers use freewriting, another exercise that can help students observe their emotional, intuitive, or physical responses to course material. It is a method of inner inquiry: you never know what you will learn until you start writing; then you discover truths that you did not know existed. Freewriting can free the writer.

It is a simple practice. You begin writing and write continuously for a set period of time, often ten to fifteen minutes. The pen should be constantly moving, with no pause to correct spelling, grammar, or punctuation. Writing teacher Peter Elbow put it this way:

> The idea is simply to write for 10 minutes (later on, perhaps 15 or 20). Don't stop for anything. Go quickly without rushing. Never stop to look back, to cross something out, to wonder how to spell something, to wonder what word or thought to use, or to think about what you are doing. If you can't think of a word or a spelling, just use a squiggle or else write, "I can't think of it." Just WRITE something. The easiest thing is just to put down whatever is in your mind . . . The only requirement is that you *never* stop. (Elbow, 1998, p. 3)

Some teachers begin with a prompt, like, "Yesterday I noticed that . . ." or "I have always been afraid to . . ." or "When I read the text, I thought that . . ." In her widely used introduction to freewriting practice, *Writing Down the Bones* (2010), Natalie Goldberg wrote, "It is a place you can come to wild and unbridled, mixing the dream of your grandmother's soup with the astounding clouds outside your window. It is undirected and has to do with all of you, right in your present moment. Think of writing practice as loving arms you come to illogically and incoherently" (p. 13).

Amy Cheng, at the State University of New York at New Paltz, begins with the premise that creativity occurs when the mind, body, and spirit are fertile, receptive. Contemplative practices encourage receptivity and fertility. Her course in studio art was designed to be experiential, embodied, and multidisciplinary in its approach and to incorporate multiple perspectives and a nonlinear path. She required her students to do a fifteen-minute freewrite every morning as well as a short meditation.

In Animals in US History, Thomas Andrews uses freewriting techniques to deepen his students' ability to think critically and historically, to help them work through their ideas about and their actions toward animals, and to give them a better understanding of the contemporary politics of human-animal relationships. In the process, the students learned about difficult issues like the cruelty inflicted on wolves and the depravity of slaughterhouses. He used freewriting following a discussion of the texts. "What is animal history?" he asked and then instructed the students in freewriting. He had found the discussion itself to be "frustratingly shallow," but the freewriting, the "hasty, stream-of-consciousness scrawlings," revealed that the students "actually understood far more than I had believed." To his surprise, the students' freewritings taken together "recapitulated the major theoretical stances and dilemma with which leading animal historians continue to grapple."

Urban Word NYC works outside the classroom with youth to develop leadership skills. At a retreat, they collaborated with the Center for Contemplative Mind in Society to join mindful silence and freewriting using certain given words: "Start writing and keep writing making sure to use the word *plastic*." After a few minutes, "Now use the word *militant*. Now *chocolate*." And so on. At the end, we all read our paragraphs aloud, and they were each wildly different from the others. In New York at their main address, called the Writers Block, Urban Word uses exercises like this in its "wordshops," student-centered environments where young writers can experiment, explore, and eventually explode their work in performance.

STORYTELLING

Writing practice can celebrate the importance of story and of the students discovering their own story and seeing it as part of a greater narrative. Stories have power. They are embedded with instructions on how to navigate a life. Stories are medicine; they transform, they heal. Martin Buber tells a story about his grandfather, who was lame. Once he asked his grandfather to tell a story about his teacher, and his grandfather related how his teacher used to hop and dance while he prayed. His grandfather rose as he spoke, and he was so swept away by his story that he began to hop and dance to show how the master had done it. From that hour he was cured of his lameness. That's how to tell a story.

An interdisciplinary class at Naropa University that included students and faculty began the semester with a contemplative exercise designed to chart their personal histories. Newsprint was taped on the walls and separated by decade. Faculty members then filled in their "lineage": the people they had studied with and the teachers of those people, and the places, events, books, and so on that influenced them in their creative journey. The students did a similar exercise while their teachers were working. Each faculty member then gave a narrative of his or her personal story.

Further uses of contemplative forms of writing are limited only by our imaginations. In the process of trying them out, maybe students will realize not only the power but also the limits of language, that words are only fingers pointing at the moon, that they are, as Joseph Conrad said, the great foes of reality. Maybe they will glimpse that timeless, unnameable reality that is beyond even the finest writing, that wholeness in the midst of the fragmentation of their lives.

CONCLUSION

Reading and writing are fundamental ways in which we express ourselves and learn from others. We often take for granted what we are doing when writing or reading, overlooking the many layers of experience and meaning conveyed.

In this chapter, we have shown how contemplative practices are being introduced into reading and writing, to illustrate how they can clarify and deepen students' experience. Through reading and writing, we share the consciousness of others across space and time. Today you may take up the *Meditations* by Marcus Aurelius, written over twenty-one hundred years ago and share his thoughts. This intimate connection is possible only if we slow down and allow ourselves to be aware of our experience as we read and write.

Resources

Michael Casey, *Sacred Reading* (Liguori, MO: Liguori/Triumph, 1996).

Peter Elbow, *Writing without Teachers* (New York: Oxford University Press, 1998).

Gary Gach (Ed.), *What Book!? Buddha Poems from Beat to Hiphop* (Berkeley, CA: Parallax Press, 1998).

Natalie Goldberg, *Writing Down the Bones* (Boston: Shambhala Press, 2005).

Annie Lamott, *Bird by Bird* (Garden City, NY: Anchor Books, 1995).

My Dante: https://blogs.commons.georgetown.edu/mydante/

Christine Valters Paintner, *Lectio Divina: The Sacred Art* (Woodstock, VT: Skylight Paths, 2011).

Ira Progoff, *At a Journal Workshop: Writing to Access the Power of the Unconscious and Evoke Creative Ability* (New York: Penguin Putnam, 1992).

Bruce Ross, *How to Haiku* (Boston: Tuttle, 2002).

Contemplative Senses
Deep Listening and Beholding

Higher education tends to focus on abstract, analytical thinking, and yet we also learn much through sense perceptions. Hearing and sight provide powerful ways for us to experience the world around us and within us. In this chapter, we examine contemplative practices that cultivate deep listening and contemplative beholding.

DEEP LISTENING

> To listen is to be willing to simply be present with what you hear without trying to figure it out or control it . . . Because truly listening requires that you do this, listening is dangerous. It might cause you to hear something you don't like, to consider its validity, and therefore to think something you never thought before . . . This is the risk of listening, and this is why it is automatic for us not to want to listen. (Fischer, 2004, p. 44)

We hear even before we are born, in the womb. Everyone with functional ears can hear. Hearing is an involuntary physical act that happens when sound waves impinge on the ear. Listening, however, takes cultivation and evolves through one's lifetime. Deep listening is a way of hearing in which we are fully present with what is happening in the moment without trying to control it or judge it. We let go of our inner clamoring and our usual assumptions and listen with respect for precisely what is being said. Very few students have developed this capacity for listening.

We spend about 45 percent of our time listening, but we are distracted, preoccupied, or forgetful about 75 percent of that time. The average attention span for adults is about twenty-two seconds. Immediately after listening to someone talk, we usually recall only about half of what we've heard and within a few hours, only about 20 percent (Listening Center, 2009).

One study found that in a spoken message, 55 percent of the meaning is translated nonverbally, 38 percent is indicated by the tone of voice, while only 7 percent is conveyed by the words used (Mehrabian, 1981). Spoken words account for only 30 to 35 percent of the meaning; the rest is transmitted through nonverbal communication that can be detected only through visual and auditory listening (Birdwhistell, 1970). Teaching students to listen fully and deeply through contemplative practice helps them succeed both in class and in the rest of their lives.

The practice of listening has many dimensions. We listen to our own minds and hearts and, as the Quakers say, to the "still, small voice within." We listen to sounds, to music, to lectures, to conversations, and, in a sense, to the written word, the text. There is a well-known image of the Tibetan poet and mystic Milarepa, sitting in his familiar listening posture, with his right hand cupped over his right ear. He is listening for the dharma, or the truth.

For all these kinds of listening to be effective, so that we understand and remember what is being heard, we require a contemplative mind: open, fresh, alert, attentive, calm, and receptive. Students often do not have a clear concept of listening as an active process that they can control, but in fact, listening and a contemplative mind can be cultivated through instruction and practice. Listening inward to ourselves is explored in chapter 5 on mindfulness. Listening to and for the text is part of the practice explored in chapter 6 on contemplative reading. In this chapter, we focus on listening outward—to sounds, music, and others. Listening outward connects us to nature, to the built environment, and to possibilities for participation with other human beings.

As a classroom practice, deep listening requires that students witness their thoughts and emotions while maintaining focused attention on what they are hearing. It trains them to pay full attention to the sound of the words, while abandoning such habits as planning their next statement or interrupting the speaker. It is attentive rather than reactive listening. Such listening not only increases retention of material but encourages insight and the making of meaning.

Through teaching listening, we are directly exploring ways in which the contemplative can have a profound influence in the academy: the role of not knowing and not judging in the process of learning, the distinction between nonaction and inaction, the power of simply bearing witness, and the role of receptivity and openness in understanding. Students quickly realize the difference when someone is actually listening to them and hearing them; they realize too the difference in their own listening to others.

MINDFULNESS OF SOUND

Early morning is especially good for listening. Try this as a homework assignment. Listen carefully as you wake up. Instead of turning on the TV, your iPod, or your computer, be still and just listen. In a rural setting, the sounds are likely to be those of birds and animals waking up. In a city, sounds of outside action begin—garbage collection, building construction, traffic. On campus, the sounds of opening doors, feet walking in the hallways, other students talking. (See "Meditation on Sound Instructions.")

Meditation on Sound Instructions

- Try to sit stable and still, like a mountain. Be relaxed and alert. Close your eyes.
- Listen to the sounds as they occur. Do not imagine, name, or analyze the sounds. As names arise, release them, and return to listening.
- Just listen with wide-open awareness.
- Let the sounds come to you and touch your eardrums.
- As thoughts, emotions, memories, and associations arise in your mind, notice them, gently let them go, and return to the sounds.
- Notice how the sounds arise and fall away.
- Do not grasp at sounds. Do not reject sounds.
- If there are no sounds, listen, and rest in the silence.

Sylvia Boorstein (1996) says it well: "You might think of the difference between radar that goes out looking for something and a satellite dish with a wide range of pickup capacity that just sits in the backyard, waiting. Be a satellite dish. Stay turned on, but just wait."

Encourage your students in their daily life to notice the positive and negative habits they might have in their approach to listening to sounds. Ask them: What helps you to listen fully, without judgment? If you are in a place that is very noisy, how can you help yourself? Must you find a quieter place or wear earplugs? Or can you be with these sounds in a different way?

In *A Natural History of the Senses* (1991), Diane Ackerman says that hearing's job is partly spatial: "A gently swishing field of grain that seems to surround one in an earthly whisper doesn't have the urgency of a panther growling behind and to the right. Sounds have to be located in space, identified by type, intensity, and other features. There is a geographical quality to listening" (p. 178).

LISTENING PRACTICES IN THE CLASSROOM

Through teaching listening, we are exploring a practice that could profoundly influence the academy. Given the activity of our discursive thinking, it is often hard for us to maintain an open receptivity to new ideas. Listening deeply can illustrate the role of not knowing and not judging in the process of learning. It can also teach the distinction between nonaction and inaction. Such listening requires discipline; it is not passive but rather requires gracious connection—the very ground for compassion. Listening also demonstrates the power of simply bearing witness. Students quickly realize the difference between someone passively listening to them and someone actually hearing them; they realize too the difference in their own witness of others.

When Michelle Francl, professor of chemistry at Bryn Mawr College, teaches Quantum States of Being: Incorporating Contemplative Practices into the Chemistry Curriculum, she uses a sound meditation that she calls "listening out" to awaken a sense of sound within space and increase the students' listening skills: "Start with the sounds closest to you—the student at the next desk rustling papers, the pumps chugging at the lab bench, the roar of the fume hoods. Slowly extend your awareness outward in circles. Let go of thoughts and emotions and return to the simple sound."

This exercise does more than allow her students to become aware of sound; they expand their awareness out beyond their immediate space. This expansion of mind helps students explore the mysteries and paradoxes of quantum theory.

In a design studio class at the University of Colorado, Peter Schneider, professor of architecture, required his students to design a contemplative space. Students planning a cell for a monk, for example, needed to understand the rituals involved and learn from the people they were designing for. Peter showed a film clip of a Buddhist monk walking very slowly and asked the students to adopt a similar practice, walking contemplatively and paying attention to sounds. After they recollected their experience through writing, he prompted them to reflect on their experience of sound as well as the architectural elements, like stairways and doorways, and to include both physiological and psychological impressions, before designing the space.

LISTENING TO MUSIC

The jazz tradition has a long legacy of artists who have used meditation and related practices to energize their creative excursions. The improvisatory core of jazz—requiring the capacity to be fully present, integrate extraordinary technical expertise with freedom and flow, and listen deeply to fellow artists—is at the heart of this connection. Jazz guitarist Pat Metheny says that listening is the key to everything good in music. Ed Sarath, who teaches Improvisation, Creativity, and Consciousness: Jazz as Gateway to Interior Domains of Learning and Teaching at the University of Michigan, proposes that educators expose their students to a range of possible practices, including the contemplative, and accept that students have to find their own way. The BFA in Jazz and Contemplative Studies curriculum has been inspired by these ideas.

Sarath began playing jazz at about the same time he began meditating in the Vedanta tradition about thirty-five years ago. He perceives "a very close relationship between improvisation and meditation practice, in that both are grounded in a heightened sense of the present moment. They also complement each other quite nicely." Sarath says that contemplative practice helps in improvisation to listen for the silence between sounds. "Students really get the connection between improvisation and meditation. They see the results in their music and can articulate them clearly. They find they are much less tense in their playing and enjoy the freedom and expansiveness that comes from being more comfortable with their minds." Through the use of contemplative practices, students experience the power of the silence between sounds and can integrate that realization into their improvisation and composition.

As part of its commitment to preparing students in academic excellence and legal expertise while providing the tools to maintain a fulfilling work-life balance, the University of Miami Law School has established the first Mindfulness in Law Program in the country. Scott Rogers, a member of the Center for Contemplative Mind's Law Program and author of *Mindfulness for Law Students* (2009), teaches mindfulness practices that help students deal with stressful situations while maintaining focus and clarity. One of these practices is listening to music. Connecting all his mindfulness practices to law, Scott quotes Plato: "Music is a moral law. It gives soul to the universe, wings to the mind, flight to the imagination, and charm and gaiety to life and to everything." He calls the exercise "Preliminary Hearing: Time for Sound Judgment." These are the instructions:

> Play soothing sounds, perhaps classical or slow-tempo music to feel calming effects. Add to this relaxing component awareness of the sound and vibration of the notes, the feelings that the music brings up within you, and other sensations that are happening in the moment as you listen. As you become aware of thoughts arising, gently bring your attention back to the music. Breathe.

After using music as a relaxing meditation, students are better prepared to the stresses of legal situations, from the deposition room to the courtroom.

At Indiana University-Purdue University Indianapolis (IUPUI), William Jackson, professor of religious studies, taught Contemplation and Music, a course on the wisdom of major religious traditions, relating musical practices to varieties of contemplation. Music, chanting, sounds, and mantras are often part of contemplative practices. The course explored religious imagination in contemplative experiences through readings, listening to music, and discussions. He related contemplation in an open-ended way to the universal spiritual uses of voice and sound, examined contemplation "as a method to develop concentration, to deepen understanding, and to cultivate awareness." The IUPUI Department of Religious Studies is careful to avoid church-state conflicts, offering courses about religious traditions, never teaching any particular religion as a favored path, and always respecting diversity. The goal of this course was to familiarize students with the importance of historical contemplative practices using music and to encourage those who were interested to explore further.

LISTENING TO EACH OTHER

> The greatest compliment that was ever paid me was when one asked me what I thought and attended to my answer.—Henry David Thoreau

> When people talk, listen completely. Most people never listen.—Ernest Hemingway

In 1998, when the Center for Contemplative Mind in Society began to explore the uses of contemplative practices in the academy, we hosted a series of off-site retreats for Yale Law School students. Because the most basic aspect of the attorney-client relationship is listening to and respecting the client's preferences, we added a mindful listening practice to the sitting meditation and yoga offered at a traditional mindfulness retreat. Lawyers often listen to clients through the defining lens of what they consider legally or strategically relevant and thus may fail to really hear what is being communicated. Similarly, the fundamental quality of contemplative practice is to listen. Learning to listen and to hear what is truly being expressed is a critical skill for lawyers. We found that contemplative listening is a powerful means to improve the attorney's relationship with clients.

The practice we introduced was already being used in legal mediation sessions by two members of the retreat's planning committee, Jack Himmelstein and Gary Friedman, both exceptional listeners. They called it "looping," or closing the loop of communication, with the listener hearing what is being said. We called it mindful listening. (See "Mindful Listening Instructions" for the step-by-step instructions.) The students found that it taught them the importance of listening to others; they reported that they were able to listen to others when they returned to law school not only for the weakness in the other person's argument but in a more caring and less judgmental (but still discerning) manner. One student wrote,

> I try to listen more when we are having a discussion in class. One of my criticisms of law school is that people seem to just make speeches in class and don't really respond to each other's questions. They think, "When I did the reading last night, I thought of this clever idea and I'm going to say it so I can get people to think that I'm smart." It's not productive to do this in conversation. I now try to really respond rather than react when people are speaking and to listen with an open mind and not be thinking about what I'm going to say next.

Another said,

> I think that I'm more sensitive now to people's different perceptions of situations. For example, I can be in a class that I'm enjoying and yet still understand why other people aren't enjoying it. It is more than just understanding it rationally, which was the way that I was before. I learned how to listen to their feelings as well as their words.

Mindful Listening Instructions

Everyone finds a partner. One person speaks; the other listens. The listener listens as carefully as possible, letting go of interpretations, judgments, and reactions, as well as irrelevant thoughts, memories, plans. When the speaker finishes, the listener repeats as closely as possible what the speaker said, until the speaker feels truly heard. The following instructions are for the person who leads the exercise:

1. *To both partners:* "One partner will spend three to five minutes speaking [decide on the time before beginning the exercise], in response to a prompt about the class content [e.g., "What I learned from that lecture was . . ."] or about an aspect of his or her life ["Right now, I am feeling . . ."].

2. *To the speaker:* "This time is yours. If you run out of things to say, you can just sit in silence, and whenever you have something to say, you may continue speaking again."

3. *To the listener:* "Your job is to listen in silence. When you listen, give your full attention to the speaker. Be curious, but don't ask questions while listening. You may acknowledge with facial expressions or by nodding your head. Try not to overacknowledge, or you may end up leading the speaker. You may feel an urge to coach, identify, chime in, or interrupt: this is normal. Just notice when this occurs, resist the temptation to act, and refocus your attention on your partner. Listen with kindness. When thoughts or emotions come into your mind, simply notice them and gently return your full attention to the speaker. If the speaker runs out of things to say, give him or her the space for silence, and then be available to listen when he or she speaks again.

4. *To the listener:* "After your partner has finished telling the story, repeat what you have been told; don't worry about memorizing—paraphrase. Have your partner correct you if you have misunderstood the story. Ask

---

questions to be sure you understand, as closely as possible, what your partner intended to say."

5. *To both partners:* "When the speaker is satisfied that she or he has been heard and comprehended, switch roles. Now it is the listener's turn to tell a story until she or he feels heard."

6. *To both partners:* "Reflect on how it feels to be listened to so closely and what it felt like to listen deeply to another. Remember to listen to the words but also the tone, the emotional undercurrent. This is an important way to stay connected at times where it may be difficult to connect to the ideas or perspective being expressed."

7. *To both partners:* End by thanking each other for listening.

In a recent English class at Holy Cross College, students were struggling with making sense of Robert Pirsig's *Zen and the Art of Motorcycle Maintenance*, which had seemed so relevant to students in 1974, when it was first published. Their teacher suggested a listening exercise. The students chose partners and took turns responding to her prompt: "This book related to something in my own life. It was . . ." The student who was not speaking listened in silence, without judgment. The book suddenly came to life for these students.

Students, like most of the rest of us, really appreciate being listened to. In the classroom, student partners may not know each other, and yet they will respond like a young engineer in a class at Google did: "I know this person for six minutes and we are already friends, yet there are people sitting in the next cubicle for months and I do not even know them." Just giving each other the gift of total attention for six minutes is often enough to begin a friendship. As Everyday Zen Foundation teacher Norman Fischer, who taught the Google class, wrote, "Listening is magic: it turns a person from an object outside, opaque or dimly threatening, into an intimate experience, and therefore into a friend. In this way, listening softens and transforms the listener."

Listening brings people closer; not listening creates fragmentation. Listening without comment is not appropriate in all circumstances, of course. There are occasions when we need to be engaged in dialogue and responses are expected. But students can use this approach to listening whenever it is appropriate and bring the qualities of mindful attention—being fully present without judgment in the moment—to all communication. Susan Burggraf, professor of contemplative psychology at Naropa University, uses a listening practice to enable students to connect with others in a more compassionate, healing way. Burggraf says her students arrive in her classroom with a largely utilitarian view of dialogue—more as a means for getting one's point across than truly speaking one's truth or hearing another's. Her challenge was to help students unlearn some of their habitual ways of listening and to relearn the kind of open, compassionate communication that may have once come naturally to them.

Burggraf borrows from the work of Gregory Kramer, whose concept of "insight dialogue" presents Buddhist contemplative practices through an interpersonal lens. Based on the observation that much of our suffering tends to come into relief through our relationships with others, Kramer's approach offers a way to work with this human truth by deepening compassion, empathy, and appreciation for one another. Though usually offered in the context of retreat or group work, the approach adapts well to an educational setting, offering a simple practice for exploring complex human problems, such as how we bridge our own inner experience and outer social life, how we negotiate the many roles we occupy, and how we shape and reshape our social identities through conversation with one another.

In Burggraf's class, students begin with a brief meditation and then do the mindful listening practice described above. They add to it a short three-step instruction to "pause," "relax," and "open," intended to remind students to bring mindfulness to the dialogue. Burggraf says that the practice of mindful listening enables her students "to infiltrate" habitual social engagement with mindfulness and awareness and to bring loving kindness into difficult dialogues. The exercise also works as a window into another key theme of Burggraf's course: the social construction of ideas and the shared nature of knowledge.

Like Burggraf, Anne Beffel explores the way contemplative exercises can enhance communication and dialogue in her contemplative art classes at Syracuse University. She gives her students these suggestions from *Right Listening* (2009, pp. 10–11) by Mark Brady:

- Listen without an agenda.
- Listen without "should'ing on people."
- Establish support for speaking truth to power.
- Stop when your energy flags.

- Avoid letting your story take over their story.

- Listen for feelings.

- Listen as a caregiver.

- Ask for more information.

- Be curious as you listen.

LISTENING IN PSYCHOTHERAPY, PHILOSOPHY, AND RELIGION CLASSES

Linda Bell, professor of psychology at the University of Houston, taught Contemplative Practice in Psychotherapy to explore the ways in which contemplative practice can contribute to psychotherapy, both indirectly through the meditative practice of the therapist and directly through application in the therapy itself. In this application, the power of the witness and the importance of nonaction are essential. She used the work of contemplative psychotherapist Mark Epstein in *Thoughts without a Thinker* (1995) and Zen teacher Thich Nhat Hanh to help students explore the subject. Like social work practitioners and other caregivers, therapists depend on excellent listening skills. This class included meditation as well as skills in meditation-supported therapy ("working/listening out of the silence"). These practices helped her students become less reactive to clients' emotions, enabled them to fully listen without immediate judgment, and allowed them space for their own inner voice to respond.

Graham Parkes, professor of philosophy at the University of Hawaii, uses listening practice to measure attention at the beginning and end of the course. On the first day of his class, he asks his students to do six attention exercises, each lasting five minutes, including listening to an audiotaped speech, watching a video, listening to a piece of music, and "just sitting" while counting their breaths. He instructs them to concentrate on the subject as intently as they can, and when their attention strays, to bring it back as quickly as possible and note with a stroke of a pen on a piece of paper each time this happens. Thus, for each exercise, each student would have an "attention-wandering" score. During the semester, they sit zazen (literally, "seated meditation," in the Zen tradition) together in the classroom at every meeting and sit at home on their own on the other five days of the week. The sittings start at five minutes in length, increasing to ten after the fourth week, fifteen after the eighth week, and twenty after the twelfth week. At the end of the semester, he asks them to repeat the exercises that they engaged in on the first day of class. All of them have had significantly better scores than on that first day—some on all the exercises, others on some of them. Only a few students have scored worse on any of the exercises. Although this is an imperfect measuring instrument, the students are gratified by the improvement in their ability to concentrate and listen.

Interested in the social effects of contemplative practice on activism, Loriliai Biernacki, professor of religious studies at the University of Colorado, taught a course on the practices of three Indian thinkers: Mahatma Gandhi, Sri Aurobindu Ghose, and Mata Amritanandayi Ma. During the Gandhi section of the course, students fasted and took vows of *satyagraha* (to speak the truth at all times). During the section on the guru Mata Amritanandayi Ma, known by the affectionate name Ammachi or Amma, they were required to attend one local group session of listening to and chanting *bhajans* (Indian devotional songs) and then to spend one hour per week singing *bhajans* either alone or in a group. They reflected on how listening to others and the singing affected their interpersonal relationships and the "social and political engagement possibilities that might arise from the practice."

These practices, including the listening, led students toward a deeper questioning of identity and the forces that construct identity; the practices "acted as a kind of antidote to the mindless adoption of ideologies." This operated especially on a personal level for many students, since the contemplative practices, including the listening and chanting, "facilitated a space to be with themselves as identities, affording a greater sense of self awareness." Students also noticed a correlation between things that was unexpected. That is, half an hour of chanting or staring at a flame might not feel calming while they were doing it, but afterward it seemed to bring a sense of calm and purpose to their actions and to influence others. The course did not directly support student social engagement or political activism, but students said that taking time to do contemplative practices caused them to think more about their actions, "inducing a greater ethical responsibility."

BEHOLDING

> Art's purpose is to sober and quiet the mind so that it is in accord with what happens in the world around it, open rather than closed, going in by sitting cross legged, returning to daily experience with a smile.—John Cage

Since the advent of literacy, academic communication and learning has favored text over image. In the process, the skills required for truly seeing something, used in the period when people learned mainly from paintings and icons or natural images, have been lost for most of us. We have benefited immensely from the vast information available to us through print, but we are missing something valuable. Reading words in a sentence is a different mental process from seeing an image. We read letters one after another in a linear sequence until a word with meaning emerges, then word after word until we have a sentence with meaning. When we look at an image, we see it all at once, as a whole.

As the scientific worldview took hold, people began to chart and map and schematize the world, and their role in relation to images became the eye that surveys at a distance. In the world of Descartes, subjects and objects, self and the world, mind and body, belonged to fundamentally different realms. The disembodied, objectifying eye became the essence of the scientific attitude and the aesthetic attitude. So we studied texts and objectified nature, and we placed art in museums or galleries or on walls, separate from daily life, in a place apart. We looked at a painting or sculpture at a distance, as an object separate from ourselves. We came to think of science and technology as essential and art as dispensable; we learned to believe that we can't live without technology but we can live without beauty.

But we are now in a new era when technology itself has reintroduced looking at both still and moving images as a primary learning method, and the reemergence of the contemplative has suggested new yet ancient ways of being with images. We have moved from image focused (sculpture, painting, icons) to text focused (post-Gutenberg) to a time of integration of the two.

Beholding Art

We need to relearn how to see. John Cage talked about paying attention to art as a way of being present in the world. After leaving an exhibit of the work of abstract expressionist painter Mark Tobey, one of the "mystic painters of the Northwest," he said that he happened to look at the pavement "and—literally—the pavement was as beautiful as the Tobey. So the experience of looking at the Tobey was instructive about looking at the pavement . . . Art became identical with life" (Cage & Retallack, 2011, p. 106).

In the academy, art historians have recently developed a contemplative way of seeing they call "beholding." *Beholding* is an old word. When the pre-Socratic philosopher Anaxagoras was asked, "Why are you here on earth?" he replied, "To behold." Milton used it to describe what had been lost in Adam and Eve's fall from grace: "How shall I behold the face henceforth of God or angel, erst [formerly] with joy and rapture so oft beheld?" When they left Paradise, when they began to think and live in a dualistic world of good and evil, Adam and Eve could no longer behold, no longer see in a sacred, whole way. Now, art historian Joanna Zeigler says, "we must learn to use our eyes again." She often quotes Henry David Thoreau, who said, "Wisdom does not inspect, but behold. We must look a long time before we can see."

Ziegler, past professor of visual arts and art history at Holy Cross and one of the Center for Contemplative Mind in Society's first Fellows, introduced the practice of beholding to her students. She didn't teach a studio class, but found a way to deepen her connection to her discipline by developing research methods that make use of studio habits like persistence and attentive observation. Her students visited the Worcester Art Museum once a week throughout the semester, at the same time, on the same day of the week, using the same mode of transportation, to look at one abstract painting for the entire semester and answer the question: What do you see? They were instructed to refrain from research, consulting secondary sources, Googling, reading the wall text, or even speaking to docents, so that they could hear their own voices. Ziegler also asked them to report on subjective features of themselves as observers: how they felt physically and emotionally and what was going on in their lives.

She left the theoretical art history until the end of the course, when students were better able to take it in without affecting their experience of their painting. During their discussions of their experience, they learned to share their perceptions and ask, "What did we see?" and "Do we have to agree on what we see before we interpret it?"

Beholding is about appreciation and relatedness rather than abstraction and distancing. Zeigler understood that through attending to and developing a feeling for great works of art, her students would become more interested and intimate with them and begin to love what they came to know. Repetition was a strong feature of her pedagogy. As her students went at the same time to the same place each day to sit before the same painting and simply look, focusing their attention again and again, they noticed the changes they saw in the painting and they also noticed changes in themselves.

Many educators would be skeptical about the value of inviting so much of their student's subjectivity into the study of their discipline (especially during those early weeks when students can find the exercise of looking at the same work pointless, irritating, or even torturous), but Ziegler found that out of subjectivity, true objectivity arose. After some time, the ordinary distractions lost their hold on the students' ability to observe; the students then went beyond their limited perspective and began to understand the limitations of all perspectives. Bringing back their wandering attention again and again to the object of beholding, the students experienced a self-transformation that took them from, "I hate this," to, "I love this." Over the thirteen-week semester, the painting did not change, of course. "The students did," said Zeigler. "Out of practice they went from antipathy to love. From dismissing it as something any kid could paint, they cultivated reverence for the work under their observation."

Translating attentiveness into care, Ziegler proposed, is the foundation for moral concern. Once the students experienced the impermanence of their own preconceptions and prejudices, they developed, Ziegler said, "the foundation of an ethical awareness, the beginning of an ethical stance." Even if they were not ready for meditation, yoga, or other traditional practices, Ziegler found that they could learn to see, to behold. And their attentiveness leads to care and the capacity to focus on what's valuable in art, nature, and human life.

Joel Upton, professor of art and art history at Amherst College, encourages his students to behold a "stupendous work of art" during his course Contemplating Monet's Painting *Matinée sur la Seine*. He asks the group to be as present as possible with the image of the Seine near Giverny in the morning, painted in 1896. At the Mead Art Museum at Amherst College, where the painting now hangs, Upton encourages the students to approach with reverence, with awe for something greater than themselves, quietly open and vulnerable. He directs them to move in close, where the brushstrokes become visible, and then move away, observing how the painting changes. Up close, the brushstrokes appear chaotic, but from a distance, they resolve into an impressionistic scene. These are just some of many contradictory elements he helps them discover through close attention: chromatic contrast between light and dark, a pull between horizontal and vertical, near and far, asymmetry and symmetry, presence and absence. The artist, Joel suggests, works toward "an intimation of the reconciliation of contradictory reality." Students learn that the artist is not the only one who needs skill and talent for this painting to come to life. The beholder does as well.

Upton identifies six steps for his students in learning to behold through an "aperture of awe":

1. Identify one painting to "behold with," that is, to "engage the work's human realization according to a unique and shared embodiment, rather than merely or exclusively to observe, analyze or situate it culturally and historically."

2. Gather basic information about the work: when, where, and by whom it was painted, its size and basic composition.

3. Analyze form, line, shape, and color, giving the subject full attention.

4. Investigate the content, or iconography, of what is represented. Students often find many possibilities here.

5. Identify the contradictions that comprise the work—for example, the tensions between horizontal and vertical aspects—as well as the deeper conflicting elements, or "paradoxes of human being," that give rise to its composition.

6. Behold the work, and seek out by way of contemplation "intimations of the reconciliation of contradictory reality," alternating focused attention and open awareness.

As students move toward the threshold of contemplative beholding, what began as a relationship between a subject (the observer) and the object (the painting) becomes closer to a relationship between subject and subject, an I and Thou encounter. The tensions that students identified in the work of art become not inconsistencies to dispel or contradictions to resolve but opportunities to break free from instrumental modes of thinking toward a dynamic artistic encounter that continues to generate new ideas.

The Practiced Eye

Beholding has been a valuable method in other disciplines as well. Don Hanlon, who teaches architecture and urban design at the University of Wisconsin-Milwaukee, used a form of beholding to sharpen students' powers of observation:

I have observed that, contrary to common belief, the most talented architects rely on an incisive observation of natural phenomena and architectural precedents more than they do on personal inventiveness. A deep understanding of composition derived from the study of existing examples can provide a designer with a repertoire of concepts and formal relationships that can be used in innumerable ways. However, contemporary students generally lack experience with the degree of concentration required to discover these formal structures. Conditioned by mass-market advertising and entertainment, most students consider frenetic activity and constant distraction to be the normal way one experiences the world.

Hanlon learned that by slowing down his students' perceptions and limiting their concentration to a single image, he could help them reveal extraordinarily complex and subtle relationships of form that dramatically enhance their ability to design:

I have studied Islamic architecture for many years because I am drawn to the crystalline clarity of its geometry. Philosophically, every part of an Islamic architectural composition is related to every other part by means of a rigorous mathematical system. However, we don't have to understand the mathematics itself. A practiced eye can perceive the system by means of proportion and correspondence. So, in the Islamic tradition, a building plan is a mandala. And that is how I use it to teach my students meditation. In this case, however, meditation upon the architectural mandala is not for the purpose of spiritual transcendence, but as a means of heightening awareness of the formal ideas that underlie superficial appearances. These ideas are startling to the uninitiated.

When there are few pressing problems to be resolved and the students are in a receptive frame of mind, Hanlon and his students sit together facing a wall of the studio on which he has mounted a simple black and white drawing of a building plan with no text or superfluous information that might distract from its basic formal organization. This is the focus of their beholding. They meditate on it for about a half an hour and then he asks, without any specific direction, for anyone to comment on any aspect of it. The students' observations are highly perceptive. They remark on how much more subtle the composition is than what they initially assumed and that the superficial simplicity of the composition seems to mask an underlying complexity. In Hanlon's experience, this is one of the greatest insights a student of architecture can achieve. He challenges them then to apply this knowledge to their own design in two ways: first, to distill their design intentions down to "a masterstroke of simplicity"; second, to achieve a comparable level of underlying complexity and subtlety that is not immediately apparent. This method has worked well. The result has been project designs that "are nearly transparent in their logic, and devoid of superfluous and gratuitous expressionism, yet deep and rich in formal implications, and entirely appropriate for their intended use."

Hanlon's pragmatic approach to contemplative practice in education, his use of beholding, or contemplative seeing, is not spiritual or transcendental but rather functional and matter-of-fact. He credits his experience growing up in a branch of the Society of Friends that emphasized a direct practical application of insights derived from meditation. Meditation was conducted collectively, and its fruits were to be used for the common good. "My students are delighted with this approach and have often commented on their great good fortune for having found a new route to creative learning. Though I have always been experimental in my teaching, the method I have discovered in this project has been a revelation."

At the Sackler Art Museum at Harvard, Ray Williams, director of education at the Harvard University Art Museums, cohosted a gathering on contemplative leadership at which he led the group in a form of beholding works of art. After a twenty-minute silent meditation in front of a sitting Buddha from eighth-century China, participants chose a question at random from a stack of cards and then walked the museum until they found a painting or sculpture that resonated with questions like, "How does this painting remind you of something important in your life?" One found a seventeenth-century Italian painting of the Virgin with the sleeping Christ Child; the child lay on a shroud, foretelling his death. Another chose a seated Abraham Lincoln, sculpted by Daniel Chester French. Once the objects were found, participants beheld them for ten minutes and then told the group how it evoked answers to the question.

Other courses have used a simple beholding exercise in nature to help students learn about perception and interconnection. Students go to a viewing place overlooking some portion of city or countryside, look at it in silence for some time, and then describe the landscape in detail. It soon becomes apparent that even though they are looking in the same direction at the same instant, they do not—cannot—see the same landscape. They may see many of the same elements—houses, roads, trees, hills—in terms of number, form, dimension, and color, but such facts take on meaning only through association; they must be fitted together according to some coherent body of ideas. In reporting and listening to others, students discover that any landscape is composed not only of what lies before their eyes but what lies within their heads. And as Ziegler wrote, they discover "that sense of connectedness with things that alone makes it possible to be connected with ourselves" (Dustin & Ziegler, 2007, p. 13).

Beholding: A New Scientific Method

Beholding exercises can also introduce students to complicated scientific concepts by having students carefully examine graphs or charts. In her Physical Chemistry course at Bryn Mawr, Michelle Francl introduces her students to solutions to the Schroedinger equation by showing them the graph in figure 7.1. This is a graph of the harmonic oscillator potential for hydrogen bromide (HBr) showing the quantum mechanical energy levels and the corresponding probability distributions for the first four states. The probability distributions are scaled to that of the lowest energy state. The horizontal axis represents the displacement of the molecule from its equilibrium length in meters. For scale, the length of an HBr molecule is on the order of 10^{-10} meters.

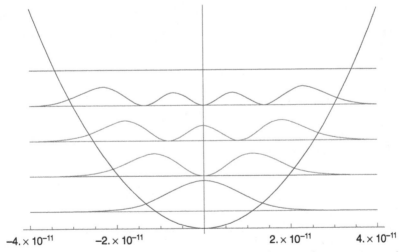

Figure 7.1 Harmonic Oscillator Potential for Hydrogen Bromide

Source: Michelle Francl to Dan Barbezat, August 28, 2012.

She asks her students to examine the figure mindfully—to simply look carefully and note what they see. After giving them some time, she asks her students to write down what they noticed. Some note that as the lines move upward, the amplitude of the waves decreases, as does the wavelength. Others note that the waves are either at their maximum or minimum at the center of the figure. Frankl then guides a discussion in which students pursue what they have seen and begin to understand why.

Through this process, students can discover the underpinnings of complicated ideas like the Bohr correspondence principle or the Shroedinger equations. Frankl says that in order to conduct this exercise, she must be willing to allow the students' observations to direct the discussion, so she cannot closely plan ahead what she will say. This is an important aspect of this kind of teaching; as the teacher, you have to balance your need to cover specific content with the time required for students' responses.

The presentation of data in figures can be informative but also quite misleading. In many areas of the curriculum, as in economics, for example, the visual display of data is used as evidence. Figure 7.2 shows one simple example. It presents the industrial production index over the 1990s; it appears that per capita values were rising at a steady, even rate. From this figure, students could draw the conclusion that industrial growth is a steady and even process.

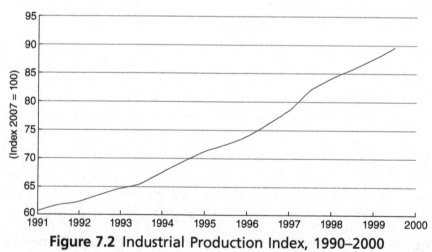

Figure 7.2 Industrial Production Index, 1990–2000
Source: Adapted from FRED, Economic Data, St. Louis Federal Reserve Bank.

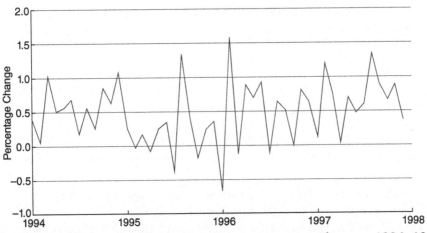

Figure 7.3 Industrial Production Index, Percentage Change, 1994–1998

Source: Adapted from FRED, Economic Data, St. Louis Federal Reserve Bank.

However, in figure 7.3, even a quick glance shows that the data suggest a great deal of variability and perhaps no growth. However, this graph displays the same data but in percentage change terms, as shown along the vertical axis. On closer inspection, you can see that the percentage change values are nearly all above zero, suggesting positive growth over the period. In addition, the spikes are very rarely over 1 percent, showing relatively steady growth over the period, just as shown in figure 7.2. A cursory look at the graph could produce very wrong conclusions. Careful attention to visual displays of data and theoretical models (often the way in which economic models, for example, are explained) provides the students a far greater understanding of the material and enables them to solve problems more creatively and make connections to other data and other models.

CONCLUSION

As students become more aware of the information coming through their senses, their learning will be enlivened and their appreciation of the world around them enhanced. Practices that cultivate deep listening can provide an important means for students to connect richly with themselves, the text, and other material for the course. Beholding exercises change the ways in which we see the world, enhancing one of our primary means for interacting with the world. Contemplative practices are effective even for deaf or blind students; the goal is not to see or hear but to increase students' ability to experience all of their senses more fully and to support them in applying that experience to their learning.

Resources

Diane Ackerman, *A Natural History of the Senses* (New York: Vintage Books, 1990).

Don Campbell, *The Roar of Silence: The Healing Powers of Breath, Tone and Music* (Wheaton, IL: Quest Books, 1989).

Norman Fischer, *Taking Our Places* (San Francisco: HarperSanFrancisco, 2003).

Sue Annis Hammond, *The Thin Book of Appreciative Inquiry* (Plano, TX: Thin Book, 1998).

Thich Nhat Hanh, *Peace Is Every Step* (Berkeley, CA: Parallax Press, 1991).

Gregory Kramer, *Insight Dialog* (Boston: Shambhala, 2007).

Kat Lindahl, *Practicing the Sacred Art of Listening* (Woodstock, VT: Skylight Paths, 2003).

Listening Center: http://www.sacredlistening.com/tlc_listening101.htm

Chade Meng Tan, *Search Inside Yourself* (San Francisco: HarperSanFrancisco, 2012).

Margaret Wheatley, *Turning to One Another: Simple Conversations to Restore Hope to the Future* (San Francisco: Berrett-Koehler, 2009).

Contemplative Movement

I train the act of being able to feel physical while getting an idea.
Ann Cooper Albright, Oberlin College

Except for athletes and dancers, students spend most of their time in their heads: thinking, studying, planning, remembering, worrying, thinking, and more thinking. While most contemporary education separates mind from body and thought from physical sensation, movement practices integrate the two. In addition, movement practice allows more kinesthetic learners to gain better access to the material of the course. "I like to think and move at the same time," wrote Ann Cooper Albright, who taught Physical Mindfulness: Embodying Contemplative Practice at Oberlin. "The term 'physical mindfulness,'" she wrote, "evokes for me the interconnected realms of embodied knowledge and critical thinking. I use it to underscore the psychic implications of one's physical being-in-the-world. I confront every day the paradigm of the separation of the mind and spiritual life from that of the body. For me, physical practice is the core of my contemplative experience."

This chapter presents several movement practices that can be used in the classroom, in a designated space like the gym or dance studio, or in the student's ordinary life, moving from place to place. They anchor awareness in the body for the purpose of increasing mindfulness, leading to insight and compassion. One of the purposes of these practices is to cultivate bodily-kinesthetic intelligence, identified by Howard Gardner as one of the five intelligences in his theory of multiple intelligences. As Gardner (2000) identifies it, "Bodily-kinesthetic intelligence entails the potential of using the whole body or parts of the body to solve problems or fashion products" (p. 42). He says that it is important for dancers and athletes but also craftspeople, surgeons, and other technically oriented professionals. Mindful or contemplative movement goes beyond increasing bodily-kinesthetic intelligence; it also supports the capacities associated with mindfulness, such as attention, curiosity, and self-awareness, which increase the potential for learning in all students and professionals.

Some practices are short and simple. Barbara Dilley at Naropa University is interested in how body and mind work together as "not one but not two." To demonstrate this, she asked her acting students to walk across a room with their minds focused on a teaspoon filled with water, trying not to spill it, in order to develop mindful awareness. In order not to spill the water, one needs to remain focused on what one's body is doing: the extension of one's arm, the evenness of one's stride, the balance of the trunk. It also helps to keep both eyes on the water and the spoon to constantly monitor one's progress. And yet if one does not want to trip and fall or move in the wrong direction, one must remain equally attentive to the larger picture—the terrain, the horizon, the movement of other bodies nearby—and move accordingly.

To give her students a kinesthetic sense of this skill, Dilley takes this analogy quite literally. Setting two bowls of water at a distance of several yards from one another and placing a spoon in each, Dilley has her students carry a spoonful of water from one bowl to the other. Along the way, they are encouraged to experiment—moving the spoon up and down and around, looking away, moving backward, lowering or raising their center of gravity—all the while exploring the elastic relationship between mindfulness and awareness. Dilley also adds other bowls, and other actors and dancers, so that individuals must remain aware of not only how their own bodies and spoons move through space but also the bodies and spoons of those around them.

Students in Andrea Olsen's Body and Earth course at Middlebury began each class lying on the wooden dance floor doing an eyes-closed body scan, noticing how long it took to get present physically, focused mentally, and cohesive energetically. Students in an economics course at Amherst College move slowly through the classroom to create a break from discursive thinking and find themselves with partners they might not have selected. Other classes used movement throughout the course to connect the students in innovative ways to the environment and to themselves as they interpret and respond to sensory experience.

WALKING MEDITATION

Fully entering the world of birth and death,
Our tears nourish all beings.
Transcending the world of birth and death.
Empty footprints going nowhere.—Thich Nhat Hanh

Walking meditation, a contemplative practice with a long history in the sacred traditions, brings close attention to the ordinary action of walking, a helpful practice for students, who usually walk often during the day. It is a way of using a natural part of life to increase mindfulness as we become aware of the movement of each step; the exercise engages students in life directly. It is not thinking or contemplating while walking (which is also delightful), but being mindful of the muscles of the body, the movement and placement of the feet, balance, and motion. Once you learn the practice, you can do it almost anywhere (see the instructions in "Mindful Walking Instructions"). It helps you feel fully present on the earth. If you are unable to walk, you can bring the same awareness to other repeated movements of the body.

The object of walking meditation is not to get to some other place but to be fully aware of what you are doing and where you are.

Mindful Walking Instructions
Steven Smith, Hawai'i Insight Meditation Center

Find a place where you can walk back and forth, about ten to twenty steps in length. Stand still, keeping your hands stationary, either behind your back, at your sides, or in front of you. Feel the sensations of standing. Be aware of contact with the ground, of pressure and tension. Feel the entire energy field of the body, how it is all participating in this standing. Feel your hands hanging down, then your shoulders weighted, next the lower back, the pelvis—each having its own part in keeping the balance of the standing position.

Bring your attention to the lower part of your body, from the hips downward, the primary foundation of standing. Staying aware, very slowly shift your weight from the left and back of your body to the right, noticing as you do how the sensations change as your balance shifts. Now hold your weight on the left for a moment, aware of the sensations in the leg, hips, thighs, legs, knees, calves, feet, toes, not particularly noticing or identifying those parts of the body but letting the awareness fill the legs. Feel hardness, tension, tightness, heat, vibration, toughness, stiffness—whatever is there.

Keeping your weight on the left side, bring your awareness to the right and feel the relative lightness, emptiness, subtler sensations on the right leg. Now, with your awareness still on the right leg, slowly shift your weight to the right side. Let the awareness seep in right down to the bone, sensing the variations of hardness and softness, toughness, and fluidity, pressure, vibration, weight.

Now bring your awareness to your left side again, and move as if you are very slowly pouring water from a full vessel into an empty one. Notice all the changes as you shift your weight to the left side. With your eyes open just enough to hold your balance, very slowly peel your right foot off the ground, move it forward, and place it on the ground. With your awareness on the right, shift your weight, bring awareness to the left, feel from your hips and buttocks down your sides, the whole range of sensations. Continue stepping slowly, keeping your awareness on the sensations. When you get to the end of the path, pause briefly and turn around. Center yourself, and be aware of the first step as you begin again.

You can do the walking meditation at different paces: brisk, normal, or very slow and meticulous. The point is not to walk slowly; it is to move mindfully. As your mind begins to quiet, you will see how you notice more when you move slowly. More becomes clear as you get to feel the interrelationship of mind and body.

If it helps you, you can say to yourself "walking/walking," or "step/step," or "right/left," using the words to encourage awareness of the sensations of walking.

After some time, you can slow down a bit and actually feel more or less two sections of walking—the lift swing and the placing. So the label might be "lift" as you lift and swing, and then "place." It is a little slower, but not so slow that you lose your balance. Lift, place, stop. Feel the stopping, feel the turning. Lift and place. It is very simple; you are really just being with walking. It is a bare awareness, feeling the flow of sensations. When you lift, move, place, notice the shift of weight, the heel peeling off your toe, even the ground. You might notice your knee bending, your calf tensing, or your thigh being taut. Sometimes you may notice your whole leg simultaneously; another time you might focus on tingling in your toe.

Holding your visual field to a minimum—six, eight, nine feet—is helpful for a period of time. Then, when you feel as if you just can't take it anymore, open up your field of vision, look around, and be aware of seeing and hearing for a while. It is important to keep a lightness of being. If you feel flooded with thoughts, stop for a moment and be aware of thoughts. Let the flood of thoughts come and go, and then go back to the walking. You begin to see that nothing is a distraction as long as you recognize what is there.

Zen Walking (*Kinhin*) Instructions

Kinhin is performed by placing your right fist, with thumb inside, on your chest and covering it with your left palm while holding both elbows at right angles. Rest your eyes about two yards in front of your feet. Count inhalations and exhalations as you walk. Count to 10 and begin again. Walk calmly and steadily, with dignity, either briskly or at a more leisurely pace.

Walking with Words

You can also walk with the phrases from the loving kindness practice (see chapter 9). On the first step, say, "May all beings be well," and on the second, "May all beings be happy."

Vietnamese Zen master Thich Nhat Hanh encourages students to walk with a light smile, to feel deeply at ease, to think that these are the steps of the most secure person on earth. The key, he says, is when you walk, know you are walking. Be in the present moment. You can use these phrases with each step:

In breath, first step	"I have arrived."
Outbreath, second step	"I am home."
Inbreath, third step	"In the here."
Outbreath, fourth step	"In the now."
And repeat.	

All of the sacred traditions teach a form of walking with words. Even if you don't choose one of these for the secular classroom, it may be helpful for students to know the history of contemplative walking. Hindu teachers often recommend a mantra. Examples include *Ram* (the name of God), *Sita Ram* (the union of the female and male principles), or *Om Namah Shivaya* (the name of Shiva, god of transformation). Buddhist walking mantras include *Om Mani Padme Hum* (evokes compassion and wisdom), *Om Tāre Tuttāre Ture Svāhā* (calls on Tara, the goddess of compassion in action, often shown in the process of stepping from her lotus throne in order to help sentient beings), and *Nam-myoho-renge-kyo* (expresses devotion to the wisdom of the Lotus Sutra). Sufi walkers and dancers use *Allah hu, allah hu, allah hu, haqq* (the name of God followed by truth) and *bismi-llāhi r-raḥmāni r-raḥīm* (in the name of God, the Most Gracious, the Most Merciful). Christians walk while repeating qualities like love, joy, or peace, or the Jesus prayer: breathing in while calling out to God (*Lord Jesus Christ, Son of God*) and breathing out while praying for mercy (*have mercy on me, a sinner*).

Meditation in Action

As an optional supplement to his Introduction to Buddhism course at the University of Montana, Alan Sponberg offered a two-credit lab called Traditions of Buddhist Meditation, which had more than seventy-five students enrolled. Sponberg was assisted by a graduate student who had directed a meditation center in Scotland. They created a website, www.wildmind.org, that included instruction (see "Wildmind Walking Meditation Instructions"), graphics indicating posture, and audio files for the various practices taught in the course.

Wildmind Walking Meditation Instructions

Walking meditation is a form of meditation in action.

In walking meditation, we keep our eyes open! We have to be aware of things outside ourselves (objects we might trip over, people we might walk into), and there are many other things outside of ourselves that we will be more aware of—the wind, the sun, and the rain, and the sounds of nature and of humans and machines.

When your body is in motion, it is generally easier to be aware of it than when you are sitting still. You can experience the body very intensely, and you can also find intense enjoyment from this practice.

In the arts, contemplative movement can stimulate and sustain creativity and artistic insight. "A girl/Alone/In the dim light/Comes walking." These are the first lines of *The Water Station*, a play by director-playwright Shogo Ohta. In 2002, drama professors Robyn Hunt and J. Steven Pearson traveled to Kyoto, Japan, where theater master Ohta taught them his method of actor training and his aesthetic approach to performance, particularly his pioneering work in silence and slow tempo, which emphasizes the moment-to-moment fact of one's "being here."

When they returned to teach at the University of Washington, they adapted his methods for their students to explore the nature of walking and other movement and stillness. They focused on the breath and how it relates to movement and acting, and they explored pace and how it relates to slow motion. The students learned to slow their movement and gesture much as one would slow a videotape; what was fast before was now done in quarter or eighth time, slow time, where, Ohta believes, "we find fresh expression to defamiliarize our daily experience—to look again." Each class begins with a thorough, full-bodied warm-up, followed by exercises that address the technical challenges of moving slowly, including balance, focus, and efficiency. Structured improvisations allow free exploration of the aesthetic principles of moving in extreme slowness. Hunt and Pearson report that their students develop improved concentration, sensitivity to the totality of thought and motion, and greater impact in performance.

Movement practices can also have cognitive effects, increasing mental clarity and precision. Barry Kroll, Rodale Professor in Writing and chair of English at Lehigh University, has developed a course called Arguing Differently, which includes challenges to traditional argument models. A contemplative component, including contemplative walking and exercises inspired by aikido, has enabled students to understand that "strategies for resolving conflict are really about conflict within." Kroll's students understand that techniques for handling external adversaries can also work for their own internal issues. Yet Kroll is wrestling with a deep responsibility to clearly and succinctly explain to administrators, colleagues, students, and parents exactly why contemplative learning is relevant to conflict resolution now that contemplative practice feels instrumental to his course. "There's a tension in me between the necessity of instrumentalizing this approach, to say that it is good because it helps me do this other thing, and another impulse I have to say that it's really good in itself. It doesn't ultimately need to be instrumental."

Kroll is also concerned about his students after they leave his classroom. What happens to a student's personal development after an intense and personal course such as this one? "Don't I have any responsibility after opening this box?" Kroll is organizing events and reunions incorporating contemplative practices and is considering ways for students to stay connected online. One of Kroll's students wrote in his journal about contemplative walking:

> Usually, I speed-walk to class. Most of the time I'm running late, so I definitely don't take the time to look around or observe my surroundings on the way. On Friday though, i left early for philosophy class so that i could take my time walking there and not have to be so rushed. With my phone in my bag and no pressure to speed-walk, it was an entirely different world. I noticed how beautiful campus looked, especially with all the different colored leaves on all the trees. The branches peacefully swayed in the wind while some leaves became detached and gracefully made their way to the ground. I looked around at the people who passed me; they all looked like they were in a rush like I usually am. One person, however, looked pretty aware of her surroundings and seemed to be decently mindful and observant. I met eyes with her and we smiled at each other. It was weird, like we knew what each other was thinking or something. I continued walking and a squirrel scurried past me. It wasn't running the way squirrels usually run though, it was taking these giant leaps and for some reason I thought it was so cute and it made me happy. I focused on my walking and realized how weird it was that it's just a process that we do so often without thinking. Mindfully putting one foot in front of the other felt better than usual. It felt like I was accomplishing something, as if walking to class was something I could check off my to-do list and feel good about. It helped take some of my stress away. When I got to philosophy I felt more in tune and ready to absorb information. It was a productive class!

TAI CHI

Tai chi ch'uan (literally, "supreme ultimate fist"), commonly known as t'ai chi, tai chi, or taiji, is a Chinese martial art known for the claims of health and longevity benefits made by its practitioners and medical studies. Tai chi is known as a soft style martial art—one applied with as complete a relaxation or "softness" in the musculature as possible, to distinguish its theory and application from that of the hard martial art styles, which use a degree of tension in the muscles.

Tai chi is best known as one of the slow motion routines that groups of people practice every morning in parks across China and, increasingly, other parts of the world. In tai chi classes, students are taught awareness of their own balance and what affects it, awareness of the same in others, and appreciation of the practical value in their ability to moderate extremes of behavior and attitude at both mental and physical levels.

Yin Mei introduced tai chi into a class on modern dance technique at Queens College, CUNY. She wanted to emphasize not the end result of movement but the flow of energy within the body, to shift her students from an external to an internal perspective. She believed that the tai chi concept of balance would provide a crucial linkage between Western understanding of physiological movement and Chinese understanding of internal motion and change. She taught the historical and theoretical aspects of tai chi, tai chi as a system of movement, and tai chi as the basis for a new approach to postmodern dance and movement. All exercises and sequences, including movements like "visiting the bottom of the sea" and "empty arm swing," were approached from a contemplative perspective, with an emphasis on energy direction, spatial projection, shape, flow, and a weighted use of the body in space.

Acting master Constantin Stanislavski said, "In every physical action, unless it is purely mechanical, there is concealed some inner action . . . they are intertwined. A common purpose brings them together and reinforces the unbreakable bond" (Stanislavski, 1961, p. 253). In Contemplation, Reflection, Action: A Somatic Approach to Acting at the University of California, Davis, Barbara Sellers-Young taught her students to integrate Stanislavski's methods with contemplative practice. For Sellers-Young, authentic acting is embodied acting. How, after all, can one truly inhabit a character or make one's presence felt on stage if one leaves one's body behind? Yet for most actors, maintaining a body-mind connection is one of their greatest challenges. To help student actors meet this challenge, Sellers-Young has developed a method that she calls "somatic contemplation." Essentially somatic contemplation entails a series of exercises aimed at "deepening and cultivating embodiment and integrating it with psychophysical action through focus on body states." As Sellers-Young describes it, the objective of this approach is to increase embodied performance through an experience of the relationship between breathing, exploration, and action, or what wu chi master James Kapp refers to as conscious action.

The course united tai chi and chi gong (a Chinese practice of aligning breath, movement, and awareness), explorations based on concepts from these disciplines, and contemporary texts from Samuel Beckett's *Act without Words*, Bertolt Brecht's *Mother Courage*, Charles Mee's *Big Love*, and Naomi Ilzuka's *Tattoo Girl*. Sellers-Young began with establishing "neutral body, or *wu chi*": "This is a dynamic alignment of your essence (*jing*), energy (*chi*), and spirit (*shen*) through the internal relationship between kinetic interdependence, opposition and circularity, which helps to create a state of being open, released, relaxed, focused, centered, and grounded. It culminates in a state of emptiness/stillness (*xiu*) that is the preparation to move between opposites—action to stillness and stillness to action."

The process unites breath, thought, and action, moving from ordinary experience to a refinement of consciousness that includes open awareness (inclusive and expansive), interest (wonderment), attention (committed contact), absorption (relevance and cognition), and understanding (integration and knowledge).

YOGA

Yoga is the settling of the mind into silence. Our essential nature is usually overshadowed by the activity of the mind.—Yoga Sutras of Patanjali

The word *yoga*, from the Sanskrit word *yuj*, means to yoke or bind and is often interpreted as "union," or a method of discipline. The Indian sage Patanjali is believed to have collated the practice of yoga into the *Yoga Sutra* about two thousand years ago. The sutra is a collection of 195 statements that serves as a philosophical guidebook for most of the yoga that is practiced today, which in the West is most often hatha yoga, a program of physical postures. Yoga is different from stretching or other kinds of fitness because it explicitly connects the movement of the body and the fluctuations of the mind to the rhythm of the breath. Connecting the mind, body, and breath helps to direct attention inward to the cultivation of awareness. Hatha yoga promotes flexibility and strength of both body and mind, contributes to vitality, cultivates balance, and calms the mind. It alleviates stress and creates a welcome feeling of wholeness and deep relaxation. And it clears the mind, leaving openness to new and creative ideas.

There are many schools of hatha yoga and many approaches to teaching. In every college town and on most campuses, you'll find yoga studios where many variations are taught. These include Iyengar, ashtanga, integral, Kripalu, and Vikram yoga styles. It is not unusual for teachers themselves to study in various schools and to blend techniques to create their own approaches.

Much of Cressida Heyes's recent work as a feminist philosopher has revolved around how our bodies are quantified, commodified, and disciplined in contemporary culture. In her former classes, students were learning how to ask the appropriate questions and answer them satisfactorily, but the material still didn't, as Heyes puts it, "feel real to them." In response, she designed a contemplative class in which rather than merely studying how power works on the body, students would explore a kind of epistemology of the body, an approach through which the body itself is a means of inquiry.

The result was a real departure from the traditional university curriculum at the University of Alberta where Heyes is Canada Research Chair in Philosophy of Gender and Sexuality: this was an upper-level philosophy course cross-listed with physical education. One day a week, students attended a seminar in which they discussed readings on the philosophy of the body. The other component of the course expanded this encounter with the material by moving it into a physical education space, where Heyes, an experienced yoga practitioner and teacher, led the students in a yoga practice.

There they would explore the "hither and yonness of their own bodies. They begin to experience their own bodies as a means of inquiry and self-knowledge," says Heyes. And they learned, through practice, to simply observe, nonjudgmentally, their own minds and bodies: "Once you are in the Warrior pose, notice how your body is leaning forward rather than simply inhabiting the space. This is how we often go through life, leaning into the future without fully being in the present." Coupled with the readings and activities of the seminar, the regular yoga practice brought students' awareness not only to the ways in which bodies in general have historically been disciplined, but also to the ways in which *their* bodies have been disciplined. To facilitate this awareness, students also kept a journal in which they reflected on their process and practice.

The course is not without its challenges. Few students who sign up for a philosophy course, even one focused on the philosophy of the body, are prepared for the kind of encounters that a course like Heyes engenders—not only with the course material but also with the students themselves. A course that challenges them to go so far beyond the bounds of traditional philosophy is bound to raise questions—and anxiety levels—for students. *If the objective is to observe my own practice without judgment,* they may wonder, *then how will the professor know if I am good enough? How will I? What place does my own visceral experience have in an environment that has taught me to leave my body at the classroom door?*

Heyes also had concerns about how to integrate the analytical and physical objectives of the course, and how to evaluate the outcomes of both. After consulting with colleagues in physical education, she decided that the final evaluation of the physical component would be a silent self-directed yoga practice called Mysore practice, which allows students the freedom to move through the poses at their own pace. Their practice would demonstrate the degree to which they had mastered the poses as well as whether they had achieved a realistic assessment of their limits, capabilities, and self-knowledge.

Yoga is useful in helping students understand ideas in a more integrated way. "Too often university students are forced to *think* their way through their courses with the idea that the world and the self can easily be understood and appreciated through the rational mind," wrote Judith Shapiro and Paul Wapner at the School of International Service, American University. To provide a complementary orientation, they designed a course that included yoga and meditation, as well as readings on the struggle to find a balance between the desire for internal peace and insight and the sense of responsibility for improving concrete conditions in a needy world. For many students, the class was "wildly successful, even life changing." Both teachers and students wished there had been more time for discussion (a common challenge when contemplative practices take part of the time usually reserved for talking). Student comments included these:

> "It is amazing to recognize and experience the interconnection between our body and our mind. I am starting to feel how the physical well-being of a person is intimately connected with his or her psychological well-being and comfort."

> "Yoga doesn't only relax my body but it clears my mind and gives me a bounce of energy."

> "Yoga is hard. There's no doubt about that. But it teaches us to be at peace even when our muscles are burning and we are tired."

> "It is our *mind* that we are relaxing. How easy it is to overlook this!"

"I have never listened to my body and what it had to say. I have discovered that the easiest way to listen to my soul and to learn who I am is to listen to my body."

In a course that focused on visual art from the Russian Orthodox and Tibetan Buddhist traditions, Deborah Haynes introduced yoga and other contemplative practices to help students learn techniques of observation and perceptual skills. Haynes has been practicing yoga since 1975. About her practice, she says, in *Art Lessons: Meditations on the Creative Life* (2003), "I learned to pay attention to deep inner experience—the obvious physical sensations . . . and the more subtle feelings of openness, vulnerability, and surrender. I learned to concentrate awareness in the *hara*, the belly, to awaken dormant energy, to discover the locus and source of the vital life force . . . These insights have informed every area of my creative life."

Dan Holland introduced yoga into his experiential seminar, Health Promotion and Disability, which included students with physical disabilities. "The yoga we will be doing," he told his class, "will involve very gentle postures done with an emphasis on awareness and breathing. Individuals are encouraged to do the postures only according to your own comfort and ability. The emphasis here is on moment-to-moment awareness as we move and breathe, not getting into the 'right' posture."

LABYRINTH WALKING

Labyrinth walking is the practice of journeying inward and then returning from the center. A labyrinth has a clearly marked path to follow; it is not a maze in which you can get lost. Labyrinths can be created with stone, tape, fabric, sticks, chalk, plants, and many other materials. Labyrinths are symbolic forms of pilgrimage; you can walk the path ascending toward understanding or enlightenment.

During the Middle Ages, labyrinths were built at a number of large European churches. The full flowering of the medieval labyrinth design came during the twelfth and thirteenth centuries with the grand labyrinths of the gothic cathedrals, most notably Chartres and Amiens in northern France and Siena in Tuscany.

Many labyrinths exist today in churches and parks to provide people with a meditative way to relieve stress. Labyrinths can now also be found in retreat centers, hospitals, prisons, airports, community centers, colleges, and at least one law school. There are approximately two thousand permanent labyrinths in the United States.

The labyrinth has been used in the classroom in many ways. Susan E. Wegner, associate professor of art history at Bowdoin College, developed a course, Art and Contemplation in Christian Europe, in which the students set up and walked a replica of the Chartres labyrinth. Cadets at West Point created a labyrinth, inviting the entire corps of cadets into its meditative space (Marilyn R. Nelson, professor of English literature at the University of Connecticut and visiting instructor at West Point: Contemplative Practice and the Muse). CUNY School of Law offers several contemplative opportunities for its students, including a labyrinth designed to teach law students how to deal with the stress of practicing law. That labyrinth is a low garden, with bricks outlining the maze. "I find that in the middle of the day, it helps me to just stop and calm down a bit," says Penelope Andrews, who teaches international law and torts. In the stressful world of litigation, this can be an important resource.

Heather Hathaway, who teaches English at Marquette University, has been using contemplative approaches in her teaching for over a decade. She cotaught a course in 1998 with Anthony Peressini, her colleague from the Philosophy Department. Since that time, they have led the honors program; Peressini is now director of the program, which includes a required sophomore contemplative practice seminar. "In my [labyrinth] course we don't even do English," said Hathaway. "We simply do labyrinth practice: we read about it, and we walk." Student response has been enthusiastic. While some were skeptical at first, by the end of the course students reported they were beginning to feel the positive effects of the practice on their daily lives. As Hathaway remarked,

> We walk a labyrinth once a week, and that has pervaded the lives of my students. Every semester I run into students who took it in previous years who ask, "Can we have another class"? They can go to the labyrinth on their own when it's open, but it was a very strong community-building enterprise every semester, and so I thought, *I'll just reserve the church for a night and get all the students on campus who've done it for the past three or four years and invite them to come and walk it. They are clamoring for that.* The great thing is seeing them change over the course of the semester from a reticent, even skeptical attitude about it, to being totally devoted. If it were not a class, they'd never, ever give themselves that opportunity to be quiet for an hour.

CONCLUSION

Movement exercises can be simple but have profound effects. Rita K. Wong, teaching at Emily Carr Institute of Art and Design, recommended some independent walking contemplations to try outside class. "I hoped for a balance between attention to self (focusing in) and awareness of surroundings (looking out, noticing both physical details of the water and land, but also mindful of the histories of the places where we live and study)." The easy, physical realization of their connection with their surroundings helped students cultivate awareness of environment. Given the profound global implications of climate change and other planetary issues, these practices could be critically important to our common future.

Resources

Howard Gardner, *Intelligence Reframed* (New York: Basic Books, 2000).

Thich Nhat Hanh, *The Long Road Turns to Joy: A Guide to Walking Meditation* (Berkeley, CA: Parallax Press, 1996).

Alfred Huang, *The Complete Tai Chi* (Rochester, NY: Inner Traditions).

Labyrinth Society, for locating labyrinths in North America: http://www.labyrinthsociety.org/

Yoga Journal: yogajournal.com

Compassion and Loving Kindness

If you want others to be happy, practice compassion. If you want to be happy, practice compassion.

Dalai Lama

Despite all the cultural stereotypes, the current generation of college students is yearning to connect in a meaningful way. Many want to find ways to use their educational experience to engage in making a difference in the world, especially in ways that address human suffering, of which they see so much. They don't know how best to do that, and they're often inarticulate about how to do it. They want to know that education is not just about writing papers and developing skills to earn a living but is really about caring for each other and making the world a livable place because they realize that soon, it may not be a livable place.

It is a contemplative premise that compassion and knowledge complement each other, As Victor Weisskopf at MIT said, "Knowledge without compassion is inhuman; compassion without knowledge is ineffective." Professors in many disciplines are introducing compassion practice into their courses as a way to help students cultivate their own compassion and connection with the world. Compassion is a mental state that is focused on others' pain or suffering and includes a wish or an aspiration to see that person relieved of that pain or suffering. Compassionate acts are generally considered those that take into account the suffering of others and attempt to alleviate their suffering as if it were their own. The Dalai Lama, a great advocate of compassion, says that it can be developed to such a degree that not only does our compassion arise without effort but it is unconditional, undifferentiated, and universal in scope. "A feeling of intimacy toward all other sentient beings, including of course those who would harm us, is generated, which is likened in the literature to the love a mother has for her only child" (His Holiness the Dalai Lama, 2001, p. 123).

Our natural capacity to care for our own welfare allows us to feel compassion for others. If we lack this sense of caring for ourselves, including our pain and suffering, we do not have the ability to care for others. And with that sense of caring for our selves, we also need to cultivate a sense of connection or identification with the other. These two—our sensitivity to our own pain and suffering and our sense of connection with the other—constitute the root of compassion, which the Tibetan Buddhist contemplative tradition evocatively calls "a loving sense of endearment toward others." In this sense, the Golden Rule, forms of which exist in nearly every culture, is based on the concept of compassion.

Compassion is not pity for another, since pity rests on a judgment of the other as weaker, and somehow slightly pathetic, and compassion is without judgment. In the Buddhist tradition, pity is known as the near enemy of compassion—its shadow, we might say—seeing others as distinct from ourselves. Understanding this difference between compassion and pity is especially important for students' service work and community engagement. Working with others requires, at its heart, a deep connection and respect rather than pity and disconnection. As universities and colleges become more engaged with the communities around them, training in compassion for students becomes very important.

While working from a sense of connection with others, we also need awareness of our own boundaries in order to sustain a compassionate relationship with the world. Part of compassion for ourselves, this awareness is important in preventing burnout while engaging in social action. These distinctions require training and attention, but the cultivation of connection and compassion may be the most important learning we can provide.

INNER CHANGE AND OUTER CHANGE

Compassion practices connect the student's academic life with the concerns of the world outside the academy. The scientific method and critical thinking traditionally seek solutions through understanding and changing the physical world, including the world of ideas, but they have not acknowledged the need for a systematic investigation of personal motives, attachments, and capacity for instinctive loving care. Contemplatives have sought to reduce pain and suffering in the world through inner transformation (which can then lead to loving kindness and compassionate action). In the foreword to Thich Nhat Hahn's iconic *Peace Is Every Step: The Path of Mindfulness in Everyday Life*, the Dalai Lama wrote, "Although attempting to bring about world peace through the internal transformation of individuals is difficult, it is the only way" (Hanh, 1991, p. vii). Jesus was led by the Spirit into the desert alone, and Muhammad fasted and meditated at Mount Hira, outside Mecca. Gandhi's insight on how to achieve Indian independence came during a retreat. Contemplative practices bring this tension between reflection and action into the light of the classroom for exploration by awakening the experience of compassion itself.

Most students prefer the idea of changing others and changing the world to actually changing themselves. But the compassion practices teach from within what the wisdom traditions all teach: you cannot give to another what you do not have. And once students are guided to look within, they see what needs to be changed. As examples in other chapters have shown, they also gain insight into the power of their cultivated relationships with others; these relationships are not fixed and static. They can develop and change in astonishing ways.

Connecting with the world around us can also mean attempting to enter and understand a totally different cultural environment. Steven Emmanuel, a professor in the Philosophy Department at Virginia Wesleyan College and Center for Contemplative Mind in Society fellow, wrote about the intrapersonal and interpersonal connections his students made through using compassion practices during a short-term service-learning trip abroad:

> It was abundantly clear that the practice had a profound impact on the way they understood themselves in their service work, and in terms of their ability to overcome the challenges of living and working under strenuous conditions for three weeks in Viet Nam. Among the challenges they noted

were being in a vastly different cultural environment where very little English was spoken, and directly confronting suffering of a kind they had never experienced in the Western world. The students described how the practice helped them to "break down the walls" of separation, the consciousness of being different; how it helped them develop a greater sense of empathy (as opposed to sympathy) and a greater capacity for compassion. Several students spoke about being able to put themselves in the shoes of the Vietnamese, to experience the world as the Vietnamese do. They also noted how this ability to be fully present in the situation helped alleviate their own anxieties and concerns. All the students noted that the experience had a transformative effect, making them feel "connected and whole."

These student responses are unusual for sojourners who have been in a new culture for a period as short as three weeks, as the typical adjustment curve for cultural adaptation spans months or even years. The fact that students reported a sense of connection and increased empathy and compassion for the Vietnamese people indicates the extent to which contemplative practices facilitated their self-awareness and enabled their growth in cultural understanding.

John Makransky, associate professor of theology, taught Meditation, Service and Social Action to master's of divinity students at Harvard University and master's students at Boston College. The meditation he teaches is adapted from Tibetan Buddhism's loving kindness practice and is accessible to those with any, or no, faith background. In addition to readings from Martin Luther King Jr., Dorothy Day, Aung San Suu Kyi, and other contemplative activists, he assigns a daily meditation practice that is "being held in the wish for well-being." Each week students write about the specific way their meditation informs the reading and the reading informs their meditation. They are also asked to reflect on how their daily meditation and reading inform their personal development and social action.

This approach has emerged from the needs of social service work, which, as discussed in chapter 3, often results in feelings of exhaustion and anger. Coming back every day to be "cradled in compassion" allows practitioners to be present for themselves and discern their own hidden strengths and underlying capacities. They do this for themselves so they can do it for others and through the process experience a greater and deeper sense of interconnection.

PRACTICES

Focused practices can cultivate and sustain connection and compassion to one's self and others. Though based on our natural inclinations, these practices can strengthen and deepen our relationship with the rest of the world. Drawing on latent and often buried senses of connection and love for this world, these practices, and others like them, allow us to reconnect with our experience of being intimately connected to this planet and all its residents.

Loving Kindness (*Metta*)

Loving kindness practice cultivates unconditional, inclusive love, a love with wisdom, without boundaries. This love has no conditions; it does not depend on whether one "deserves" it; it is not restricted to friends and family; it extends out from personal categories to include all living beings. There are no expectations of anything in return. We begin with loving ourselves, for unless we have a measure of this unconditional love and acceptance for ourselves, it is difficult to extend it to others. Then we include others who are special to us and, ultimately, all living things, even the most ordinary things. We hold them all with a sense of reverence. Gradually both the visualization and the meditation phrases blend into the actual experience, the feeling of loving kindness (See "Loving Kindness Instructions.")

This is a meditation of care, concern, tenderness, loving kindness, friendship—a feeling of warmth for oneself and others. The practice is the softening of the mind and heart, an opening to deeper and deeper levels of the feeling of kindness, of pure love. It does not depend on relationships, on how the other person feels about us.

Loving Kindness Instructions

Take a very comfortable posture. One of the aims in this meditation is to feel good, so make your posture relaxed and comfortable. Begin to focus around the solar plexus, your chest area, your "heart center." Breathe loving kindness in and out from that area, as if all experience is happening from there. Anchor your mindfulness only on the sensations at your heart center.

Begin by generating this feeling of kindness toward yourself. Continuing to breathe in and out, use either these traditional phrases or ones you choose yourself. Say or think them several times:

"May I be free from inner and outer harm and danger."
"May I be safe and protected."
"May I be free of mental suffering or distress. May I be happy."
"May I be free of physical pain and suffering. May I be healthy and strong."
"May I be able to live in this world happily, peacefully, joyfully, with ease."

Next, move to a person who most invites the feeling of pure unconditional loving kindness. The first person is usually a mentor, a benefactor, an elder, a parent. Repeat the phrases for this person: "May she be safe and protected."

After feeling strong unconditional love for the benefactor, move to a person you regard as a dear friend and repeat the phrases again, breathing in and out of your heart center.

Now move to a neutral person, someone for whom you feel neither strong like nor dislike. As you repeat the phrases, allow yourself to feel tenderness, loving care for their welfare.

Now move to someone with whom you have difficulty, hostile feelings, or resentments. Repeat the phrases for this person. If you have difficulty doing this, you can say before the phrases, "To the best of my ability I wish that you be . . ." If you begin to feel ill will toward this person, return to the benefactor and let the loving kindness arise again. Then return to this person.

After the difficult person, radiate loving kindness out to all beings.

May all beings be safe, happy, healthy, live joyously.

Compassion Practice: Just Like Me

Just Like Me is a practice for seeing the similarity between ourselves and others, an important prerequisite for experiencing compassion. (See "Compassion Practice: Just Like Me Instructions.") It is a powerful practice, reminding us how often we discount others, forgetting they are fellow human beings who want to be free from pain and suffering, "just like me." During this practice, one experiences being vulnerable as well as being strong, receiving as well as giving. By bringing the whole of oneself forward to meet another person, a true connection takes place.

Compassion Practice: Just Like Me Instructions

Ask participants to sit in pairs and guide them with this script or with other phrases that seem appropriate to the group:

Become aware that there is a person in front of you. A fellow human being, just like you.
  Now silently repeat these phrases, while looking at your partner:

This person has a body and a mind, just like me. This person has feelings, emotions, and thoughts, just like me. This person has at some point been sad, disappointed, angry, hurt, or confused, just like me. (You can say these one at a time.) This person has in his or her life experienced physical and emotional pain and suffering, just like me. This person wishes to be free from pain and suffering, just like me. This person wishes to be safe, healthy, and loved, just like me. This person wishes to be happy, just like me.

Now, let's allow some wishes to arise:

I wish for this person to have the strength, resources, and social support to navigate the difficulties in life. I wish for this person to be free from pain and suffering. I wish for this person to be happy.
  Because this person is a fellow human being, just like me.

Tonglen

This practice is a method for connecting with suffering—ours and that which is all around us everywhere we go. It is a method for overcoming fear of suffering and for dissolving the tightness of our hearts. Primarily it is a method for awakening the compassion that is in all of us, no matter how cruel or cold we might seem to be. In the Tibetan tradition, it is called *tonglen*, which means "giving and receiving." (See "Compassion Practice: Transforming Suffering [*Tonglen*] Instructions.")

Compassion Practice: Transforming Suffering
(*Tonglen*) Instructions

We begin the practice by taking on the suffering of a person we know to be hurting and whom we wish to help. For instance, if you know of a child who is hurt, you breathe in the wish to take away all the pain and fear of that child. Then, as you breathe out, you send the child happiness, joy, or whatever else would relieve his or her pain. This is the core of the practice: breathing in others' pain so they can be well and have more space to relax and open, and breathing out, sending them relaxation or whatever you feel would bring them relief and happiness.

Students sometimes have difficulty doing this practice because it brings them face to face with their own fear, resistance, or anger. At that point you can change the focus and instruct them to do *tonglen* for what they are feeling and for millions of others just like them who at that very moment are feeling the same unhappiness and misery. Maybe the pain is hard to name, but they can feel it—a tightness in the stomach, a heavy darkness. Instruct them to just contact what they are feeling and breathe in, taking it in for themselves and for all of us, and sending out relief to all the people who are caught with that same emotion.

COMPASSION FROM MANY TRADITIONS

These practices can be drawn from diverse sources. Larry Fine taught a comparative course at Mount Holyoke College in which students investigated contemplative practices in five traditions. He taught the Jewish practices (from

Kabbalah and Hasidism), and guest speakers taught others: Christian, Hindu, and Islamic. One of the unifying themes in the course, loving kindness in the various traditions, proved to be the aspect of practice that students found most appealing, simulating, and challenging. He said, "I believe that it touched some students in very personal ways and brought the subject of our study into the orbit of their experience in a direct and immediate way."

COMPASSION AND DISTANCE LEARNING

While we might think practices require intimate and close interaction, they can be taught and practiced effectively even at a distance. As early as the year 2000, Alan Sponberg at the University of Montana was already exploring distance learning on the Internet for his Buddhism in Religious Studies course. He was interested in how the Internet can "be a place to develop concentration, to deepen understanding, and to cultivate awareness." The contemplative practices were a two-credit "lab" course offered as an optional supplement to his Introduction to Buddhism course. The students were introduced to several forms of meditation, including loving kindness practice. An online introduction precedes the practice instructions. In it, he says:

> Think about someone who has upset, irritated, or angered you. Imagine that
> in a past life this person has been the most loving and caring mother to you
> conceivable. Imagine that this person made every sacrifice possible to shield
> you from danger, comfort you in sadness, and attend to your every need.
> Then think about how grateful you would have been to this person when
> they were taking such care of you when you were a child. Now try this with
> as many people as possible who have upset, hurt, or angered you in the past.

Although many teachers do not think practice can be taught effectively without personal presence, Sponberg felt optimistic about the educational potential of the Internet, although he agreed that in a class on a subject like meditation, personal contact is even more vital than in other classes. This class was a combination of live class time and Internet time. As a result, he became convinced that meditation can be taught, and taught well, online and that the medium has distinct applicability and even advantages for those with no ready access to either university courses or traditional meditation instruction.

ENGAGED DEMOCRACY

Many students are entering the professions and the workforce without the capacity to lead an integrated life in a democratic civil society where they can make intelligent and compassionate contributions. To introduce theories and practices of democratic deliberation and at the University of Alberta, David Kahane used a range of practices to help students explore habitual modes of engaging with injustice and suffering and develop compassion for self and others. He told his students that they would learn "ways people can come together across differences of perspective, identity, and power to collaboratively solve problems." The class practiced loving kindness meditation and read from texts that included Ram Dass and Paul Gorman, *How Can I Help? Stories and Reflections on Service*, Pema Chodron, *Practicing Peace in Times of War*, and Michael Edwards and Stephen Post, *The Love That Does Justice: Spiritual Activism in Dialogue with Social Science*.

While conflict can and often does arise between and among individuals, the most threatening forms rise between collectives: nation-states, ethnic groups, religious sects, and ideological organizations. Leslie Thiele, professor of political science at the University of Florida, whose research focuses on environmental ethics and politics and the intersection of political philosophy, psychology, and cultural studies, used loving kindness practice along with interdisciplinary scholarship and experiential encounters to explore the relationship of community to conflict. He hoped that students would gain a deeper and more nuanced understanding of the human capacity for community and the role it plays in global affairs and personal lives. Each student had to choose a campus group or organization toward which he or she had experienced fear, distrust, unease, or hostility. For example, a student concerned about environmental protection might choose the Marketing Club of the Business School. After practicing loving kindness for that group, the student then created an opportunity to connect with compassion and understanding to one of its members. After the encounter, the students in the class wrote papers explaining what they learned and proposing a plan for introducing mindfulness and loving kindness practice to the resolution of a national or international conflict. Students reported that they found the practices challenging but appreciated them as both a new experience and "a means for gathering insight and centerness."

COMPASSION, VIOLENCE, AND STRESS

Compassion practice often opens up useful discussion on suffering in the world, the role of the media in revealing (or distorting) that suffering, and the challenges of responding. After integrating practice into an anthropology course, Meditation and Media Violence, Alan Klima, a Center for Contemplative Mind in Society fellow, teaching then at the University of California, Davis, wrote, "While there are persuasive and important arguments about how mass media technology conspires to eliminate perception of real pain and suffering through compassion fatigue and other processes, this disempowers the viewer, especially students who do not yet have much experience of making change in the world. By introducing meditation, the course was able to open up to a wider field of discussion on this matter." He added that the combination of compassion meditation and the class materials was able to "render the familiar unfamiliar, and the unfamiliar strangely relevant to the familiar" and that "many students began to articulate their own ethical practice of viewing violence."

For many students, historical events can be seen as not merely temporally distant but emotionally distant as well. A course at Bryn Mawr, Crossing the Threshold of Pain's Legacy, taught by Linda Susan Beard in the Department of English, included contemplative pedagogy to "help students find ways of encountering the literature of shared human horror—literature of the transatlantic slave trade, the European holocaust, and South African apartheid—and to bring deeper, more inclusive, and humane understandings to it." Beard used a 1930s photograph of a lynching: smiling fathers and sons with arms linked for the picture. In the foreground is a black man who has been castrated and is being burned alive. "The experience of contemplative seeing is not about fossilizing or reifying. I ask them to look in the faces of everyone in a photograph, particularly the people who are smiling, and I ask, 'What terror might lurk behind those smiles?' I am hoping that my students and I will go beyond mere analysis to something much deeper, compassionate understanding. And for that, we have to see our own faces in the photograph too . . . The focus is less on what a person has done and more on the subversive question Toni Morrison asks in *The Bluest Eye*: 'Why?'" This innovative approach connects the students directly to the material of the course and establishes the means for them to more deeply understand their connection with these past events.

Professor Fran Grace's Seminar on Compassion at the University of Redlands is one of several academic courses taught in the campus Meditation Room.

Eight weeks into the course, after the students had already worked with several different meditation methods, she introduced the most challenging meditation: taking and giving meditation (*tonglen*), in which the meditator exchanges his or her peace with the suffering of others. At first, the students resisted this new practice. Among the protestations were these:

> "If I willingly breathe in the pain of others—like disease and dying—won't that make me sick? Didn't Gandhi, or one of the other exemplars we've studied, say that you become what you think about? I don't want to think about disease!"

> "I don't want to breathe in more stress! Isn't this class supposed to be helping us with inner peace?"

> "This meditation makes me feel depressed. And I haven't even tried it yet."

However, after working with the meditation for a week, the students became convinced of its power to transmute suffering. Many students used it to connect with others who had a similar suffering, such as this student who suffered from constant stress:

> The biggest suffering for me right now is stress, and so I focused on that for my meditation. I allowed myself to feel that overwhelming stress . . . tightening in my shoulders, a sort of constriction in my throat and a tensing of my facial muscles . . . Then I thought of all my friends who are equally being pushed from all sorts of directions and pulled in so many uncomfortable ways . . . I added my family, acquaintances, and the other people I had seen before, like a homeless man on the streets digging through newspapers. All the stress and pain together created a big, dark cloud, and I slowly tried to bring it into my heart, allowing it to pierce and pop my narcissistic feelings. I then began to cultivate a sense of great happiness inside of me. I felt a white strong light growing from my heart and then radiating out from all corners and sections of my body. I brought the rays of light to people I knew . . . An overwhelming calm came over me, a great feeling of satisfaction and joy spread from all parts of me. I felt a high that I do not think I have ever felt before. (Grace, 2009, p. 8)

COMPASSION IN THE SCIENCES

Not only have compassion practices been used throughout the humanities, they have also made a contribution to learning in science courses. How does research in social neuroscience, affective science, and social psychology inform our understanding of empathy and compassion? This was one of the questions that framed a seminar Al Kaszniak at the University of Arizona taught. As part of learning about historical perspectives on compassion from science and contemplative traditions, students practiced loving kindness and compassion and read texts including Joan Halifax's on *Being with Dying* and a study by Cendri A. Hutcherson, Emma M. Seppala, and James J. Gross titled "Loving-Kindness Meditation Increases Social Connectedness." They also discussed factors that hinder the expression of kindness and compassion. The discussion was facilitated through watching a clip from the Attenborough film *Gandhi*, focusing on the instructions Gandhi gives to a distraught person. Building on the discovery of mirror neurons (neurons that sympathetically fire in reaction to seeing movement in another), Kaszniak had students relate the scientific discoveries to their own practices through conversations and journaling.

COMPASSION AND CONNECTION

Compassion exists in relationship, which includes relationships in the classroom. The majority of Contemplative Mind fellows reported that "incorporating contemplative practice into their courses changed the nature of their relationship with their students in a positive way. The process and intention of creating a space of openness and trust often led to a deepening of the relationships between the students and between the students and teachers. Even professors who usually had good relationships with their students noted that these relationships tended to go deeper and developed much earlier in the course (Scribner, 2000).

SunHee Gertz, a professor in the English Department at Clark University, said that since teaching with contemplative practices, she has allowed herself to become more compassionate in the classroom, offering undergraduate students opportunities to reflect or meditate close to midterm exam time and introducing contemplative practices to students in her graduate studies course. She insists that her use of contemplative practices is something "I never would have tried without the program offered by the center—never! I had a distinct division between academic work and my personal life. So it just underscores for me the need for permission to recognize that spiritual side of yourself, or experiencing peace, or whatever words you want to use for it."

Kathleen Biddick of Temple University has always tried to encourage community within her classroom, but she related that it was the "deepest ever" in her contemplative practices course: "The community was much deeper and more open, and created an intimacy that was extraordinary." In reflecting on this course compared to her previous ones, Biddick recognized that "there seems to be a great thirst for such classroom experiences among undergraduates. In their course evaluations, the students reiterated their enjoyment and appreciation of the classroom community they built."

In anecdotal reports, many students find these classes to be a refreshing experience, with a new appreciation of their teachers, which for some teachers creates an opportunity in the classroom to take risks and explore in more experimental ways and to connect what they are teaching to other aspects of life.

There was also an increase in compassion in the way students related to each other. After a student retreat, one Yale Law School student wrote:

> After we got back, I was writing a brief for a class. There was lots of research to be done, and I felt a bit behind. I was worried about it. I pulled an all-nighter and got all this research done. One of my friends asked me the next day, "How is your research going?" I had actually found a lot of cases. Before, I would have been very contractual and would have said, "Well, if you show me some of your cases, I'll show you some of mine." But then I stepped back and thought, "Well, you know really, what does it matter? Give him the stuff, he needs it, and maybe it will make his brief better than yours, but it's not that big a deal and you probably ultimately will build a better friendship of this, which is what it is really about."

An example of increased awareness of the needs and rights of others came from a Contemplative Practice, Health Promotion, and Disability on Campus course taught by Daniel Holland, a Contemplative Mind in Society fellow at the University of Arkansas. Students with disabilities, who are at particularly high risk for chronic stress, loneliness, and attrition and who encounter more obstacles in gaining peer support and group membership than nondisabled peers, reported significant improvement in their ability to cope with daily stressors after practicing mindfulness, yoga, and journaling. But perhaps of even more interest, a large number of students who did not identify themselves as having a disability or chronic illness indicated that they had gained a more positive perspective regarding those who do.

In her class on contemplation and environmental writing at the University of St. Thomas, a student in the class committed suicide during the semester, and the others needed to grieve. The professor, Mary Rose O'Reilley, was grateful that it had happened in her contemplative class, which created space for what was needed. "As I write this, tears again. We cried all the time in class, made a rule, *Cry and keep talking. Cry and keep writing.* We called it *crying practice.* And I learned that the single most important thing a contemplatively centered classroom teaches the teacher is not a pedagogical recipe but *pedagogical flexibility.*"

CONCLUSION

Of all the qualities cultivated in contemplative education, compassion and connection are perhaps the most important. As we collectively face the global problems of poverty, gross inequity, racism and other forms of prejudice and intolerance, environmental degradation, and climate change, we have little hope of surviving without unprecedented levels of cooperation and care for each other. Education at all levels must foster this connection if we are to use the tools and techniques that are being developed to foster human and ecological flourishing on our planet.

Resources

Karen Armstrong, *Twelve Steps to a Compassionate Life* (New York: Knopf, 2010).

Sylvia Boorstein, *Pay Attention for Goodness Sake* (New York: Ballantine Books, 2002).

Pema Chodron, *Practicing Peace in Times of War* (Boston,: Shambhala, 2006).

Pema Chodron, *Start Where You Are: A Guide to Compassionate Living* (Boston: Shambhala, 1994).

Ram Dass and Paul Gorman, *How Can I Help? Stories and Reflections on Service* (New York: Knopf, 1985).

Michael Edwards and Stephen Post, *The Love That Does Justice: Spiritual Activism in Dialogue with Social Science* (Arcata, CA: Unlimited Love Press, 2008).

Matthew Fox, *A Spirituality Named Compassion: The Healing of the Global Village, Humpty Dumpty, and Us* (Rochester, NY: Inner Traditions International, 1999).

Joanna Macy, *World as Lover, World as Self, Active Hope: How to Face the Mess We're In without Going Crazy* (Berkeley, CA: Parallax Press, 1991).

John Makransky, *Awakening through Love* (Somerville, MA: Wisdom Publications, 2007).

Sharon Salzberg, *Loving Kindness: The Revolutionary Art of Happiness* (Boston: Shambhala, 1995).

Guest Speakers, Field Trips, and Retreats

chapter
TEN

Practicing contemplative methods in the classroom on uncomfortable chairs under fluorescent lights is possible, as the examples in this book demonstrate, but practicing in a space that celebrates nature or contemplative design and encourages calmness, clarity, and insight can be a powerful experience that frequently takes the practice deeper. Field trips provide the opportunity for experiencing such environments, from the stillness of a Japanese garden to engagement with monks in a monastery committed to meditation and service. One professor took his students to Vietnam to experience suffering and the contemplative calm that can accompany the relief of suffering.

Guest speakers or teachers can also deepen connections with the contemplative world outside the classroom, placing the practices in a larger cultural context. Guests who represent contemplative traditions or teach practice can enrich the class; they can offer guidance that the class teacher may not be able to. Some professors invited guests to lecture on the philosophy or history of a practice; some guest teachers taught meditation and other practices, relieving the professor of that responsibility. Inviting guests can provide expert introduction to a variety of practices in many traditions. Since personal practice is so important, these visitors can provide important opportunities for students to examine and expand their own practices.

Steven Nuss, associate professor of music at Colby College, wanted to find ways to help students bridge the historically constructed divide between academic pursuits in music and science and contemplative practices. He designed Contemplating Music through Contemplative Practice, which emphasized active engagement in contemplative practices. There was no assumption of conversion to or belief in particular theologies or in the spiritual or physical efficacy of any contemplative practice, but the students were unanimous in their feeling that one could not just talk or theorize about contemplative practice: at whatever level, with whatever level of conviction, and despite any misgivings or self-consciousness, contemplative practice definitely needed to be practiced.

To complement the students' practice, Nuss invited guest speakers. Christiane Guillois, a noted local authority on Zen meditation and hatha yoga, offered sessions on each of these practices. Shakuhachi artist Carl Dimow performed for the class. James Martin, author of *The Jesuit Guide to (Almost) Everything*, provided valuable insights into the mechanics and psychology of the Roman Catholic Rosary and the Liturgy of the Hours. Three Colby professors also visited the class: Nikki Singh (religious studies) provided explanations of the intersections between Hindu iconography and mantra recitation. Anindyo Roy (English) gave a presentation on complementary and competing cultural constructions of the Divine. Ankeney Weitz (art history) offered insights into the historical evolution and meaning of Hindu and Zen Buddhist iconography. The class also took a field trip to a local Russian Orthodox church to observe the mechanics of the liturgy and make a firsthand detailed study of the altar screen.

Can contemplative practice, which cultivates seeing things as they really are, prevent actions with destructive outcomes? In a course on life-changing decisions made by poets, artists, Manhattan Project scientists, and suicide bombers, Carole Cavanaugh at Middlebury College taught her students to track their own decision making in the journals they kept on their daily practice of mindfulness. Early in the course, students had the optional but strongly encouraged opportunity to attend a weekend retreat at Blue Cliff, a monastery founded by Thich Nhat Hanh in Pine Bush, New York, for people who wish to cultivate the art and practices of engaged Buddhism through mindful living. The students had the opportunity to learn mindfulness and talk with monastics about their own life-changing choices. Each student wrote a personal essay on the retreat experience.

Inés Hernández-Avila, professor of Native American studies at the University of California, Davis, used meditation and other contemplative practices in her course, Ometeotl Moyocoyatzin and Ancient Nahuatl Contemplative Practice. Her intent was to demonstrate how Native American religious traditions have within them contemplative practices that honor both the individual and the community, both personal and collective autonomy. She was especially interested in exploring with her students, and in her research, how creativity is linked to autonomy, and how both of these, in effect, are nurtured by contemplation. Throughout the course, she emphasized the importance indigenous peoples give to their relationship to the earth, how the earth is sacred, and how the earth sings, dances, teaches, heals, and bears witness.

The course included guest speakers and field trips. One guest was Felipe Molina, coauthor with Larry Evers of *Yaqui Deer Songs/Maso Bwikam* (1987), who spoke to the class and visited with the students. He participated in the meditation at the beginning of class and then led the students through his own version, where he asked them to close their eyes and take the time to thank each of their organs as he named them and noted what they did for them. He spoke about teaching in the Yoeme (or Yaqui) traditional way and related his experiences as someone who evolved into a master deer singer, one who sings traditional Yaqui poetry as another dances wearing a deerskin and antlers in a "deer dance," one of the most important vehicles of Yaqui cultural survival. He and Juan A. Avila Hernăndez, a Yoeme historian and deer singer, sang several songs for the students, as Felipe explained that they were calling the Deer Spirit into the classroom; in their last song, they sang for the deer to return to his place in the Flower World. Felipe's text was brought into being with these songs, and the students were able to see how sacred song and dance are themselves forms of contemplative practice. Felipe and Juan allowed the students to look at and touch the instruments they used, all of which represented parts of the deer, such as his breathing and his heartbeat. Prior to Felipe's visit, Juan had already come to talk to the students about Yoeme history from both a scholarly perspective and the oral tradition, from the perspective of what is called the Elders' Truth. The relationship between the Nahuatl and Yoeme understandings of the word—the sacred word, the spiritual word, and the creative word—were brought to life in these visits.

There were several field trips, including one to another elder's home for a sweat lodge ceremony. Bill Wright is a traditional Patwin spiritual leader, called by many an Indian doctor. The university sits on ancestral Patwin land. Students were not required to attend the ceremony, and some did not go, but many attended. It was a positive experience for the students who went, an introduction to an ancient contemplative practice original to this hemisphere. The ceremony consisted of four rounds, with songs and prayers for each round, as well as doctoring by Bill Wright.

In Linda Patrik's course on social justice ethics at Union College, students studied how nonprofit organizations used contemplative practices for engaging in social justice work. The course was structured around four field trips to non-profit organizations that use contemplation in tackling the social justice problems of incarceration, gender discrimination, violence in the schools, and discrimination against Native Americans and other minorities: the National Prison Sangha Project based in Woodstock, New York; the Audre Lord Project in Brooklyn, New York; the Oneness-in-Peace Center in Hudson, New York; and the Grafton Peace Pagoda in Grafton, New York. A guest also spoke to the class about the Urban Grief Project, a volunteer effort to provide immediate grief counseling after inci-dences of gun violence in Albany, New York. The five nonprofit organizations represent different spiritual traditions and use different contemplative methods in their social justice work. The range of contemplative methods was fairly broad, from the quiet sitting practices of Zen Buddhism to the dynamic dance and drumming practices of black churches, from the walking practices of Catholicism and Nipponzan Myohoji to the night sky contemplative practices of Islam. Because students were introduced to a wide range of contemplative methods, they not only explored the ethical theories and contemplative practices of unfamiliar spiri-tual traditions but also learned about the contemplative dimensions of their own religious traditions. Many of the students were excited to experience their own religion—Catholic, Jewish, Muslim, or black church—in a new way by study-ing the contemplative methods connected to their tradition. Each student wrote a term paper about the applied ethics of altruism or the contemplative methods of one of the nonprofit organizations. In conjunction with their research for their term papers, students formed groups of five, and each group designed a website for one of the nonprofits (for an example, see https://sites.google.com/site /groupaudrelorde/home).

Exploring the connection between practice and social change in a religion department, Rebecca Gould at Middlebury College described her course, Practicing for Life: Contemplative Practice and Social Change, in this way:

> This course is a scholarly endeavor that includes an invitation into experiential education. We will examine the lives of those who have dedicated themselves to various kinds of social change (such as peace work, civil rights, and environmental protection). Many individuals who have taken up the call for social change have also maintained some kind of contemplative practice. We will examine the relationship between contemplative practice and transformational work with attention to such figures as King, Gandhi, Pema Chodron, Thich Nhat Hanh, and Thomas Merton. Students also will be asked to participate regularly in some forms of (non-religious) meditation practice.

The course included two field trips of two nights each. The field trips were opportunities to do some intensive learning by following the patterns of monks at the Weston Priory and the teachers and students at Karmê Chöling.

The visit to Weston Priory, a community of Benedictine monks in Vermont, was first. There was no requirement to attend any religious services, and students could use that time alternatively for reading and personal reflection. Gould did advise them that the more they attended the various services, the better they would understand Benedictine monastic life, and most of the students went to most of the five services each day. They also did outdoor labor together for several hours and ate silent meals of home-harvested food with the monks. A highlight was the opportunity to interview the monks. Students asked probing questions, and the monks responded in kind with their own questions.

After reading Thich Nhat Hanh and Joanna Macy on Buddhism and ecological issues, they traveled to Karmê Chöling. In rural Vermont, Karmê Chöling is a Shambhala meditation retreat center and community for people from all walks of life "to connect with their basic goodness and the basic goodness of others." It was founded by Tibetan teacher Chogyam Trungpa. Experienced teachers there led meditative practice and introduced students to the challenge of longer and more frequent meditation sessions, which provided good fodder for discussion. In addition, Gould worked with the leader to create a "question night" so that some of the younger, long-term residents and staff could talk about their own lives and practice, including what brought them there.

Both experiences required rising very early, not typical for students, but these students—of many faiths and none—were even positive about the 5:00 a.m. matins chanting service at the priory. The field trips also enabled the students to have casual time with each other and to experience their professor in a more informal mode, wearing jeans and talking about her sheep. Gould said, "I was both proud and inspired that without my prodding, the students were talking about the reading, processing what they had just experienced, and beginning to tie together the threads of the course."

Contemplative practices, including field trips, may seem natural methods for courses in social justice or music or Native American studies, but do they a have a place in mathematical inquiry? At Florida Atlantic University, Jacqueline Fewkes and Terje Hoim found that one way to explore the connection to the contemplative is through the cultural study of mathematics. Their course, Ethnomathematics: A Contemplative Approach, addressed how mathematical knowledge has been constructed within a variety of value systems, with culturally specific meanings and spiritual implications. Practices included in-class contemplation exercises, a mandala creation exercise, journal writing, and a field trip to the Morikami Japanese Gardens in Boca Raton, Florida. A number of different meditation gardens at the site provided good locations for contemplation, and the students spent time in them cultivating mindfulness. As a group, they then did origami exercises and reflected in this calm place on how to think differently about the relationship of culture and mathematics.

In Contemplative Practices in Zen Buddhist and Hellenistic Philosophies, a course taught by Graham Parkes at the University of Hawaii, students engaged in contemplative practices and kept a journal documenting their experiences. They were required to sit zazen together in the classroom at every meeting and at home on their own. During the last week of the semester, to deepen their practice and witness practice outside the academic setting, they attended a formal twenty-five-minute sitting at the Diamond Sangha Zen Center in Honolulu.

Leigh E. Schmidt at Princeton University developed a seminar on the cultural history of American spirituality that focused on critical engagement with primary and secondary texts and included experience with a range of contemplative practices. The class allowed Schmidt and his students to confront the tension between insider (practitioners in a tradition) and outsider perspectives. That tension was especially highlighted through a visit to Pendle Hill, a Quaker retreat center for contemplation on the outskirts of Philadelphia, one of the most influential retreat centers in the making of twentieth-century American spiritualities. Having spent much time reading such Quaker luminaries as Thomas Kelly and Douglas Steere, the class was ready to meet the living heirs of that contemplative tradition. The dean at Pendle Hill, along with one of the community's spiritual nurturers, met with them for an afternoon of extended discussion. They also toured the grounds, including the primary worship space, the library, and two unoccupied hermitages. Meeting with people who took the centering practices of contemplation so seriously was instructive for the students. They ended the day with a trip to Theosophical Society founder Madame Blavatsky's Philadelphia home, which has been turned into a trendy restaurant with an occult bookstore. It seemed to them an appropriate place to end the seminar, poised between history and contemporary practice.

Stephen Prothero's Hinduism in America course at Boston University explored the transplantation and transformation of the ideas, institutions, and practices of Hinduism in the United States, including the ways that Asian Americans and European Americans alike have adapted Hinduism to American circumstances and in the process changed the course of American religious history and the history of Hinduism. Prothero and his students visited Hindu sites in the Boston area and then analyzed their experiences.

Of the various methods Prothero used in this course, he says that the site visits were particularly productive: "I told the students that they were to go as participant observers. In other words, they were there to participate as long as they felt comfortable doing so and to observe." The visits gave students a flavor of spiritual practice and an opportunity to engage in it without mandating any particular practice or rite. One Catholic student, respectful of other traditions and eager to learn about Hinduism, went to a devotional service at a Hare Krishna temple. She participated in *aarti*, a fire rite, but then decided to be just an observer when she felt she might be doing something contrary to her Catholic faith. The students' experiences differed widely, from being deeply moved to being "bored to tears," which gave them the opportunity to discuss what makes a spiritual experience rich or shallow.

Steven Emmanuel's students at Virginia Wesleyan College went beyond the local field trip model to spend twelve days in Vietnam as part of his course, Peaceful Steps: Service Learning in a Global Context. They were exposed to a different cultural environment and a different kind of suffering from what they knew. Before leaving, the students learned mindful breathing in order to be more aware of the thoughts and feelings that would arise in response to their service experience, give structure to the process of reflecting on their experience, cultivate a sense of interconnectedness with those they would serve, and develop a greater capacity for deep listening and compassionate action. In Vietnam, they visited monasteries and learned how the monks perform community service. The students then participated in projects in Da Nang and nearby Quang Nam province. When they returned, they processed what they had seen and done. They said that the practice had helped them break down walls of separation and the feeling of being different. It helped them develop a greater sense of empathy and compassion. They also noted that being "fully present" helped to alleviate their anxieties and concerns. They said it made them feel more connected and whole. Emmanuel says that the idea of mindful service is a relatively unexplored area that holds much potential for curricular development.

All of these teachers reported that they particularly enjoyed these courses, reflecting that the field trips contributed in interesting ways to the students' understanding of the material. Many also said that by traveling to a place together and practicing together, they got to know each other better than they would have in the classroom, which significantly enriched the experience of the class.

Although these field trips were not actually pilgrimages, most were journeys to sacred destinations (monasteries, gardens, temples) and had the potential for the kind of awakening that one can experience through pilgrimage.

CONCLUSION

Pilgrimage is a journey not only to a destination but into the lives of others, and into community and the world and what we can possibly share with others and learn from them. "Going out," said John Muir, is "really going in." It can shake the pilgrim or student out of conventional ways of seeing and knowing. For students in contemplative courses, what we are calling field trips could help them, as Rilke had said, "dive into your increasing depths where life calmly gives out its own secret."

Resources

Phil Cousineau, *The Art of Pilgrimage: The Seeker's Guide to Making Travel Sacred* (Newburyport, MA: Conari Press, 2012).

Jack Kelly and Marsha Kelly, *Sanctuaries: The Complete United States—a Guide to Lodgings in Monasteries, Abbeys, and Retreats* (N.p.).

Conclusion

In this book, we have explored the many ways in which contemplative approaches can transform classrooms and provide a new context for teaching and learning. The development of these practices has been amazing to witness, and we are proud to be part of such a vibrant and meaningful community. We could not possibly have covered all the various practices or all the many amazing examples and practitioners. We hope, though, that the examples will provide a powerful introduction to this fine work and lead to a greater transformation of postsecondary education.

SIMPLE YET RADICAL CHANGE

In the United States, markets allocate goods, with consumers and producers determining prices and providing signals for the allocation of resources. And for many, many goods and services, these markets tend to work very well. However, for goods and services that benefit our entire society, we support them through donations and subsidies. In 2011, Americans gave nearly $300 billion in charitable contributions: 117 million US households, 12 million corporations, 99,000 estates, and 76,000 foundations gave to charities during the year (Nichols, 2012). We provide such support because we believe in the missions of these institutions and want to increase the impact of their programs.

In addition to giving directly, we subsidize a whole host of services and activities provided often, but not always, by the government and financed through taxes. Usually these are services that produce benefits to society at large, outside of those who are directly consuming or producing them. Economists call these benefits "positive externalities" and recognize that free markets likely underprovide these goods without any intervention: subsidizing them increases their use and contributes to the welfare of society at large.

As in many other nations, education in the United States is subsidized. Making basic education available provides the necessary (but not sufficient) conditions for a well-informed population so that a representational democracy can operate, and we maintain a society of individuals who have the basic skills required to join the labor force, act responsibly, and have the tools necessary to meet the many global challenges facing us today. We subsidize education because we believe that it provides profound benefits to our society, challenging students to create lives of meaning and purpose and providing them with the tools to sustain this process for themselves and others. To the extent that we in higher education have forgotten this important mission, we risk collapsing into a fee-for-service industry in which we simply convey information and train narrowly for the workforce.

Virtually all private and public institutions, both two year and four year, subsidize their students' educations through donations, grants, or public funding. For example, in 2009, Connecticut's fifty-five thousand community college students paid for 21 percent of the total cost of their education—the highest rate in the past twenty years (Thomas, 2010). At private liberal arts colleges and large universities, subsidies are provided at just about every level; for example, the Harvard Law School website states that "every student enrolled at Harvard Law School receives an implicit subsidy from the School's endowment and the annual gifts made to the Law School by generous benefactors, in that the tuition fee covers only about 60 percent of the total cost of providing a quality legal education to each student."

Why don't we expect students to pay the full cost of their education? If the only goal of postsecondary education were to provide accurate information and vocational training, then most students would simply pay the full cost and receive the return in terms of higher income throughout their careers, just like an investment in a financial market. If all schools are doing is training for the labor market and signaling to future employers, then subsidies do not make sense. Sure, some subsidies would be available in recognition of profound differences in preparation and access, but we would not have reason to subsidize all students. An education that provides skills to serve the labor market is vital for individuals, the economy, and our society. Providing the means to engage in meaningful work is obviously important.

However, the reason we continue to subsidize postsecondary education is to produce benefits beyond those that simply accrue to the individual student through vocational training and employment. Education must create environments for students to inquire and challenge themselves about the meaning of their lives and the lives of others; this is the primary mission of education. Our courses must offer challenging reflections on how the material relates to students' values, allowing them to discern the nature of the impact they want to have in the world. We must return to this mission and attend to it throughout our classes, student services, career counseling—all aspects of higher education. This is precisely what contemplative modes of learning encourage.

Christina Elliott Sorum, writing about this issue from the perspective of liberal arts in 2005, said, "It seems to me that our mission—why we teach what we teach—is muddled, especially with regard to the questions of whether we should or can teach values and of why the liberal arts are relevant beyond the teaching of skills" (Sorum, 2005, p. 27). From the vantage point of 2013, as this book is being written, I (D.B.) agree with her statement: "It is no longer clear to our students—I fear, in part, because it is not clear to us—that the liberal arts prepare us to be better persons and better citizens and leaders in today's world" (p. 38).

This mission of challenging our students to inquire into what it means to be a good citizen of the world must be supported and subsidized, since all beings benefit from it. We subsidize our students' education since that is how we create and support a vibrant and ethical society. We have the means to do this: to complement our teaching by integrating students' sense of engagement and purpose directly into their studies. We believe the practices we have outlined and described in this book can be the vehicle toward this essential goal.

The first step in this process is for students to become clear about what is most deeply meaningful to them. What are their values? It is vital that we provide exercises and time for students to reflect on how the material in their courses affects and challenges their own sense of meaning. Along with guidance in this inquiry, students need to be supported in learning to attend to the implications and consequences of their actions; without an understanding of the impact our behavior has on ourselves and on others, we are destined to create harm and suffering. This requires clarity and sustained attention; expedient gains from abandoning meaning seem so alluring, and actions based in violence, lust, or greed have such obvious costs. But once this inquiry is established and supported, students can begin to focus on their intention and alter behavior that is not in accord with it.

To support our students in the discovery of what means most deeply to them and provide them the tools to live out that meaning in the world is the primary mission of education. Analytical thinking, fostered and developed so well by academic institutions, also benefits from the complement of these contemplative approaches—enabling students to relate their learning directly to their own lives and act in ways that they value, deepening their understanding of the material they are studying. We need to renew our commitment to creating institutions that foster this inquiry throughout all of their activities.

While this book has stressed classroom teaching, all facets of postsecondary education contribute to learning. The comprehensive resources provided by institutions are a key strength of residential colleges and universities. The many professionals throughout higher education are essential to the educational mission—not tangentially connected to the core of learning—and without them, one of the most powerful arguments for the continuation of residential education will be lost. The intentional integration of course work and broad student services provides a full educational environment; increasing attention to student services creates an integrated field of experience across students' curricular, residential, and social lives. After all, everything is education—every action and interaction is an opportunity for learning and cultivation. There is no such thing as "extracurricular" activities: every act is cultivating something. The question we must ask is: What is being cultivated?

The fullness of their education is expressed through students' whole lives, through the ways in which they actually live. If we cannot create greater connections between traditional curricular activities and "extracurricular" activities, we will have lost a great opportunity to foster communities of well-being and greater connection among our students. As important as it is to create classroom environments in which students inquire deeply into meaning, connection, and purpose, we must also collectively pay attention to the time students are not in class. Students are actually in class only about fifteen hours a week. Apart from sleep (if they sleep!), there remain about one hundred hours in the week. Many of these non-class-time hours are taken up with lab work, reading, and homework, but what of those hours not spent on activities directly related to courses? It is at these times that students interact with one another, establishing, in effect, a rich laboratory that engages their action and learning in their communities. Paying keen attention to what students are cultivating during this time will support their development of living rich, meaningful lives. Certainly, for residential colleges and universities, this is a major question and challenge.

Fortunately, colleagues in health, counseling, community engagement, residential life, administration, athletics, career services, and development are developing methods of integrating contemplative practices into their work with students. Through their work and our united purpose of challenging and fostering student change, we can build institutions that will transform education. Joined together with an intention to create environments in which students develop and sustain meaning and connection, we can provide a powerful purpose for educational institutions. We look forward to the continued collaboration across all facets of our work together.

RESOURCES

Support for the development of contemplative practices is available from many sources. We hope that the suggestions we have made throughout this book help in this regard. We cannot stress enough how important it is to have significant experience with the practices that you introduce to your students. With regard to developing practices for the classroom, a number of resources are helpful.

○ The Center for Contemplative Mind in Society focuses on higher education and has created an association for those interested in these practices and includes members from all aspects of higher education. Information about membership can be found at www.contemplativemind.org/programs/acmhe. The center sponsors a yearly conference, an academic retreat, and a week-long curriculum development program. These are geared to the development of contemplative practices in all aspects of higher education. More information, along with reports, lectures, and recordings, for example, are available at its website, www.contemplativemind.org.

○ Harold Roth and colleagues have developed a contemplative studies program at Brown University that sponsors lectures, conducts summer session courses, and provides an integrated major for students covering areas in the sciences, humanities, and the creative arts. The Contemplative Studies Initiative pursues an active program of contemplative scientific research through the Clinical and Affective Neuroscience Lab, the Translational Neuroscience Lab, and the Laboratory for Clinical and Perceptual Learning. Student lab members present their research in a biannual research symposium and publish scientific articles of their work. More information is available at www.brown.edu/academics/contemplative-studies.

○ Naropa University, in Boulder, Colorado, has a low-residency master's contemplative education program, designed to foster contemplative pedagogy for K–12 teachers as well as college instructors. More information on this program can be found at www.naropa.edu/admissions/explore/contemplative-education.php.

○ The Mindfulness in Education Network sponsors annual conferences and acts to connect practitioners from all aspects of education in the use of contemplative modes of teaching and learning. You can find more information at www.mindfuled.org.

WELL-WISHING

We hope that this book has provided useful information for the fostering and deepening of contemplative modes in higher education. Through these practices, may you transform yourself and your students' lives, providing a means to sustain lifelong inquiries into meaning and action.

AFTERWORD

Arthur Zajonc

Over the past twenty years, a quiet revolution in higher education has been taking place to which this book contributes. Students at colleges and universities around the world are increasingly settling their bodies, stilling their minds, calming their emotions, and schooling their attention by means of contemplative practices. Insight and compassion practices complement those designed to strengthen attention and emotional balance so that complexity can be sustained until the epiphany we experience as direct and deep apprehension occurs. In this book, the fruits of twenty years of faculty experimentation with contemplative practices in the classroom and beyond have been gathered together by Daniel Barbezat and Mirabai Bush. They have offered reader-practitioners the guidance they need to make contemplative pedagogy part of any course or to use meditation in student life and counseling.

American higher education today too often neglects the crucial role of reflection where the tempo of intelligence slows and the lines of a poem or the colors of a painting evoke feelings and perceptions inaccessible to rapid analysis alone. Contemplative exercises are a crucial form of experiential learning where time is taken to pause and the individual or entire class drops into silence in order to release their attention from conventional preoccupations, redirect it, and then live fully into the content at hand. As Rainer Maria Rilke wrote to the nineteen-year-old Franz Kappus on July 16, 1903, the answers to questions are important only if you can live them: "And the point is, to live everything." Contemplative engagement permits us to do exactly that: to live the poem, the painting, the natural phenomenon, poverty. If we fail to animate our ideas, to bring them to life through inner experience, we will be imprisoned in abstractions, and our knowing will lack the vitality of truly embodied understanding.

Mirabai Bush and Daniel Barbezat have masterfully guided us into the territory of quiet reflection and contemplative engagement, which leads to an intimate form of understanding that is the central aspiration of all inquiry: direct perception or insight. To my mind, such knowing overarches the split between fact and value, the scientific and aesthetic. We experience contemplative knowing not as the manipulation of an equation or the descent into technique alone but as the means by which we can know things whole; it is a knowing that is at once entirely personal and at the same time objectively true. No scientist has made a discovery any other way; no artist has achieved greatness by any other means. No education is complete without learning the discipline and delight of contemplative engagement, inquiry, and insight, and I know of no better guides than my colleagues and friends Mirabai and Dan.

Arthur Zajonc is professor emeritus of physics, Amherst College, and president of Mind and Life Institute.

REFERENCES

Ackerman, D. (1991). *A natural history of the senses.* New York, NY: Random House.

Ambrose, S. A., Bridges, M. W., DiPietro, M., Lovett, M. C., & Norman, M. K. (2010). *How learning works: Seven research-based principles for smart teaching.* Hoboken, NJ: Wiley.

Apfelbaum, E. P., Norton, M. I., & Sommers, S. R. (2012). Racial color blindness emergence, practice, and implications. *Current Directions in Psychological Science, 21,* 205–209. doi:10.1177/0963721411434980

Arum, R., & Roksa, J. (2010). *Academically adrift: Limited learning on college campuses.* Chicago, IL: University of Chicago Press.

Astin, A. W., Astin, H. S., & Lindholm, J. A. (2010). *Cultivating the spirit: How college can enhance students' inner lives.* San Francisco, CA: Jossey-Bass.

Awbrey, S. M. (2006). *Integrative learning and action: A call to wholeness.* New York, NY: Peter Lang.

Axelrod, R. (1988). The evolution of cooperation. In A. Gromyko & M. Hellman (Eds.), *Breakthrough: Emerging new thinking: Soviet and Western scholars issue a challenge to build a world beyond war* (pp. 185–192). New York, NY: Walker & Company.

Barker, D. (2009). Zen wheelbarrows and collard greens. In M. Schut (Ed.), *Food and faith: Justice, joy, and daily bread.* New York, NY: Morehouse Publishing.

Berlia, B. (2012). *Embodied learning: Integrating the body into feminist pedagogy.* Unpublished manuscript.

Birdwhistell, R. L. (1970). *Kinesics and context: Essays on body motion communication.* Philadelphia: University of Pennsylvania Press.

Birnie, K., Speca, M., & Carlson, L. E. (2010). Exploring self-compassion and empathy in the context of mindfulness-based stress reduction (MBSR). *Stress and Health, 26*(5), 359–371. doi:10.1002/smi.1305

Bonilla-Silva, E. (2006). *Racism without racists: Color-blind racism and the persistence of racial inequality in the United States.* Totowa, NJ: Rowman & Littlefield.

Boorstein, S. (1996). *Don't just do something; sit there*. San Francisco, CA: Harper One.

Brady, M. (2009). *Right listening: Contemplative practices for fostering kindness and compassion*. Langley, WA: Paideia Press.

Cage, J. (1961). *Silence: Lectures and writings*. Middletown, CT: Wesleyan University Press.

Cage, J., & Retallack, J. (2011). *Musicage: Cage muses on words * art * music*. Middletown, CT: Wesleyan University Press.

Childs, C. (2007). *The animal dialogues: Uncommon encounters in the wild*. New York, NY: Little, Brown.

Chugh, D., & Bazerman, M. (2007). Bounded awareness: What you fail to see can hurt you. *Mind and Society*, *6*, 1–18.

Collins, B. (1998). *Picnic, lightning*. Pittsburgh, PA: University of Pittsburgh Press.

Csikszentmihalyi, M., & LeFevre, J. (1989). Optimal experience in work and leisure. *Journal of Personality and Social Psychology*, *56*(5), 815–822.

Cutler, H. (2009, May 1). The mindful monk: The Fourteenth Dalai Lama bridges the gap between East and West. *Psychology Today*. http://www.psychologytoday.com/articles/200105/the-mindful-monk

Cytowic, R. E. (2002). *Synethesia: A union of the senses*. Cambridge, MA: MIT Press.

Cytowic, R. E. (2003). The clinician's paradox: Believing those you must not trust. *Journal of Consciousness Studies*, *10*(9–10), 157–166.

Damasio, A. (2000). *Descartes' error: Emotion, reason and the human brain*. New York, NY: Penguin Books.

Davidson, R. J., Kabat-Zinn, J., Schumacher, J., Rosenkranz, M., Muller, D., Santorelli, S. F., Urbanowski, F., . . . Sheridan, J. F. (2003). Alterations in brain and immune function produced by mindfulness meditation. *Psychosomatic Medicine*, *65*(4), 564–570.

Dawkins, R. (1989). *The selfish gene*. New York, NY: Oxford University Press.

Dewey, J. (1986). Experience and education. *Educational Forum*, *50*(3), 241–252. doi:10.1080/00131728609335764

Dreyfus, G. (2013). Is mindfulness present-centred and non-judgmental? A discussion of the cognitive dimensions of mindfulness. In J. Williams & J. KabatZinn (Eds.), *Mindfulness: Diverse perspectives on its meaning, origins and applications* (pp. 41–54). London: Routledge.

Dustin, C. A., & Ziegler, J. E. (2007). *Practicing mortality: Art, philosophy, and contemplative seeing*. London: Palgrave Macmillan.

Dyrbye, L. N., Thomas, M. R., & Shanafelt, T. D. (2006). Systematic review of depression, anxiety, and other indicators of psychological distress among U.S. and Canadian medical students. *Academic Medicine*, *81*(4), 354–373. Retrieved from http://journals.lww.com/academicmedicine/Fulltext/2006/04000/Systematic_Review_of_Depression,_Anxiety,_and.9.aspx.

Easterlin, R. A. (1974). Does economic growth improve the human lot? Some empirical evidence. In P. David & M. Reder (Eds.), *Nations and households in economic growth: Essays in honor of Moses Abramovitz* (pp. 89–125). New York, NY: Academic Press.

Easterlin, R. A. (1995). Will raising the incomes of all increase the happiness of all? *Journal of Economic Behavior and Organization, 27*(1), 35–47. doi:10.1016/0167 −2681(95)00003-B

Eck, D. L. (1993). The challenge of pluralism. *Nieman Reports, 47*(2).

Elbow, P. (1998). *Writing without teachers* (2nd ed.). New York, NY: Oxford University Press.

Epstein, M. (1995). *Thoughts without a thinker.* Cambridge, MA: Basic Books.

Evers, L., & Molina, F. (1987). *Yaqui Deer Songs/Maso Bwikam: A Native American Poetry.* Tucson: University of Arizona Press.

Falk, A., & Knell, M. (2004). Choosing the Joneses: Endógenous goals and reference standards. *Scandinavian Journal of Economics, 106*(3), 417–435. doi:10.1111/j.0347 −0520.2004.00370.x

Feig, K. G. (1979). *Hitler's death camps: The sanity of madness.* New York, NY: Holmes & Meier, 1979.

Fischer, N. (2004). *Taking our places: The Buddhist path to truly growing up.* New York, NY: HarperCollins.

Foucault, M. (1988). *Madness and civilization: A history of insanity in the Age of Reason.* New York: Random House.

Frank, R. H. (1988). *Passions within reason: The strategic role of the emotions.* New York, NY: Norton.

Freire, P. (1970). *Pedagogy of the oppressed.* New York, NY: Continuum Press.

Gadamer, H. G. (1976). *Philosophical hermeneutics.* Berkeley: University of California Press.

Gardner, H. (2000). *The disciplined mind: Beyond facts and standardized tests, the K–12 education that every child deserves.* New York, NY: Penguin Books.

Gardner, H. (2004). *Frames of mind: The theory of multiple intelligences.* New York, NY: Basic Books. Retrieved from http://search.ebscohost.com/login.aspx?direct=true&db =psyh&AN=2004–18831–000&site=ehost-live.

Ghiselin, M. T. (1974). *The economy of nature and the evolution of sex.* Berkeley: University of California Press.

Ginsberg, A. (2001). *Deliberate prose: Selected essays, 1952–1995.* New York, NY: Harper Perennial.

Gintis, H., Bowles, S., Bowd, R., & Fehr, E. (2003). Explaining altruistic behavior in humans. *Evolution and Human Behavior, 24,* 153–172.

Goldberg, N. (2010). *Writing down the bones: Freeing the writer within* (Exp. ed.). Boston, MA: Shambhala.

Goleman, D. (2006). *Emotional intelligence.* New York, NY: Bantam Books.

Gould, S. J. (1996). *The mismeasurement of man.* New York, NY: Norton.

Grace, F. (2009). Breathing in suffering, breathing out compassion. *Spirituality in Higher Education Newsletter, 5*(2), 8.

Greenwald, A. G., & Banaji, M. R. (1995). Implicit social cognition: Attitudes, self-esteem, and stereotypes. *Psychological Review, 102*(1), 4–27. doi:10.1037/0033–295X.102.1.4

Hahn, T. N. (1991). *Peace is every step: The path of mindfulness in everyday life.* New York, NY: Bantam Books.

Halifax, J. (2008). *Being with dying: Cultivating compassion and fearlessness in the presence of death.* Boston, MA: Shambhala.

Hamilton, W. D. (1964). The genetical evolution of social behavior. *Journal of Theoretical Biology, 37,* 1–52.

Hayes, S. C., Barnes-Holmes, D., & Roche, B. (2001). *Relational frame theory: A post-Skinnerian account of human language and cognition.* New York, NY: Springer.

Haynes, D. J. (2003). *Art lessons: Meditations on the creative life.* New York, NY: Basic Books.

Heiliwell, J., & Putnam, R. (2004). The social context of well-being. *Philosophical Transactions of the Royal Society of London. Series B: Biological Sciences, 359*(1449), 1435–1446. doi:10.1098/rstb.2004.1522

His Holiness the Dalai Lama. (2001). *Ethics for the new millennium.* New York, NY: Riverhead Books.

His Holiness the Dalai Lama. (2011). *Beyond religion: Ethics for a whole world.* New York: Houghton Mifflin Harcourt.

Hölzel, B. K., Lazar, S. W., Gard, T., Schuman-Olivier, Z., Vago, D. R., & Ott, U. (2011). How does mindfulness meditation work? Proposing mechanisms of action from a conceptual and neural perspective. *Perspectives on Psychological Science, 6*(6), 537–559. doi:10.1177/1745691611419671

Hutcherson, C. A., Seppala, E. M., & Gross, J. J. (2008). Loving-kindness meditation increases social connectedness. *Emotion, 8*(5), 720–724.

Immordino-Yang, M. H., & Damasio, A. (2008). We feel, therefore we learn: The relevance of affective and social neuroscience to education. In M. H. Immordino-Yang (Ed.), *The Jossey-Bass reader on the brain and learning* (pp. 183–198). San Francisco, CA: Jossey-Bass. Retrieved from http://search.ebscohost.com/login.aspx?direct=true&db=psyh&AN=2007-19412-012&site=ehost-live.

Jacobs, T. L., Epel, E. S., Lin, J., Blackburn, E. H., Wolkowitz, O. M., Bridwell, D. A., Zanesco, A. P., & Saron, E. D. (2011). Intensive meditation training, immune cell telomerase activity, and psychological mediators. *Psychoneuroendocrinology, 36*(5), 664–681.

Jain, S., Shapiro, S. L., Swanick, S., Roesch, S. C., Mills, P. J., Bell, I., & Schwartz, G.E.R. (2007). A randomized controlled trial of mindfulness meditation versus relaxation training: Effects on distress, positive states of mind, rumination, and distraction. *Annals of Behavioral Medicine, 33*(1), 11–21.

James, W. (1890). *The principles of psychology.* New York, NY: Holt.

Kahneman, D., & Deaton, A. (2010). High income improves evaluation of life but not emotional well-being. *PNAS, 107*(38), 6489–6493.

Kahneman, D., & Tversky, A. (1984). Choices, values, and frames. *American Psychologist, 39*(4), 341–350. doi:10.1037/0003–066X.39.4.341

Katz, H. N. (1997, August). Personal journals in law school externship programs: Improving pedagogy. *Thomas M. Cooley Journal of of Practical and Clinical Law,* 1–25.

Kavale, K. A., & Forness, S. R. (1987). Substance over style: Assessing the efficacy of modality testing and teaching. *Exceptional Children, 54*(3), 228–239.

Kerouac, J. (1993). "Essentials of spontaneous prose." In *The portable beat reader.* New York, NY: Viking Press.

Knight, J., Song, L., & Gunatilaka, R. (2009). Subjective well-being and its determinants in rural China. *China Economic Review, 20*(4), 635–649.

Konow, J., & Earley, J. (2008). The hedonistic paradox: Is Homo economicus happier? *Journal of Public Economics, 92*(1–2), 1–33.

Kroll, K. (Ed.). (2010). *Contemplative teaching and learning.* New Directions for Community Colleges, no. 151. San Francisco, CA: Jossey-Bass.

Kuhn, P., Kooreman, P., Soetevent, A., & Kapteyn, A. (2011). The effects of lottery prizes on winners and their neighbors: Evidence from the Dutch postcode lottery. *American Economic Review, 101*(5), 2226–2247.

Langer, E. J. (1989). *Mindfulness.* Cambridge, MA: Da Capo Press.

Langer, E. J. (1997). *The power of mindful learning.* Reading, MA: Addison-Wesley.

Lazar, S. W., Kerr, C. E., Wasserman, R. H., Gray, J. R., Greve, D. N., Treadway, M. T., McGarvey, M., et al. (2005). Meditation experience is associated with increased cortical thickness. *NeuroReport, 16*(17). Retrieved from http://journals.lww.com /neuroreport/Fulltext/2005/11280/Meditation_experience_is_associated_with _increased.5.aspx.

Lewis, H. R. (2006). *Excellence without a soul: How a great university forgot education.* New York, NY: Public Affairs Press.

Linden, G., Kraemer, K., & Dedrick, J. (2009, March). Who captures value in a global innovation network? The case of Apple's iPod. *Communications of the ACM, 52*(3), 140–144.

Listening Center. (2009). *The sacred art of listening.* http://www.sacredlistening.com /tlc_listening101.htm

Luttmer, E.F.P. (2005). Neighbors as negatives: Relative earnings and well-being. *Quarterly Journal of Economics, 120*(3), 963–1002.

Lutz, A., Brefczynski-Lewis, J., Johnstone, T., & Davidson, R. J. (2008). Regulation of neural circuitry by compassion meditation: Effects of meditative expertise. *PLoS One, 3*(3), e1897.

Lutz, A., Dunne, D., & Davidson, R. J. (2007). Meditation and the neuroscience of consciousness: and introduction. In P. D. Zalazo, M. Moscovitch & E. Thompson

(Eds.), *The Cambridge handbook of consciousness*. Cambridge: Cambridge University Press.

Lutz, A., Slagter, H. A., Rawlings, N. B., Francis, A. D., Greischar, L. L., & Davidson, R. J. (2009). Mental training enhances attentional stability: Neural and behavioral evidence. *Journal of Neuroscience, 29*(42), 13418–13427.

MacLean, K. A., Ferrer, E., Aichele, S. R., Bridwell, D. A., Zanesco, A. P., Jacobs, T. L., King, B. G., & Saron, C. D. (2010). Intensive meditation training improves perceptual discrimination and sustained attention. *Psychological Science, 21*(6), 829–839.

Marx, K., & Engels, F. (1902). *Wage-labor and capital*. New York, NY: Labor News Company.

Mehrabian, A. (1981). *Silent messages: Implicit communication of emotions and attitudes*. Belmont, CA: Wadsworth.

Merton, T. (1995). *The intimate Merton*. New York, NY: HarperCollins.

Merton, T. (1997). *Learning to love: Exploring solitude and freedom*. San Francisco, CA: HarperSanFrancisco.

Mitchell, S. (1990). *Parables and portraits*. New York, NY: Harper.

Murray, M., & Byrne, R. (2005, July). Attention and working memory in insight problem solving. In *Proceedings of the Cognitive Science Society* (pp. 1571–1575). Happauge, NY: Nova Science.

Neff, K. D. (2003). The development and validation of a scale to measure self-compassion. *Self and Identity, 2*(3), 223–250. doi:10.1080/15298860309027

Neisser, U., Boodoo, G., Bouchard, T. J., Boykin, A. W., Brody, N., Ceci, S. J., Halpern, D. F., . . . Urbina, S. (1996). Intelligence: Knowns and unknowns. *American Psychologist, 51*(2), 77–101.

Nicklaus, J. (2005). *Golf my way: The instructional classic, revised and updated*. New York, NY: Simon & Schuster.

Nichols, M. (2012). U.S. charitable giving approaches $300 billion in 2011. *Reuters*, June 19. http://www.reuters.com/article/2012/06/19/us-usa-charity-idUSBRE85I05T20120619.

Nielsen, L., & Kaszniak, A. W. (2006). Awareness of subtle emotional feelings: A comparison of long-term meditators and nonmeditators. *Emotion, 6*(3), 392–405.

Nisbett, R. E., & Wilson, T. D. (1977). Telling more than we can know: Verbal reports on mental processes. *Psychological Review, 84*(3), 231–259. doi:10.1037/0033-295X.84.3.231

Ogilvy, J. P. (1996, Fall). The use of journals in legal education: A tool for reflection. *Clinical Law Review*, 55–101.

O'Reilley, M. R. (1998). *Radical presence: Teaching as contemplative practice*. Portsmouth, NH: Heinemann.

Overgaard, M., & Sørensen, T. A. (2004). Introspection distinct from first-order experiences. *Journal of Consciousness Studies, 11*(7–8), 77–95.

Pace, T.W.W., Negi, L. T., Adame, D. D., Cole, S. P., Sivilli, T. I., Brown, T. D., Issa, M. J., & Raison, C. L. (2009). Effect of compassion meditation on neuroendocrine, innate immune and behavioral responses to psychosocial stress. *Psychoneuroendocrinology, 34*(1), 87–98.

Parker, P., & Zajonc, A. (2010). *The heart of higher education A call to renewal.* San Francisco, CA: Jossey-Bass.

Pascual-Leone, A., Amedi, A., Fregni, F., & Merabet, L. B. (2005). The plastic human brain cortex. *Annual Review of Neuroscience, 28,* 377–401.

Piaget, J. (1973). *To understand is to invent: The future of education.* New York, NY: Grossman Publishers.

Potok, C. (1967). *The chosen.* New York, NY: Ballantine Books.

Putnam, R. (2000). *Bowling alone.* New York, NY: Simon & Schuster.

Rilke, R. M. (1993). *Letters to a young poet.* New York, NY: Norton.

Roberts-Wolfe, D., Sacchet, M., & Britton, W. B. (2009, March 26). *Changes in emotional memory recall following mindfulness meditation vs music training: Implications for affective disorders.* Paper presented at the 13th Annual Research Symposium on Mental Health Sciences, Brown Medical School, Providence, RI.

Rodgers, C. (2002). Defining reflection: Another look at John Dewey and reflective thinking. *Teachers College Record, 104*(4), 842–866.

Rogers, S. (2009). *Mindfulness for law students. Using the power of mindfulness to achieve balance and success in law school.* Miami, FL: Mindful Living Press.

Rosser, S. V. (1992, September–October). The gender equation. *Sciences,* 46.

Roth, H. (2008). Against cognitive imperialism: A call for a non-ethnocentric approach to cognitive science and religious studies. *Religion East and West, 8,* 1–23.

Roughgarden, J. (2009). *The genial gene: Deconstructing Darwinian selfishness.* Berkeley: University of California Press.

Schwitzgebel, E. (2004). Introspective training apprehensively defended: Reflections on Titchener's lab manual. *Journal of Consciousness Studies, 11*(7–8), 58–76.

Scribner, D. R. (2000). *Fellows survey.* Retrieved from contemplativemind.org

Searle, J. (1992). *The rediscovery of mind.* Cambridge, MA: MIT Press.

Shapiro, S. L., Brown, K. W., & Astin, J. A. (2008). *Toward the integration of meditation into higher education: A review of research.* Northampton, MA: Center for Contemplative Mind in Society.

Shapiro, S. L., Brown, K. W., & Biegel, G. M. (2007). Teaching self-care to caregivers: Effects of mindfulness-based stress reduction on the mental health of therapists in training. *Training and Education in Professional Psychology, 1*(2), 105–115.

Shapiro, S. L., Schwartz, G. E., & Bonner, G. (1998). Effects of mindfulness-based stress reduction on medical and premedical students. *Journal of Behavioral Medicine, 21*(6), 581–599. doi:10.1023/A:1018700829825

Siegel, D. J. (2007). *The mindful brain: Reflection and attunement in the cultivation of well-being*. New York, NY: Norton.

Simmer-Brown, J. (2011). Training the heart responsibly: Ethical considerations in contemplative teaching. In J. Simmer-Brown & F. Grace (Eds.), *Meditation and the classroom: Contemplative pedagogy for religious studies* (pp. 107–120). Albany, NY: SUNY Press.

Singer, T., Weng, H., Klimecki, O., & Wager, T. (2011). *Neural substrates of compassion*. Paper resented at the International Symposia of Contemplative Studies, Denver, CO.

Slagter, H. A., Lutz, A., Greischar, L. L., Nieuwenhuis, S., & Davidson, R. J. (2009). Theta phase synchrony and conscious target perception: Impact of intensive mental training. *Journal of Cognitive Neuroscience, 21*(8), 1536–1549.

Slagter, H., Lutz, A., Greishar, L., Francis, A. D., Nieuwenhuis, S., Davis, J. M., & Davidson, R. J. (2007). Mental training affects distribution of limited brain resources. *PLoS Biology, 5*(6), 1228–1235.

Stanislavski, K. (1961). *Creating a role*. New York, NY: Routledge.

Sorum, C. E. (2005). The problem of mission: A brief survey of the changing mission of the liberal arts. In *Liberal arts colleges in American higher education: Challenges and opportunities* (pp. 26–39). New York, NY: American Council of Learned Societies.

Stanley, D., Phelps, E., & Banaji, M. (2008). The neural basis of implicit attitudes. *Current Directions in Psychological Science, 17*(2), 164–170. doi:10.1111/j.1467–8721.2008 .00568.x

Sternberg, R. J. (1985). *Beyond IQ: A triarchic theory of human intelligence*. CUP Archive.

Stevenson, B., & Wolfers, J. (2008, Spring). Economic growth and subjective well-being: Reassessing the Easterlin paradox. *Brookings Papers on Economic Activity*, 1–102.

Straight, B. (2002). From Samburu heirloom to new age artifact: The cross-cultural consumption of Mporo marriage beads. *American Anthropologist, NS, 104*(1), 7–21.

Tang, Y.-Y., Ma, Y., Wang, J., Fan, Y., Feng, S., Lu, Q., Yu, Q., et al. (2007). Short-term meditation training improves attention and self-regulation. *Proceedings of the National Academy of Sciences, 104*(43), 17152–17156. doi:10.1073/pnas.0707678104

Taylor, M. C. (2010). *Crisis on campus: A bold plan for reforming our colleges and universities*. New York, NY: Knopf.

Thomas, J. R. (2010, December 8). Community colleges provide returns for students, but state subsidies lag. *CT Mirror*. http://www.ctmirror.com/story/community-colleges -provide-returns-students-state-subsidies-lag.

Thompson, E. (2001). Empathy and consciousness. *Consciousness Studies, 8*(5–7), 1–32.

Titchener, E. B. (1901). *Experimental psychology: A manual of laboratory practice*. New York, NY: Macmillan.

Trivers, R. L. (1971). The evolution of reciprocal altruism. *Quarterly Review of Biology, 46*, 35–47.

Van Dam, N. T., Sheppard, S. C., Forsyth, J. P., & Earleywine, M. (2011). Self-compassion is a better predictor than mindfulness of symptom severity and quality of life in mixed anxiety and depression. *Journal of Anxiety Disorders, 25*(1), 123–130.

van den Hurk, P.A.M., Giommi, F., Gielen, S. C., Speckens, A.E.M., & Barendregt, H. P. (2010). Greater efficiency in attentional processing related to mindfulness meditation. *Quarterly Journal of Experimental Psychology, 63*(6), 1168–1180.

Varela, F., Thompson, E., & Rosch, E. (1991). *The embodied mind.* Cambridge, MA: MIT Press, 1991.

Vermersch, P. (1999). Introspection as practice. *Journal of Consciousness Studies, 6*(2–3), 17–42.

Wadlinger, H. A., & Isaacowitz, D. M. (2011). Fixing our focus: Training attention to regulate emotion. *Personality and Social Psychology Review, 15*(1), 75–102.

Wallace, B. (1999). The Buddhist tradition of Samatha: Methods for refining and examining consciousness. *Journal of Consciousness Studies, 6*(2–3), 175–187.

Wallace, B. A. (2007). *Contemplative science: Where Buddhism and neuroscience converge.* New York, NY: Columbia University Press.

Welch, C. (2002). Appropriating the didjeridu and the sweat lodge: New age baddies and indigenous victims? *Journal of Contemporary Religion, 17*(1), 21–38.

Whitehead, A. N. (1929). *The aims of education.* New York, NY: Free Press.

Wilson, T. D., Lisle, D. J., Schooler, J. W., & Hodges, S. D. (1993). Introspecting about reasons can reduce post-choice satisfaction. *Personality and Social Psychology Bulletin, 19*(3), 331–339.

Wilson, T. D., & Schooler, J. W. (2008). Thinking too much: Introspection can reduce the quality of preferences and decisions. In R. H. Fazio & R. E. Petty (Eds.), *Attitudes: Their structure, function, and consequences: Key readings in social psychology* (pp. 299–317). New York, NY: Psychology Press. Retrieved from http://search.ebscohost.com/login.aspx?direct=true&db=psyh&AN=2007-02438-018&site=ehost-live.

Winkielman, P., Berridge, K. C., & Wilbarger, J. L. (2005). Unconscious affective reactions to masked happy versus angry faces influence consumption behavior and judgments of value. *Personality and Social Psychology Bulletin, 31*(1), 121–135.

Winston, G. (1999). Subsidies, hierarchy and peers: The awkward economics of higher education. *Journal of Economic Perspectives, 13*(1), 13–36.

Zajonc, A. (2008). *Meditation as contemplative inquiry: When knowing becomes love.* Aurora, CO: Lindisfarne Press.

Zajonc, A. (2011, March 17). *Thinking like Einstein. meditative life.* Retrieved from http://www.psychologytoday.com/blog/the-meditative-life/201103/thinking-einstein.

Zajonc, R. B. (1980). Feeling and thinking: Preferences need no inferences. *American Psychologist, 35*(2), 151–175.

Zylowska, L., Ackerman, D. L., Yang, M. H., Futrell, J. L., Horton, N. L., Hale, T. S., Pataki, C., & Smalley, S. L. (2008). Mindfulness meditation training in adults and adolescents with ADHD. *Journal of Attention Disorders, 11*(6), 737–746. doi:10.1177/1087054707308502

INDEX

Page references followed by *fig* indicate an illustrated figure.

on compassion, 15–16, 58, 66; on happiness through compassion, 174; in internal transformation of individuals, 176; *A Policy of Kindness* by, 51; reading a prayer written by the, 119; on unconditional nature of compassion, 175

Damasio, A., 15, 32

Dante, 121, 122

Dass, R., 183

Davidson, R. J., 22–23, 30

Dawkins, R., 58, 66

Day, D., 177

Deaton, A., 54, 55

Dedrick, J., 29

Deep listening, 137–139

Deeper understanding: contemplative reading for, 111–122; *lectio divina* practice for, 14, 111–116, 117; strategies for facilitating, 14

Descartes, R., 49, 149

Dewey, J., 5, 8

Dhikr (Islamic "remembrance"), 96

Diamond Sangha Zen Center (Honolulu), 194

Didjeridus or *didgeridoo* (instrument), 70

Digital contemplative reading, 121–122

"Digital natives," 129

Dillard, A., 118

Dilley, B., 160

Dimow, C., 190

DiPietro, M., 8

Distance learning instruction, 182

Diversity (variation), 73

Divina Commedia (Dante), 121

"Diving into the Wreck" (Rich), 117

Dreyfus, G., 95–96

Drucker, P., 103

Dunn, K., 9

Dunn, R., 9

Dunne, D., 30

Dustin, C. A., 155

Dutch postal code lottery study, 57

Dyrbye, L. N., 27

E

E-mail habits, 104–105

Earley, J., 63

Earleywine, M., 32

Easterlin, R., 54, 55, 56, 66

Eck, D., 79–80

Economic contemplative pedagogy: Easterlin paradox and the relative income hypothesis, 54; exploratory exercises, 59–65; measure of well-being and income, 54–57; mechanisms of selfishness, kindness, and compassion, 57–59

Economic well-being, 51–52

Economics students: contemplative exercise goals for, 53; use of contemplative practice for, 51–65; creating cooperative environments and agency for, 52–53

Edwards, M., 183

Einstein, A., 17

Elbow, P., 133

Embodied Mind (Varela, Thompson, and Rosch), 106

Emily Carr Institute of Art and Design, 173

Emmanuel, S., 176–177, 196

Emotional regulation: brain-imaging studies on meditation impact on, 29; how contemplative exercises can improve, 14–16

Emotional well-being: Axelrod's cooperation study and, 57–58; Easterlin paradox and relative income hypothesis on, 54; exploratory exercises on, 59–65; meditation impact on health and, 27–29; perspective on gains of others as detracting from own, 56–57, 59–65, 66; positive affect, blue affect, stress, and life evaluation measures of income and, 54–57. *See also* Happiness

Emotions: compassion, 14–16; how meditation impacts the, 27–29; learning process and role of, 32

Empathy: how contemplative exercises can increase, 14–15; how reflection embeds, 98; importance of education in cultivating, 15–16

Empathy and Consciousness (Thompson), 6

"Empathy fatigue," 16

Engaged democracy, 183

Engels, F., 55–56

Epstein, M., 147

Essentials of Spontaneous Prose (Kerouac), 125

Ethical awareness, 151

Milarepa (Tibetan mystic), 138
Milton, J., 150
Mind and Life Institute, 205
Mindful Attention Awareness Scale, 32
The Mindful Brain (Siegel), 98
Mindful learning. *See* Learning
Mindful listening, 46–47, 143. *See also*
    Listening
Mindful teaching, 98. *See also* Teachers
Mindful Walking Instructions, 161–162
Mindful writing, 132–133
Mindfulness applications: to law schools,
    106–108; a mindful look at personal
    identity, 100–101; mindfulness and the arts,
    101–102; mindfulness as self-management,
    102–103; mindfulness for reflective
    scientists, 103–105; mindfulness of sound,
    139–140; witnessing, welcoming, and being
    present, 98–100
Mindfulness-based stress reduction (MBSR):
    focused attention for, 95; programs for, 24,
    31
Mindfulness for Law Students (Rogers), 107,
    142
Mindfulness in Education Network, 203
Mindfulness (Langer), 4
Mindfulness of sound, 139–140
Mindfulness practice: *Anapanasati sutta*
    (Buddha) on mindfulness of breathing,
    106; beholding, 47–48; body awareness for
    increasing, 159–161; as both a process and
    an outcome, 95; Chinese character for, 95;
    classroom applications of, 98–105; as
    creating a space for learning, 98;
    instructions on conducting, 97;
    introduction to basic, 45–46; mindful
    eating, 46; mindful listening, 46–47, 143;
    shoveling snow presented as, 96; students
    with disabilities and, 108–109
Mirror neurons, 186
The Mismeasurement of Man (Gould), 13
MIT, 174
Mitchell, S., 132
Molina, F., 191
Moral concern, 151
Morikami Japanese Gardens (Florida), 194
Morrison, T., 184

Morton, T., 74
Moskal, J., 128
Mother Courage (Brecht), 168
Motivation: how teacher intention can impact
    student, 75–76; strategies for encouraging
    student, 76
Mount Holyoke College, 181
Movement. *See* Contemplative movement
Mporo marriage beads, 70
Muhammad, 112, 176
Muir, J., 196
Multiple intelligences theory, 13, 160
Muraqabah (the Islamic contemplation of
    scripture), 96
Murray, M. A., 12
Music: listening to, 141–142; relationship
    between meditation and improvisation of,
    141–142
"My Dante" (interactive website), 121

N
Naropa (Tibetan Buddhist scholar), 112
Naropa University (Boulder, Colorado), 71, 77,
    120, 129, 132, 135, 146, 160, 203
National Prison Sangha Project (New York),
    192
Native American studies, 191, 194
A Natural History of the Senses (Ackerman),
    140
Nature-related reading, 118
Neff, K. D., 31
"Neighbors and Negatives: Relative Earnings
    and Well-Being" (Luttmer), 56
Neisser, U., 13, 15
Nelson, M. R., 127, 128, 132–133, 172
Neuropsychology of synesthesia, 37–38
New Directions for Community Colleges,
    89
Nichols, M., 199
Nickaus, J., 25–26
Nielsen, L., 28
Nipponzan Myohoji, 192
Nisbett, R., 35
Norman, M., 8
Northwestern Law School, 108
Norton, M. I., 73
Nuss, S., 190

pedagogy used to build professional skills for, 39–40; mindfulness practice introduced to, 45–47; walking meditation practice introduced to, 50

Society of Friends, 154

Soetevent, A., 57

Sommers, S. R., 73

Song, L., 57

Sorum, C. E., 200

Sound: Meditation on Sound Instructions, 139; mindfulness of, 139–140

Speca, M., 5, 31

Speckens, A.E.M., 25

Sponberg, A., 164, 182

St. Cloud University, 83

St. Joseph's University, 9

Stairs, A., 100–101

Stanislavski, C., 167

Stanley, D., 75

State University of New York, 102, 134

Steere, D., 195

Sternberg, R., 13, 15

Stevenson, B., 54

Stoic *meletai* practices, 22

Storytelling, 135

Straight, B., 70

Stress: mindfulness-based stress reduction (MBSR) for managing, 24, 31, 95; students with disabilities at risk for, 187

"Strong reciprocity" norm, 59

Students: acknowledging backgrounds of your, 68–69; changing their relationship to the curriculum, 6–9; contemplative practices supporting self-monitoring by, 8–9; demonstrating teacher intentions to, 72; as "digital natives," 129; evaluating participation of, 76–78; experiencing their own engagement with contemplative pedagogy, 83–84; increasing variation and inclusion of, 73–75; keeping contemplative practices separate from religious beliefs of, 78–81; lifetime value of higher education provided to, 199–202; personal practice of the contemplative practices, 91–94; teacher intention and motivation of, 75–76

Students with disabilities: at risk for stress, 187; compassion and connection with, 187; mindfulness work with, 108–109; yoga work with, 171

Subliminal cues research, 35–36

"Subliminal perception," 35

Suffering: role of compassion in responses to, 184–185; *tonglen* for transforming, 45, 48–49, 181, 185

Sufi "noble connection" practice, 22

Suu Kyi, A. S., 177

Suzuki, S., 118

Syracuse University, 101

T

Tafakkur (the Islamic contemplation of nature), 96–97

Tai chi (martial art), 166–168

Tanahashi Kazuaki, 95

Tang, Y.-Y., 23

Tattoo Girl (Ilzuka), 168

Taylor, M., 7–8

Teacher intention: demonstrating them to students, 72; student motivation relationship to, 75–76

Teacher preparation: confronting your own preexisting beliefs and biases, 74–75; deciding how to approach student evaluation, 76–78; developing an experiential sense of the material, 83–84; establishing context of students' backgrounds, 68–69; for framing language to introduce contemplative exercises, 81–83; for handling the variation and pluralism of students, 73–75, 80–81; by implementing the contemplative practices, 67–68; respect for traditions, 69–71. *See also* Contemplative pedagogy

Teachers: intention of, 72, 75–76; mindful teaching by, 98. *See also* Mindful teaching

"Telling More Than We Can Know: Verbal Reports on Mental Processes" (Nisbett and Wilson), 35

Telomerase (enzyme), 28–29

Temple University, 119, 187

Theosophical Society, 195

"Third-person learning," 105

Thomas, M. R., 27

Thompson, E., 6, 106

If you enjoyed this book, you may also like these:

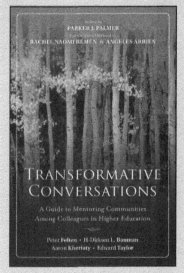

Transformative Conversations
by Peter Felten,
H-Dirksen L. Bauman,
Aaron Kheriaty, Edward Taylor
ISBN: 9781118288276

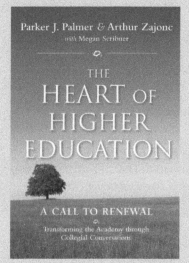

The Heart of Higher Education
by Parker J. Palmer
and Arthur Zajonc
ISBN: 9780470487907

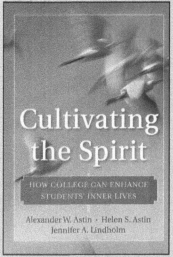

Cultivating the Spirit
by Alexander W. Astin,
Helen S. Astin,
Jennifer A. Lindholm
ISBN: 9780470769331

Learner-Centered Teaching,
Second Edition
by Maryellen Weimer
ISBN: 9781118119280